What Nobody Told You About

The Return Of Christ

David John Sörensen

What Nobody Told You About the Return of Christ

ISBN: 979-8-9960884-0-9

Printed in the United States of America
Published by Hope for Humanity PMA

Visit us at: www.TheReturnToChrist.com

Dedication

I dedicate this book to all the true children of God
who do not bow to corruption for the sake of monetary gain,
but who are willing to follow Christ as their example,
who laid down His life to bring humanity
into the fullness of the glory of God.

TABLE OF CONTENTS

INVOCATION

A Call To The Brave

Dear Reader,

I am excited that you have picked up this book.

The truths you will discover here have the power to radically transform your life. They will open your eyes and your heart to behold the glory of the Lord Jesus Christ in ways you never thought possible. Ancient chains of deep deception will be shattered, and you will be enabled to rise up in the fullness of who you are: a royal child of the Most High God, called to reign with Christ the King.

This book is not for cowards and traitors who prefer position, popularity, and profit over truth. It is for those who burn with a desire to see all lies and deception fall to the ground and who hunger and thirst to know the Lord Jesus Christ in all His majesty.

It is a *call to the brave*—those who have the courage to break through the hordes of hell that fight with all their might to prevent us from fully knowing Christ in all His glory (2 Cor. 10:5).

I encourage you to pray continually as you read, for this book exposes some of the most powerful strongholds that have blinded and enslaved God's people for a very long time. It reaches into the very heart of the enemy—into the core of the strategy of the Great Deceiver.

When these strongholds are challenged and the eyes of God's sons and daughters begin to open, intense spiritual warfare is unleashed.

The Spirit of God is initiating a new worldwide reformation in His Church, and no true reformation comes without a battle. The only way to be victorious in this spiritual warfare is to radically lay down all ego, pride, and selfish agendas, and choose to be a true follower of Jesus Christ who listens to His voice with an open ear and a tender heart.

When we submit to any form of compromise for self-preservation, we automatically surrender crucial ground to the enemy of our soul, resulting in loss of victory and failure in our mission.

Because of the profound and serious truths that will be uncovered in this book, I invite you to pray with me before continuing your reading.

After all, it is not through the words of men or worldly wisdom that His truth is revealed, but by His Spirit. We can only be awakened to the truth of Christ when His Spirit works deep inside of us.

So please take a brief moment to pause and sincerely pray this prayer with me. I even encourage you to pray it out loud, if you are willing.

Heavenly Father,

You are Light, and in You there is no darkness at all.
You are pure truth, without any trace of deception.

I ask You to reveal all truth to me and to set me free
from every hidden deception I am not yet aware of.

Let the light of Your Holy Spirit shine brightly upon me,
so that I may clearly see the truth and wholeheartedly embrace it.

Deliver me from every evil that secretly holds me,
and lead me into the fullness of Your glory.

In Jesus' name,
Amen.

Choose to be
a true follower
of Jesus Christ,
a student of
the Master;
one who listens
to the voice of
the King of kings
with an open ear
and a willing
heart.

The Return To Christ

It is time for a reformation. Not merely an adjustment to a flawed doctrine, but a far deeper, more radical transformation. A reformation that strikes at the very core of our being; the beating heart of the Church, the essence of Christianity itself. A reformation in which the Church returns to her Savior, her Master, her King, and abandons the idols, demons, and deceivers of this world.

For far too long, the Father of Lies has infiltrated and hijacked the Christian Church. His deceptions have not merely weakened or oppressed us — they have done far worse. They have turned us away from Jesus Christ Himself. We have forsaken His words, ignored His message, abandoned His mission, and turned our hearts from Him. Never in the history of the Church has such devastating deception taken root so deep that we have, in practice, betrayed our Beloved Lord and enthroned His enemy in His place.

The dark lies of Satan have been exalted as "unquestionable truth," while the crystal-clear message of the Lord Jesus Christ has been trampled underfoot as though it were filthy dirt.

The result is a Church so indescribably confused, so unimaginably crippled, so devastatingly disempowered, that it is barely recognizable as the glorious Body of Christ.

Despite countless revival meetings, healing conferences, Bible camps, Christian television programs, and millions of church services, the Church has become more irrelevant than ever.

Historically, the Church used to be the most powerful force of transformation. In every nation where the early Christians came, they ended the worship of demons and the practice of human sacrifice. They ended slavery and oppression and established churches, hospitals, and orphanages in every town and city, transforming human culture from unspeakable darkness to unprecedented light. Where the Church came, darkness had to flee, and a new day dawned for the people of the land. Today, the situation has flipped: the Church no longer casts out evil, but is being invaded by the very demons it once expelled.

It may sound like an exaggeration, but only to the deaf and blind who don't hear or see the reality of the world today. When our heart is truly connected with the heart of Jesus Christ who stands in the very center of our world, seeing the devastation all around Him, then we weep with Him, as we feel His intense agony over what is happening.

His fiery Spirit of Truth is burning again in the hearts of those who hear His heart cry and who respond with tears of despair.

Overcome with His fire of love, they release a shout louder and more powerful than their own soul could ever release. It's a battle cry of the Most High that resounds deep inside the souls of those who have not abandoned the Lord their God. They share in His suffering as they burn with a relentless desire to see our world set free again from the dark chains of evil.

They see a glowing horizon, a new day dawning, a light beginning to spread over the lifeless landscapes.

The Lord is moving on with the truth. He is speaking to the spirit of His true servants. And He is calling His Bride back to Himself—*without compromise.*

This is the sound you will hear in this book: a cry of truth, a roar of revelation, a whirlwind of transformation that exposes the lies that have led the Church astray.

This is not just a book to share some insights. It is a call to war, a crusade against the forces of hell that have flooded the Church.

I am calling all who long for a new day where the Bride of Christ will once again stand at His side in all her beauty and radiance, to change this world into a majestic habitation for the King of glory, to have the courage to read this book to the end. Don't allow anything to stop you. Not even your own inner struggles.

Just. Keep. Reading. All. The. Way.

Let the blazing light of the truth shatter the chains around your mind and elevate your spirit to soar to the heights of the Most High God, where you will behold His glory as never before.

May we all rise up with a desire so strong that we will not bow for the demons of our time, the liars in our churches, the deceivers in our midst, and we will slay dragons with a boldness given by Christ Himself, who defeated the Great Dragon of old.

His example calls us to follow where He goes. Not to a corrupted religion, but into a kingdom that is burning with the fire of the heavenly hosts who wage war against the forces of hell.

We are called to join their battle and bring the Church back to its Master, Savior, and Lord: Jesus Christ, the King of kings, the Name above all names, and the One who will once again make us His glorious hope in this world.

When we turn from evil and return to Jesus Christ, the Lord of lords, our lives will be changed — touching and transforming all other lives that come near to us, igniting a wildfire of deliverance in our world.

This book is the declaration of that new day — a dawn where truth pierces the clouds of confusion, and the glory of the Lord rises upon His people more than ever before.

"Arise, shine; for your light has come,
And the glory of the Lord has risen upon you.
For behold, darkness covers the earth,
And deep darkness the peoples;
But the Lord will rise upon you,
And His glory will appear upon you.
Nations will come to your light,
And kings to the brightness of your rising."
—Isaiah 60:1–3

The reformation begins here.

This is...

The Return To Christ.

David John Sörensen
TheReturnToChrist.com

FOREWORD

A Deep Passion For The Truth

What if most of what you've been taught about the return of Christ is wrong—and the truth is *far greater, far more powerful, and far more present* than you ever imagined?

It takes real courage to challenge the status quo of mainstream Bible teaching. And when I think of David John Sörensen, one word rises above the rest: *courageous.*

I was introduced to David several years ago through an online theology discussion group where I serve on the leadership team. This group is devoted to equipping ministers who teach a Christ-centered, biblical worldview. It didn't take long before I recognized something rare: we shared a deep, uncompromising passion for the Truth that sets people free, and a desire to communicate that truth in a way people can truly grasp and live out.

Over the years, through many conversations, messages, and calls, we have explored the Scriptures together, uncovering the powerful reality of Christ's present reign in His Church. Again and again, we were confronted with the same urgent truth: believers must awaken to their current Kingdom authority on the Earth.

Yet so many have been taught to wait... to delay... to expect everything to change only at some distant future return of Christ. But Jesus Himself declared that He would come within the lifetime of His first-century disciples.

This book will open your eyes.

It will ground you in Scripture and empower you to realize that you are not waiting for Christ to return—you are called to live in the reality of His presence now. There is no gap. No separation. In Christ, Heaven is not distant but accessible. His power, His presence, and His goodness are available here and now.

Although David has already impacted many lives through his published works in Europe, it is my great honor to introduce his very first book in the United States: *What Nobody Told You About the Return of Christ.*

I believe this book will become a classic—one that finds its way into homes, hearts, and ministries across the world. A resource not only for personal transformation, but for equipping others with truth that restores clarity, purity, and power to the Body of Christ.

Many are already familiar with the depth and intensity of David's work through his platform, StopWorldControl.com, where he boldly exposes deception, confronts darkness, and shines light on truth with unwavering conviction. This book carries that same spirit—but with even greater focus, depth, and purpose. It is the fruit of a divine assignment:

to reveal the living reality of Jesus Christ among His people with clarity, authority, and compassion.

I am always inspired when someone breaks beyond the confines of religious tradition, refusing to bow to the fear of man, and instead presses into the depths of God's Word to uncover hidden treasures. David has done just that. He has laid out compelling, Scripture-based evidence upon which others can build a strong, unshakable foundation for a life of purpose and impact.

Get ready to be challenged. Get ready to be awakened. And above all, get ready to step into a new level of boldness and courage.

Dr. Cindye Coates, Th.D.
Professor of Theology
Author of "The Fulfilled Prophecies Of Jesus"

Get ready

to be challenged.

Get ready

to be awakened.

And above all—

get ready

to step into

a new level

of boldness

and courage.

2:41

CHAPTER 1

A Voice Like Thunder

This book is the direct result of the Lord Jesus Christ speaking to me in a loud, audible voice that resounded like rolling thunder. Let me assure you: hearing His voice like that is nothing short of life-altering. The sheer power in His voice penetrates every fiber of your being, touching places no human word could ever reach. It transforms you for all eternity.

The Lord has spoken to me audibly several times. The first time, I was lying on my bed, pondering scriptures from Isaiah that I had read. Suddenly, His voice exploded all around me. It sounded like a violent blast of thunder—full of power, authority, and terrifying majesty. Yet, mingled with that severity was a blazing current of joy and love that danced like living fire. I was amazed.

But what shook me wasn't only the majesty of that voice—it was the words He thundered into my spirit. Like a lightning strike they hit me:

"You will be My prophet!"

I leapt off my bed in absolute terror and bolted down the stairs into the garden, gasping for air. *"I did not just hear that!"* My whole body shook. To me, prophets were wild-eyed fanatics—mean, scary doomsayers who munched on bugs, dressed in animal skins, and shouted curses over everyone. Yikes! I had zero interest in joining that club.

But the divine calling haunted me...

One day, while talking to our pastor, I casually shared what was on my heart: "We shouldn't interrupt worship with announcements. It prevents people from having a deep encounter with God. The Lord longs to draw us deeper into His presence, and that can only happen if worship flows unhindered." The pastor looked at me strangely, and said slowly: "David, I consider you a true prophet in this church."

If he had stabbed me with a knife, I wouldn't have been more shocked.

The problem is, this wasn't a one-time event. Over the years, similar moments kept coming—until one day I'd had enough. After trying to push this calling away, burying it in the deepest, darkest corner of my soul so I could forget about it entirely and live a "normal Christian life," I came to a disturbing conclusion: *it was impossible to outrun God.*

Over time, I learned that being God's mouthpiece isn't as horrifying as I feared. It doesn't mean thundering doom on everyone or being mean and vicious all the time. On the contrary, the Lord allowed me to feel what He feels and think what He thinks. In most cases, it was an overwhelming, almost crushing sense of unspeakable love for people who are hurting—a deep, indescribable longing in the heart of God to see His children restored and radiant in His love.

Sometimes I was overcome by an indescribable pain when, in the middle of a Church service, I would suddenly feel His intense longing to heal the people in that gathering. He yearns with all His heart to touch His children and transform their lives—*but He is being blocked by leaders more interested in running a show than hosting His presence.*

On several occasions, the Lord allowed me to experience a sliver of His agony over humanity. It was unbearable and left me undone in tears, often for many hours.

Once, I cried an entire night, until, in the morning, I wondered if I was losing my mind. It's not normal to weep for hours on end, fall asleep exhausted, and then wake up only to begin weeping again with even greater intensity. I asked the Lord what was happening, and He gave me a scripture: Nehemiah 1:3-4.When I looked it up, I was astonished.

It spoke of the prophet Nehemiah, who wept for many days, mourning because the people of God had been carried off into exile and the city of God lay in ruins. Suddenly, I understood that the Lord was allowing me to experience something similar—being overcome by His intense anguish over the state of His children worldwide. He weeps over us with a sorrow no words could ever express.

The Return Of Christ

Over the years of walking with the Lord—drawing close to His heart, hearing His very breath, tasting His passion, and carrying His burden for humanity and the Church—He began to speak to me about a subject that burns brighter than almost anything else in His heart. The theme of His return, the end of the age, and the dawning of the new creation. What He showed me shook my life upside down. It rattled me so violently that I had to cling to Him with everything inside me.

The Lord unveiled how Satan—the most cunning deceiver of all beings in all of eternity—has woven lies into the very fabric of the Church. Lies so devastating, so confusing, so masterfully misleading that they have left much of the Body of Christ disoriented, weakened, and in ruins.

Even churches that are full of passion for the Lord and His kingdom, burning with desire to see their nations transformed by His glory, fail in their daring endeavors, because they are sabotaged from within by deceptions that cripple even the most zealous believers.

When our mind is controlled by crippling deceptions, it doesn't matter how much fire we carry inside. Ultimately, we will stumble and fall over and over again, until the cords that bind us within are broken, and we are finally able to see clearly, without being led into hidden pitfalls again and again.

And the worst deceptions in Church history pertain to His return and the end of the age.

Nothing has destroyed Christians more than false beliefs about the coming of Christ and the new creation.

When our life is built on a false belief and a crooked expectation, it distorts everything we think and do. It sabotages every aspect of life, whether we realize it or not.

It was about this very situation that the Lord spoke to me once again—not with the gentle voice I hear daily in my heart, as a friend and companion—but with His thunderous, audible voice. Usually, our communion is intimate, a daily fellowship deep within my spirit. He whispers, guides, encourages, and comforts. But on rare occasions, when He really needs to get through to me, He thunders so loudly that I am marked forever, changed for all eternity.

The reason the Almighty speaks to me with such incredible force, is because His heart burns with passion to reveal His wonderful plans for His people. His eternal desire is that His beloved children would be released into *the full measure of His glory.*

But it is only when we are delivered from deception—every lie, every false teaching, every crafty distortion—that we can step into this glorious fullness and experience the breathtaking majesty of the Most High God, who loves us beyond comprehension.

Christ gave His very life so that we could become everything He has imagined us to be. That is why it breaks His heart to see so much of His Church wandering in the wilderness, far from the royal destiny He prepared for us. The Lord yearns with a burning desire to lead us out of this desert into the abundance of His life and goodness.

So I plead with you, dear reader: open your heart wide to the Heavenly Father. Open yourself to His beautiful dreams for you. He longs with everything that is within Him to lift you out of the enemy's snares and carry you onto the heights of His overwhelming goodness. If you will allow Him, He will astonish you beyond your wildest imagination with what He has prepared for you.

That is why I want to invite you—before you read another page—to again join me in prayer. It is critical that we posture ourselves before the Lord of Glory, opening our hearts so His brilliant light can pierce the darkness within our minds and souls. Only then will we be illuminated by the blazing truth that sets us free from the insidious infiltrations of the Prince of Darkness.

Never forget: this dark entity is the *master of disguise.* He has masqueraded even as the very Word of God, twisting and hijacking Scripture in order to cripple the people of God. He has done it so cunningly that most of the Church has not even realized it.

That is why it is absolutely imperative that we take a bold stand in the Spirit right now, to rebuke this "Father of Lies" and to submit ourselves wholly and completely to the authority of Jesus Christ, who alone is the embodiment of pure truth.

So please pray again with me, with all your heart. I even encourage you to pray these words aloud, as a bold declaration. Feel free to use your own words, if you prefer.

Prayer For Truth

Heavenly Father,

Thank You for loving me with such fiery passion
that You gave all You have and all You are
to rescue me from all deception.

Fill me now with Your Spirit of Truth,
so that I may hear Your heart
and see Your light clearly.

I rebuke every spirit of deception, every lying spirit,
and every influence of the Father of Lies
that seeks to keep me blinded and confused.

I submit myself wholly
to the authority of the Lord Jesus Christ.

He gave His life and shed His blood
to deliver me from the grip of Satan,
and I embrace His saving power for me.

Lord Jesus Christ, be my King.
Be my Lord.
Be my Shepherd and Guide.

You alone are my God—there is no other.

Lead me into all truth
and into the fullness of Your freedom.

Amen.

EVOLUTION
ORIGIN of SPECIES
DESCENT of MAN

CHAPTER 2

The War On Truth

Have you ever noticed how the truth is not very popular in our world? On the contrary, it seems that lies are always mainstream, while truth is consistently pushed aside.

Look at science: the mindset of mainstream science is that all humans are dressed-up monkeys who accidentally started walking upright. This absurd belief is imposed upon everyone in the world as an unquestionable fact. As a result, our existence is deemed meaningless, and humans are considered beasts without intrinsic value. This concept robs the children of the Almighty Father of their dignity and identity. It plunges humanity into the abyss of despair and depravity—born without purpose.

However, despite being utterly destructive, the theory of evolution has become the solid foundation of the western world, and woe to he who dares raise a questioning finger.

As children of a deeply loving Creator we know how wrong that doctrine is. We are not the result of absurd chance, accidental events, and meaningless natural processes. No! Humankind is a brilliant masterpiece created by Almighty God. We are priceless in value, divine in nature, and royal in identity. Our lives are rich in purpose and loaded with hidden treasures that await expression.

But the theory of evolution steals our identity and reduces us to meaningless lumps of clay that are only born to die again. This results in a human race that falls prey to countless traps: addictions, broken relationships, perversion, obesity, and burnout are all the result of the human mind being blinded to who we truly are. We have lost our identity as royal children of the Most High, and we stumble about like beasts without understanding.

Although truth empowers us while deception cripples us, it is not the healing truth that reigns in our world, but the poison of deception.

As a result, it can be difficult for those with a burning desire for truth to attain the object of their passion. Anyone daring to venture out from underneath the cloud of darkness is faced with demons erupting on all sides, even—often especially—in those closest to us. As if truth has to be kept hidden by all means and at all costs, even at the pain of betraying loved ones. How many spouses have stood up against their precious partners with a raging fury, forbidding them to investigate critical matters? How many colleagues suddenly turned into fiery foes, viciously attacking their otherwise favourite companions the moment they dare to touch the forbidden realm of truth?

Once one of us has the courage to reach beyond the invisible prison of deception that encloses the entire human race, the attacks come from all sides, even from within. "How dare you question this? What wicked person are you to ask these questions? Who do you think you are? Shut up and sit down!" Inner voices can be the worst enemies of those who heed the high calling of searching for what is so desperately hidden from all of us.

It makes it hard to choose what is right.

Who is willing to pay the price?

Our foremost example is Jesus Christ, who was the least mainstream of all who ever walked the face of the Earth. Nobody had a clue what He was talking about, and even His closest friends failed to comprehend His mission. The popular expectation was that the Jewish Messiah would overthrow the Romans and restore Israel to become a mighty military nation. Jesus had a tough job explaining to His Jewish followers that He was not a political or military leader who would set up a violent kingdom. He was in every way the exact *opposite* of that. But nobody believed Him. They all wanted a military, political Israel. Christ was greatly misunderstood, yet He kept speaking the truth, knowing that one day the Spirit of Truth would manage to open their eyes.

Meanwhile, He was killed.

It can take time before the truth breaks through.

The question is: are we willing to be like Jesus Christ and stick to the truth, even if we are misunderstood, rejected and hated for it?

That was the choice I had to make one cold, lonely night.

The street was empty, the air biting against my skin, and the only light came from a flickering lamp post above me. Its pale glow cast long, trembling shadows on the pavement where I stood, utterly alone. In my hand I held a phone, carrying the voice of a pastor. This spiritual leader did something I never imagined anyone would ever do: he invited me to honestly consider what I believed about the return of Christ. His words struck me with a force I could not resist. What flowed from his lips was uncompromising truth that would alter the entire course of my life. Here is a rough summary of what reached me that night:

> "David, you do understand that we are living in the *new covenant*, right? This covenant is all about Jesus Christ dwelling *within us*. He is no longer distant. He abides inside us at all times, wherever we go. We are His home, His temple, His dwelling place. This is the essence of the new covenant:
>
> **The Lord is no longer far away, but He is always with us. He lives in us, and He lives through us.**
>
> That is why Jesus died on the cross, to make this union a reality. That is why He was tortured and crucified: to restore His presence with us forever."

I could not agree more. This has been my greatest passion since the day I encountered Christ as the most beautiful reality of my life: *His abiding presence with me.* He transformed me from a stuttering boy, scarred and silenced by horrific events in my childhood, into a man who now testifies boldly of the unfailing love of Jesus Christ.

When we organize conferences, the presence of the Lord often manifests so powerfully that many people experience divine healing and life-changing deliverance. One day, a young boy came to our church with his face covered in warts. Surgery had been scheduled to remove these growths, but it would have left his face permanently scarred. Yet, in that meeting, the presence of the Lord Jesus was so strong that the boy's face was completely transformed and his skin became soft and pure, like the tender face of a newborn child.

Throughout my childhood, I had many encounters with the presence of God. One night, a powerful angel stood beside my bed and lifted me into his arms. He carried me to Heaven, where I was led into a gathering of the heavenly elders before the Most High. They asked me a question about my destiny. I answered—and in an instant, I was back in my body.

In my young adulthood, severe trauma pushed me away from God, and I wandered for a few years through the dark realms of the godless world. Yet like the prodigal son, I crashed, burned, and was welcomed back into the Father's arms of compassionate love.

One day, as I prayed on my knees, the ceiling above me disappeared, and I beheld the eternal glory of Heaven. From that majestic realm, two enormous hands reached down and lifted me up. I was home again! Angels danced around me, and my life was forever transformed.

At the Royal Academy of Arts, my peers exclaimed: "You've changed from a devil into an angel!"

From that moment on, my heart belonged to Him forever.

But I still carried a terrible handicap: *I could not speak.* Sometimes, when I tried to call someone on the phone, not a single sound would come out. If I went to buy coffee, I would come home with milk because I could not say the word "coffee." It was unbearable.

One night, in deep agony, I banged my head against the wall, crying out because of my inability to speak. Finally, I collapsed to my knees before my bed and opened my Bible. Through my tears, I could see only one verse illuminated on the page, as if all the rest had gone dark:

> **"He will yet fill your mouth with laughter**
> **and your lips with shouts of joy."**
> —*Job 8:21*

It was God's promise that He would heal my speech.

Years later, I was baptized in the Spirit of God, and His power engulfed me in a tremendous way. During that encounter, I saw the Lord Jesus Christ walk up to me. His radiance filled the room, and my body trembled with His divine power. He spoke to me and commissioned me to be His servant. I was never the same again.

Still, my speech problem remained. When I was asked to speak in churches, I would stand before the congregation in tears, unable to utter a single word. Then suddenly my body would begin to vibrate, my limbs would tremble, and His overwhelming presence would engulf me.

In that moment, words of life would suddenly began to flow from my lips. Healings took place. People ran forward, confessing their sins. Demons screamed as they were cast out, and supernatural signs broke forth in our meetings.

One day, as I proclaimed the lordship of Jesus Christ—the Name above every name—a man suddenly rose from his wheelchair.With tears streaming down his face, he cried, "I am standing for the first time in years!" His nurse came running and confirmed it: this man was walking for the first time in years. I took him by the arm, and together we walked through the auditorium, praising Jesus with loud voices.

Those were the kinds of manifestations of the presence of the Almighty Lord of Heaven and Earth I was used to: glorious workings of deliverance, healing, and transformed lives. Not by power, not by might, but by the Spirit of the Lord.

And the glory of His presence manifested—not because of my abilities, but in spite of my severe handicap.

So when this pastor spoke to me on the phone about the essence of the new covenant—the presence of the Lord Jesus Christ with us, dwelling within us and working through us—I was all ears.

Indeed! Jesus is not far away in some unreachable place; He is right here with us, in our midst, every day.

But then the pastor continued:

> "Now, David, do you also realize that the popular doctrine about the return of Christ essentially claims we will be *sent back* into the dark ages of the old covenant? In that covenant, the Lord was *not* present with His people. He was *far away*, hidden behind the walls of a distant stone temple, separated from His beloved ones. There was no daily communion with His presence. He was set apart from the people, while they lived distant and disconnected from Him. That was the reality of the old covenant."

That was indeed a dark, cold night, just as Apostle Paul described it: a covenant where God was somewhere "out there," distant, untouchable, and hidden in a faraway temple.

And then he spoke words that shattered the solid foundation of my popular theology...

"Do you understand, dear David, that the popular doctrine of the return of Christ literally teaches that when He comes, we will be dragged back into the same shadows of the old covenant? According to this belief, Christ will return *in a physical body* to take up residence *in a stone temple* in Jerusalem—thousands of miles away from us. If we want to see Him, we'll have to book flights and cross continents. Then we'll stand in suffocating crowds, waiting for hours in mile-long lines, just to catch a fleeting glimpse of the King of kings—maybe a quick wave from a balcony if we're lucky—before being shoved aside so the next wave of desperate pilgrims can have their turn. And then, off we go again—thousands of miles back home, cut off from His presence, until our next exhausting journey. Exactly like the dark days of the old covenant, when God's glory was locked away in a stone temple, far removed from His people.

Are you aware that the Lord Jesus Christ shed His very blood to end that dreadful reality of the old covenant? Do you understand that He bled and suffered on the cross to bring an end to that age when the presence of God was always distant from His people? Do you see that Jesus gave everything—His life itself—so that He could be with us, everywhere we are, always and forever? That is why He has made *us* His temple.

We are now His dwelling place. Never again will He be far away in some distant sanctuary.

This is why He died, why He poured out His blood—to make His abiding presence with us a reality for all time.

But the widespread belief about the second coming essentially denies all of this. It suggests that Jesus gave His blood for nothing. Because, according to this doctrine, when He returns everything will be reversed back into the old covenant. Once again, the presence of God will be *far away from us,* and we will have to travel thousands of miles just to briefly visit Him in a stone temple in Israel. No longer would we be His temple, where He dwells daily in intimate fellowship. No—under that doctrine, we would be thrust back into the shadows of the old covenant, where Christ is once again 'somewhere out there,' in a faraway land called Israel, sitting in a physical temple, thousands and thousands of miles away from us."

There I stood under the eerie glow of a lonely streetlight. No one else around. Just me, the darkness, and the Lord.

I knew exactly what was happening. This pastor had asked me a question that every one of us must eventually face in life. A hard question. A dangerous question. A question that determines who we truly follow. The question was this:

Would I shut my ears, end the conversation right there, and retreat back into safety—pretending I had never heard these devastating words? Or would I be honest and have the courage to truly consider what this man of God had explained?

I knew this was no light matter. Asking questions about the return of Christ can feel like suicide. It is one of those taboo subjects in the Church. You believe what you are told, and you keep silent. Raising objections is not allowed. But why? Why are there topics in Christianity locked away, forbidden to examine, beyond the reach of honest investigation? Does not the Bible itself call us to search for truth as for silver and gold? Is it not the hallmark of a true child of God to seek understanding and wisdom, for this is what it means to fear the Lord (Proverbs 2:4-6)? Why, then, is it considered heresy to ask questions about the return of Christ?

That night, I had a raw conversation with the Lord Jesus:

> "Lord, You know I have often said I would die for You. I have dedicated my entire life to You. Time and again, at altar calls, I have run to the front, laying my life before You, declaring I am willing to follow You no matter the cost. And now, here I stand—faced with a choice that cuts to the core. Lord, I can simply ignore what this brother has spoken and continue my ministry as if all is well, or I can allow You to speak to me about this topic, knowing that it could cost me everything—my reputation, my finances, my position, my standing as a respected preacher."

After a short but fierce struggle, I came to a trembling conclusion:

> "Lord Jesus, I don't know where this will lead me, but I know what this pastor has told me is so profound, so fundamentally true, that it could open doors with consequences beyond anything I can imagine. Yet, I cannot suppress truth for the sake of safety. Come what may, I present myself fully to You."

"Have Your way with me. Lord, if there is anything You need to show me about the doctrine of Your return that is false or twisted, then open my eyes."

I walked away from that phone conversation with a pure heart. I had chosen the right thing to do. At that moment I knew nothing yet about anything you will read in this book. All I knew was that this pastor hit an absolute home run when he said:

"Never will God allow any form of distance to be created between Himself and us again, after Jesus has suffered to make sure that we would always be in His presence."

If a doctrine—no matter how popular it is—creates distance between us and our dearest beloved Lord, then there is something not right with that theology. This is a key the Lord gave me:

"Any doctrine that creates distance between you and Me is false. Any doctrine that brings you closer to Me is true."

If Christ died to be forever present with us, wherever we are—making us His dwelling place, His temple, where He lives and from where He spreads His love and healing to the world around us—then why do we believe a doctrine that says Christ will return to Israel and sit in a stone temple, thousands and thousands of miles away from us, so that we would have to travel just to briefly meet Him from a distance?

Do we have the courage to honestly ask this question?

My personal answer to the Spirit of Truth was a daring "Yes!" In response, He led me on an adventurous journey of biblical discovery, uncovering what the Scriptures truly reveal about the "return of Christ."

When the Lord invited me to walk this path with Him, He said:

"David, I am going to reveal to you the greatest treasure of all time— the most powerful riches in all of creation. This is what the angels have longed to look into. This is what the apostles laid down their lives for. This is what the demons fear the most. This is why I gave My life for you. This is what the heavenly Father has been preparing for His beloved ones. This will empower you, bless you, heal you, and lift you up more than anything else. This is the treasure of Heaven."

This is what the angels
long to look into.
This is why Christ
gave His life for you.
This will empower you,
bless you, heal you,
and lift you up more
than anything else.
This is the treasure
of Heaven.

JESUS IS
COMING
SOON!

CHAPTER 3

The Greatest False Prophet in History

The popular doctrine of the "Second Coming" or the "Return of Christ" is an essential part of modern-day evangelical Christianity. Hundreds of millions of sincere Christians believe that Christ will return physically to Earth to set up His kingdom in the nation of Israel. Then He will put an end to evil, make all things perfectly well, solve all our problems, and create a wonderful paradise—all in the twinkling of an eye.

This amazing promise—that all evil, all suffering, all sickness, all fear, and all terror will disappear once Christ sets foot on Earth—has inspired billions of believers to focus their entire life on this fantastic event! The old world of darkness will be gone, and a beautiful new creation will emerge—*just like that!*

Countless books have been written to prepare the Church for this mighty moment of divine deliverance. Thousands of conferences have been organized, where millions of people heard their popular pastors proclaim the coming of Christ any moment now. Every well-known Evangelical preacher predicted, with great fervency and deep conviction, that the return of Jesus Christ would surely occur during their lifetime. They passionately preached it from their pulpits, daringly declared it on radio and television, taught it in mass conferences, and wrote numerous books to prepare mankind for this absolutely amazing apocalypse.

However, as time went by, one generation followed another, and all these powerful preachers peacefully passed away, a sobering reality dawned on the minds of the honest observers. No matter with how much zeal these fantastic forecasts were spoken, and how widely they spread, ultimately *none of them came to pass.* Every single prediction about the imminent rapture and return of Christ proved to be false. Nothing of the sort happened. *Never. Nowhere.*

The spectacular book "Late Planet Earth" by Hal Lindsey, which sold 35 million copies and assured an entire generation of Christians that Christ would return during the 1980s to set up His kingdom on Earth, came to nothing. The mega mind-blowing "Left Behind" series that turned the authors into Evangelical millionaire celebrities by describing how the world would look after the Rapture, proved to be worthless.

Tens of thousands of fervent prayer warriors at the International House of Prayer in Kansas City have been praying day and night for decades on end, for Christ to return to Earth. They, however, woke up in shock as they stared the harsh reality in the face that their highly enlightened charismatic leader Mike Bickle turned out to be a merciless abuser of women. One moment he was on the platform of IHOP insisting everyone needed to prepare for the imminent return of Christ, and the next moment he was in bed with one of the ladies of his church.

Not a single one of the many prophecies uttered by the prophets at the world-famous IHOP ever came to pass, and the whole castle of deception came crashing down.

The toxic tsunami of faulty forecasting continues unchecked, as the internet is buzzing with countless videos, articles, and books that constantly announce the same apocalyptic events. If they don't happen as predicted, the date is simply moved a year ahead. Year after year, again and again, the coming of Christ is prophesied to happen during every single year: 1900, 1901, 1902, 1903, ... 1920, 1921, 1922, 1923, ... 1970, 1971, 1972, 1973, ... 1990, 1991, 1992, 1993, ... 2000, 2001, 2002, 2003, ... 2021, 2022, 2023, 2024, 2025, 2026, 2027,... and so on, and so on, and so on.

Thousands times thousands of predictions have been made from countless pulpits that all proved to be false—*every single one of them!* No matter how wonderful the pastors were who announced the imminent return of Christ, they were all wrong. *Nothing happened.*

We now observe the absurd phenomenon that the Church has become the greatest false prophet in the history of mankind.

Today we find ourselves in the disturbing reality that nobody on the face of the Earth releases so many false prophecies as... the Evangelical Church!

We have uttered more erroneous revelations than anyone else since the creation of the world. That is not an achievement to be proud of, to say the least.

Naturally, this widespread wave of whoppers has crushed the credibility of Christianity in our time. Wikipedia features extensive lists of famous false prophecies about the end of the world—most of them made by popular Christian ministers! That is extremely serious.

What is even more grave is that nobody is ever held accountable for their phony predictions. And so the treacherous tsunami of faulty forecasting continues unhindered and unchecked.

This level of fraud is not without consequences. The false prophecies are causing crippling confusion in the lives of countless precious children of God. Millions never prepare for retirement and end their lives in deep poverty and disillusionment. Parents fail to dream big for their children, believing "the end of the world" is upon them. Youngsters refuse to study for their future, thinking all God requires of them is to pray for a rapture to take them away. Christian leaders all over the world end up in burnout because they believe the end is near and they need to run as fast as they can to save a few last souls.

But not only has the massive misguidance mangled millions of beloved believers, it has also dramatically decreased the effectiveness of God's people in the Earth. For many centuries, Christians used to be the forerunners in the world, who pushed back the powers of darkness and established the Kingdom of God wherever they went. They built the very first schools and hospitals, established caring for the poor and the elderly, and put an end to public slavery, cannibalism, and human sacrifice. Throughout the centuries, the followers of Jesus Christ created a world that is safer, healthier, and wealthier than it had ever been. Public slaughter and torture were cancelled, and the global oppression by magic, sorcery, and demon-worship was largely stopped. A significant portion of mankind encountered—for the first time in history—the true God of love and goodness. Historically, the Church has always been an unstoppable army of love and deliverance that put a halt to the works of evil and established the Kingdom of God. They created a brighter future for the next generations.

But, since the rise of false predictions about the end of the world and the return of Christ, the increasing influence of God's people was severely sabotaged. Millions of believers stepped away from their place of authority and impact in the world. "If Christ is about to wipe out the Earth, why would we spend any effort trying to heal it?"

The focus of the Church shifted from impacting our world to escaping it. The once brave warriors of Christ who powerfully expelled darkness from our societies are now hoping to "get the hell outta here" as quickly as they can.

As a result of this shift in theology, Christians in general have become the *least relevant* and *least effective* people in our world. We have indeed been "left behind," but not in the way the popular books told us...

The Church stepping away from her call to reign with Jesus Christ also opened the gates of our cultures wide for the ancient powers of darkness to return to our once Christianized nations. Demonic forces that had been pushed back by our Christian ancestors are once again poisoning our societies.

The Church observes this influx of evil passively, thinking it is a "sign of the end times" and therefore inevitable. Instead of rebuking the renaissance of darkness, many even applaud it because they were led to believe it is evidence that Christ will return very soon now.

Never before in the history of the Church did a doctrine cause such devastation as the widespread idea of the Rapture and the Second Coming. Still, most Christian leaders stubbornly refuse to spend even a few minutes of their lifetime pondering the terrible condition of Christianity. Where did we go off track? What caused us to miss the mark so badly? Is it truly the will of God that His people are the worst deceivers and false prophets in all of history? Does Christ revel in the crippling confusion of His people, who run back and forth, stumbling over one another, constantly proclaiming the end of the world without ever doing anything truly impactful for humanity? Is it truly the message of the Bible that all Christians, throughout the course of history, should wait their entire lives for an "imminent" event that never happens, causing them to waste their lives in useless anticipation, instead of powerfully marching forward, fulfilling their God-given dreams?

Are we truly meant to live our lives in this kind of intense confusion, fueled by a toxic tsunami of false prophecies, without even the remotest form of accountability?

Is it acceptible that pastors and preachers, ministers and authors, Christian celebrities and influencers can go about announcing earth-shattering end-time events that never come to pass, without ever having to face the dire consequences of their mad messaging?

Or, should we come to a screeching halt and look each other deeply in the eyes while we pound our chests in conviction, understanding how far we have gone into the depths of darkness, running to our doom without ever giving it a second thought?

I say doom for a reason, because millions of precious children of the Most High God have been led to their doom, ending their lives in devastating disillusionment, painful poverty, and fatal failure, because everything they had built their lives on proved to be fundamentally false. They neglected their children, ruined their marriages, and ignored the future of their loved ones because they believed the world was doomed and that everything would end "any moment now."

With every new world leader, we cry, "He is the antichrist!" just as we yell during every catastrophic event, "The end of the world is near!"

Many churches are like ships without a compass, lost at sea during the storms raging in our world. Their captains constantly shout, "Christ is about to save our ship any moment now," only to end up crashing against the hidden rocks of the shorelines, drowning most aboard.

We have become the local village idiots, the least respected individuals on the face of the Earth. The real world sees us and laughs their heads off. Such morons! Always running around like madmen, crying doom and the end of the world without ever having a truly transforming impact on our communities. We hide in the buildings we erect, singing songs of deliverance while the people outside of the shiny doors are dying on the steps of our sanctuaries.

What has happened to the Christian Church? Where did we lose track of the truth? What made us so vulnerable to this incredible wave of destructive deception that has been terrorizing the minds of billions of God's children for so long?

The only way we can find out what went wrong is if we have the humility and honesty to return to Jesus Christ, sit quietly at His feet, and learn to listen.

Not shout this and that, wave our Bibles in the face of Christ, and object to what He says. But *kneel down and listen*. Become students of the Master all over again—hear what the King has to say about the end of the world, His return, and the future. Only when we do that can we learn the lessons we all need so desperately. Shall we do that, please? Can we stop our mad apocalyptic rat race and sit down at the feet of the King of kings, listening to what He has to say?

Kneel down

and listen.

Become a student

of the Master

all over again.

Hear what the King

has to say about

the end of the world,

His return,

and the future.

CHAPTER 4

Coming On The Clouds

When Jesus Christ walked the Earth, He made an absolutely astonishing announcement: He would appear on the clouds of heaven, in the glory of His Father, accompanied by armies of angels and blazing fire. At that moment, He would be revealed as King of kings and take His rightful place in the Kingdom of God.

Read how Christ announced this incredible event:

"For the Son of Man is going to come
in the glory of His Father with His angels,
and will then repay every person according to his deeds."
— *Matthew 16:27*

"Then will appear in heaven the sign of the Son of Man,
and then all the tribes of the earth will mourn,
and they will see the Son of Man coming
on the clouds of heaven with power and great glory."
— *Matthew 24:30-31*

Without a doubt, this is the most spectacular prediction anyone has ever made! No wonder His followers were eager to know when this magnificent moment would take place:

"Tell us, when will these things be,
and what will be the sign of your coming
and of the end of the age?"
— *Matthew 24:3*

Now, what do you think? Would Jesus look them in the eye, see their burning passion to know *when* this glorious manifestation of His majesty would take place, and then turn around... to stone-cold *lie* to them? Would He make such dramatic announcements... only to use them to *deceive* His dearest friends?

There is not a single atom in my entire being that believes the Lord would ever do such a thing. No. I know wholeheartedly that He gave them an answer they could build on. He would not lead them astray and send them wandering off into the woods with wrong directions. He is the light of the world, the shepherd of our souls, the friend in times of need, the lamp on our path, the one who leads us *out* of darkness—not *into* it. So when the disciples asked Jesus to please tell them *when* He would come on the clouds, He gave them a solid and reliable answer:

"For the Son of Man is going to come
in the glory of His Father with His angels,
and will then repay every person according to his deeds.
Truly I say to you, there are some
of those who are standing here
<u>who will not taste death</u> until they see
the Son of Man coming in His kingdom."
— *Matthew 16:27-28*

Hold on a second... Did Jesus say that some of His followers would *live* to see His coming on the clouds? Really? How can that be? We have always been told the exact opposite: that *we* are the ones who will see Jesus coming, thousands of years later. Not those very first followers of Jesus... they died many centuries ago! No, no! His coming was not for the *first* disciples of Jesus. His coming is for the *last* disciples of Jesus. It is for us who live thousands of years later, and many thousands of miles away from Jerusalem.

Why did Jesus promise His first followers in Jerusalem that *they* would surely live to see Him coming?

And He didn't just toss it out casually—He used the emphatic: "Truly, I say to you..."

Whenever Christ used "Truly, I say to you" He wanted His listeners to know they were hearing absolute truth. It was like saying:

> **"Now listen to me, and listen well.**
> **Some of you will absolutely live**
> **to see Me coming on the clouds!"**

That is an *absurd* statement! We all know it can't be true, because we've heard our entire lives—in every single church we ever visited and on all Christian television—that *we*, the 21st-century modern Church, will be the ones to see Christ coming.

But wait... maybe there is a way out of this crisis caused by the Scriptures. Perhaps it was just an isolated moment where Jesus had a brain glitch. Maybe He'd eaten something bad and His mind was playing tricks on Him. I mean, He was human, right? He shared in all our human experiences. It happens to the best of us.

Let's quickly read the other passages where Christ mentioned the timing of His coming. Surely He made it clear in other passages that it would be a generation in the far-distant future—thousands of years later—who would be the ones to see Him coming, and *not* those first disciples. So let's dive back into the Scriptures.

Look, here's the moment when Jesus was preparing His disciples to go and proclaim the gospel throughout all of Israel:

> **"But whenever they persecute you in one city,**
> **flee to the next; for truly I say to you,**
> **you will not finish going through the cities of Israel**
> **until the Son of Man comes."**
> — *Matthew 10:23*

Oh no—He did it again! Jesus guaranteed His first disciples that He would come on the clouds before they even finished going through all of Israel. How on Earth is it possible that Jesus made such outrageous statements? Was Jesus glitching twice during His ministry? Was He allergic to olives, or perhaps dates? Maybe His brain malfunctioned when He ate fish?

We need to find out. So let's keep searching for those verses where He said His coming was for a very distant future—more precisely, for the 21st-century Christians in America. It has to be in the Bible somewhere—because that's what every pastor, preacher and prophet proclaims!

Alright, here's Matthew 23–25. What did Jesus say to His Jewish followers in Jerusalem?

> **"Truly I say to you, this generation will not pass away until all these things take place."**
> — *Matthew* 24:34

For the third time, Jesus left no room for doubt: His *first* followers would be the ones to witness His coming. He urged *them* to stay ready, for though it would surely occur *within their lifetime*, the precise day and hour would remain unknown:

> **"For this reason you must be ready as well;**
> **for the Son of Man is coming at an hour**
> **when you do not think He will."**
> — *Matthew* 24:44

This is absolutely unbelievable! How can this even be?

Our entire lives we've been told that Christ will come on the clouds in *our* time, thousands of years later. But when we read what Jesus said, we see that He repeatedly told His first followers in ancient Jerusalem to prepare, because *they* would experience His coming.

Read what He told them:

> "Take heed that no one deceives **you."**
> **"You** will hear of wars and rumors of wars."
> "See that **you** are not troubled."
> "They will deliver **you** up to tribulation and kill **you**."
> "**You** will be hated."
> "Let **those who are in Judea** flee to the mountains."
> "Therefore **you** also be ready."
> — *Matthew* 24

When Jesus was alone with His closest friends, He didn't suddenly change His story and reveal that His return would actually be thousands of years later. *He stayed consistent.* Talking to Peter about John, He said:

> **"If I decide to let him live until I return, what concern is that of yours?"**
> — *John* 21:22

CHRIST LOOKED THE JEWISH BELIEVERS STRAIGHT IN THE EYES AND BURNED HIS WORDS INTO THEIR HEARTS: **THEY** HAD TO BE READY FOR HIS COMING.

Jesus said John would live to see His coming!

And Jesus didn't just say it to His friends—He said it to His enemies. Standing before the Jewish High Council, who were about to condemn Him to death, He told them:

> **"I say to you, hereafter you will see the Son of Man**
> **sitting at the right hand of the Power,**
> **and coming on the clouds of heaven."**
> — *Matthew 26:64*

Do you even know what this means? In Jewish culture, the expression "coming with power on the clouds of heaven" was a well-known idiom meaning *executing divine judgment*. What Jesus bluntly told those Pharisees to their face was nothing less than:

> "You think you can kill me, hey? But wait a little, you guys...
> because before you know it, I will come as God to judge you!"

No wonder the high priest lost his mind and went into a full-blown rage, ripping his clothes and shouting, "Blasphemy! Kill Him!"

> **"Then the high priest tore his robes and said,**
> **'He has blasphemed! What further need do we have**
> **of witnesses? See, you have now heard the blasphemy;**
> **what do you think?' They answered, 'He deserves death!'**
> **Then they spit in His face and beat Him with their fists;"**
> — *Matthew 26:65-67*

Maybe some of you reading this are also just about ready to lynch me for quoting what the Lord Jesus Christ *actually said* about the timeframe of His coming—rather than obediently parroting the false prophecies that claim *we* are the ones who will see Jesus coming.

Well, go ahead. Rip your clothes, find a rope, and pick your favorite tall tree. You wouldn't be the first to try. Several people on social media have already called for my death. "David John Sörensen deserves the death sentence"—yes, that's literally what some "nice Christians" posted on Facebook. Others have sent me hate-filled emails so venomous I half expected them to have a sulfur odor to them, as if they came straight from hell.

Christ guaranteed
the Jews in Jerusalem
that **THEY** were the ones
who would see Him
coming on the clouds.

I spent most of my life in Bruges, Belgium—a city where, centuries ago, "heretics" were burned alive by religious authorities. Yes—Christians burned Christians. They tortured, mutilated, and murdered fellow believers simply for daring to question the officially sanctioned Church narrative. Brutal murder, cruel torture, violent massacre—all performed in the name of God.

I must admit, I'm glad to be alive in the 21st century and not the 1600s. I wouldn't have lasted long.

But let's not be intimidated by diabolical retaliation. Let's return to the words of Jesus Christ—and carefully consider the time indications He Himself gave concerning His coming on the clouds.

This is when Jesus Christ said He would come again:

- **The Jews in Jerusalem had to prepare for His coming.**
  — *Matthew 24*

- **Some of His audience would live to see it happen.**
  — *Matthew 16:28*

- **He would surely come during that generation.**
  — *Matthew 24:3*

- **The disciples wouldn't have enough time to go through Israel before His coming.**
  — *Matthew 10:23*

- **The Jewish Council would witness it.**
  — *Matthew 26:64*

- **Apostle John would still be alive.**
  — *John 21:22*

Stand on your head, jump, argue, and twist it all you want—the truth of Scripture does not move: Jesus Christ never said His coming on the clouds would be for a distant generation, thousands of years after He spoke those words. Whenever Jesus spoke about His return, He drove it home with the strongest language—"verily, verily"—declaring that the very people standing before Him would experience it. He pressed it on them with urgency: be ready. There was no doubt.

What Say The Apostles?

But what did the apostles say? Perhaps they are the ones responsible for the modern doctrine that claims Christ would not come during the first century, but He will return in our time—thousands of years later?

After all, what we believe must be stated *somewhere* by at least some of the authors of the Bible, right? Why else would we all believe what we believe? Let's investigate what the apostles told the first churches:

> **"For yet a little while, And He who is coming will come and will not delay."**
> — *Hebrews 10:37*

> **"But this I say, brethren, the time is short."**
> — *1 Corinthians 7:29*

> **"The night is far spent, the day is at hand."**
> — *Romans 13:12*

> **"The end of all things is near."**
> — *1 Peter 4:7*

What the heck?! The apostles were just as crazy as their Master!

They said the same thing—Jesus would come *during their lifetime*. His coming was "near," He would "not delay," the time was "short," and it would only be "a little while."

So much for hoping the apostles would balance things out and tell everyone it was actually thousands of years away. Nope—they doubled down. In fact, most of their letters to the early churches revolved around this very event, constantly encouraging the first followers of Jesus that *they* would absolutely experience the Lord's coming—and that it was, indeed, right around the corner.

James told the very first believers in Jerusalem:

> **"Establish your hearts,**
> **for the coming of the Lord is at hand.**
> **Behold, the Judge is standing at the door!"**
> —*James 5:8, 9*

John went even further:

"Dear children, this is the last hour."
— *1 John 2:18*

Paul literally assured the first churches in Corinth that Jesus would keep *them* steady and strong until the day of His coming:

"...you eagerly await the unveiling of the Lord Jesus, the Anointed One. He will keep you steady and strong to the very end, making your character mature so that you will be found innocent on the day of our Lord Jesus Christ."
— *1 Corinthians 1:7-9*

The Christians in Corinth were expecting the coming of Christ during their lifetime—and Paul had no intention of talking them out of it. On the contrary, he confirmed their urgent expectation and even added a promise: the Lord would keep them steady and strong to the very end, so they would be found innocent on the day of the Lord Jesus Christ.

Paul gave the same encouragement to another group of Greek believers in Thessaloniki. They were suffering under the cruel hands of those who rejected Christ—just as the apostles themselves were persecuted by the Jews. Knowing their troubles, Paul sent a message that lifted their spirits and filled them with fresh hope:

"[The Lord] will pay back trouble to those who trouble you and give relief to you who are troubled, and to us as well. This will happen when the Lord Jesus is revealed from heaven in blazing fire with his powerful angels in flaming fire taking vengeance on those who do not know God, and on those who do not obey the gospel of our Lord Jesus Christ."
— *2 Thessalonians 1:6-8*

What wonderful, comforting words! The trials of the very first Christians in Thessaloniki would come to an end. No longer would they be crushed under the harsh feet of their merciless oppressors. There was hope! And when would this relief come? Paul left no doubt:

"This will happen when the Lord Jesus is revealed from heaven in blazing fire with his powerful angels."
—2 Thessalonians 1:7

Paul didn't just affirm their expectation that Christ would come during their lifetime—he promised it would bring *the end of their troubles.* He even tied it to the apostles' own persecution, making it clear that he and the other apostles would also live to see this liberating event.

When we combine all the time indicators given by the apostles, we see they all agreed that Christ would come during their own lifetime:

- **The first Christians and the apostles would find relief at the coming of Christ.**
  —2 Thessalonians 1:6-8

- **They were eagerly waiting for Christ.**
  —1 Corinthians 1:7

- **Christ would keep them strong until His coming.**
  —1 Corinthians 1:8

- **It would only be a little while; He would not delay.**
  —Hebrews 10:37

- **The Judge was already at the door.**
  —James 5:9

- **They were in the last hour.**
  — 1 John 2:18

- **The time was short.**
  —1 Corinthians 7:29

- **The day was at hand.**
  —Romans 13:12

- **The end was near.**
  —1 Peter 4:7

The apostles assured the first Christians that **they** would absolutely live to see Christ come on the clouds with His angels.

CHAPTER 5

A Mighty Revelation

All right, all right, we get it: Jesus and His apostles were lying lunatics. They predicted something that—according to what we have been taught—*never happened.* What a bummer. But we have one last card up our sleeve: the mighty book of Revelation! Surely every respectable preacher, pastor, and prophet of our time knows that the book of Revelation tells us, time and again, that *we*—Christians who live in the 21st century—will absolutely experience the end of the world, the rule of the Antichrist, the Rapture, and the coming of the Lord Jesus, right? I mean, that's what all the big books, the mega movies, and the Christian conferences have been telling us, on and on and on. It's what has been broadcast on every Christian TV and radio station, and what every pastor has been preaching from the pulpit:

"The book of Revelation shows us how we—21st century Christians—will all be raptured outta here, really soon!"

But is that also true? Did Apostle John write his dramatic prophecies with the American Church in mind—two thousand years later? Perhaps it's time we take a good, honest look at the book of Revelation, shall we?

First, we must understand what the book of Revelation is actually about. We have been told it is a terrifying apocalyptic horror story predicting the end of the world and the rise of the Antichrist.

Every study, book, TV program, or movie about Revelation seems obsessed with the same theme: *the Antichrist, the Antichrist, the Antichrist*—as if Revelation were his big Hollywood premiere.

Right? Wrong!

Read the title of the book: *"The Revelation of Jesus Christ."*

Revelation is not about unveiling the Antichrist; it is about unveiling Jesus Christ.

We must understand that Jesus Christ came to end the era of the old covenant and establish a whole new covenant. In this new covenant God's presence is no longer confined to a building; *we* are now His temple. The law is no longer carved into stone but written *on our hearts* by the Spirit. The city of God is no longer a fortress of stone—*we* are the living dwelling place of the Lord. This breathtaking shift—from separation to union, from law to grace, from death to life—was accomplished by Jesus Christ. He ended the old and brought forth the new:

"Behold, I am making all things new."
— *Revelation* 21:5

John called his book "Revelation" or "Apocalypse" because *apokalypsis* means *to unveil.* It is an unveiling of Jesus Christ who is enthroned as King of kings in the new covenant. John was shown visions of the spiritual conflict surrounding this decisive transition, as the old order passed away with great upheaval—just as Jesus foretold when He said not one stone of the temple would be left upon another. In its place a brand new realm emerged, in Jesus Christ, during which the believers are now the temple of God.

Now, no more sacrifices are needed. Now, God's presence walks with us wherever we go. Now, we have access to the holy of holies. Now, we belong to the New Jerusalem—the living Bride of Christ. Now, the mysteries of Heaven are being unveiled to the sons and daughters of God.

Revelation is not a book of doom and despair. It is the unveiling of Jesus Christ and the brand new reality He created for us to live in.

It is nothing less than a master crime that the entire worldwide Church has been told that this book is about worldwide calamity in the twenty-first century—where mankind will be devoured by demons, New York will be swallowed by the sea, Satan will rule the world as a supreme global leader, and all Christians will be brutally beheaded.

As you will see in the rest of this book, these horror stories are the result of a shameless abuse of the Word of God—driven by profit. Authors and filmmakers, ministries and Christian television networks have made billions of dollars by spreading wild, fantastical end-times scenarios, combined with a never-ending tsunami of false prophecies about the so-called rapture and return of Christ, while never speaking a single word about what the book of Revelation is actually about.

Fear sells. And fear based on so-called "Bible prophecy" has become one of the greatest money-making machines imaginable. Countless profiteers have used it to build enormous fortunes—while waving the Bible before the eyes of gullible believers.

Truth is not popular; deception is. So they sell out to the highest bidder. And they brazenly call it "spreading the Gospel of Jesus Christ," while they literally do the opposite: they *hide* the true Gospel and replace it with insane fairy tales that destroy the lives of countless beloved children of God. The judgment on these platforms will be severe.

But Apostle John was not like them. He was a sincere follower of Jesus Christ, and he didn't write made up myths to become a widely praised mega-pastor. He chose the opposite: John gave a clear account of what the Spirit of God showed him, and he made it crystal clear *when* all these events would take place.

"The Revelation of Jesus Christ, which God gave Him to show His servants—things which must shortly take place."
— *Revelation 1:1*

"Blessed is he who reads and those who hear the words of this prophecy, and keep those things which are written in it, for the time is near."
— *Revelation 1:3*

John felt such urgency in his spirit that he kept repeating it:

"Do not seal the words of the prophecy of this book, for the time is at hand."
— *Revelation 22:10*

Apostle John shatters every end-times fabrication spread today by countless deceiving voices, stating plainly and simply that the events he described would happen *shortly*, for the time was *at hand.*

Now, did John change his mind as he kept writing the book of Revelation? Did he grow more cautious in his strict time indications near the end? Not at all—he maintained his unwavering sense of imminence:

> **"And the Lord God of the holy prophets sent His angel to show His servants the things which must soon take place."**
> — *Revelation 22:6*

There is no denying it: not only did the Lord Jesus Christ repeatedly affirm that His coming on the clouds would surely be witnessed by His first followers, and not only did the apostles confirm that the Lord was "at the door," they were living in "the last hour," and that this would soon end their troubles—but even Apostle John, the most beloved friend of Christ, stressed it again and again.

All the events described in the book of Revelation were "at hand"; they would happen "very soon," because "the time was near." He urged those early churches to "hold on," because the Lord would "come quickly"!

> **"Because you have kept My command to persevere,**
> **I also will keep you from the hour of trial...**
> **Behold, I am coming quickly,**
> **so cling tightly to what you have,**
> **so that no one may seize your crown of victory."**
> — *Revelation 3:10*

> **"And the Lord God of the holy prophets**
> **sent His angel to show His servants**
> **the things which must shortly take place.**
> **'Behold, I am coming quickly!'"**
> — *Revelation 22:6, 7*

> **"And behold, I am coming quickly,**
> **and My reward is with Me,**
> **to give to everyone according to his work."**
> — *Revelation 22:12*

To read these urgent time indications and then turn around and proclaim that Christ was saying it would be a very long time—thousands of years—is the worst form of Bible abuse we can ever be guilty of.

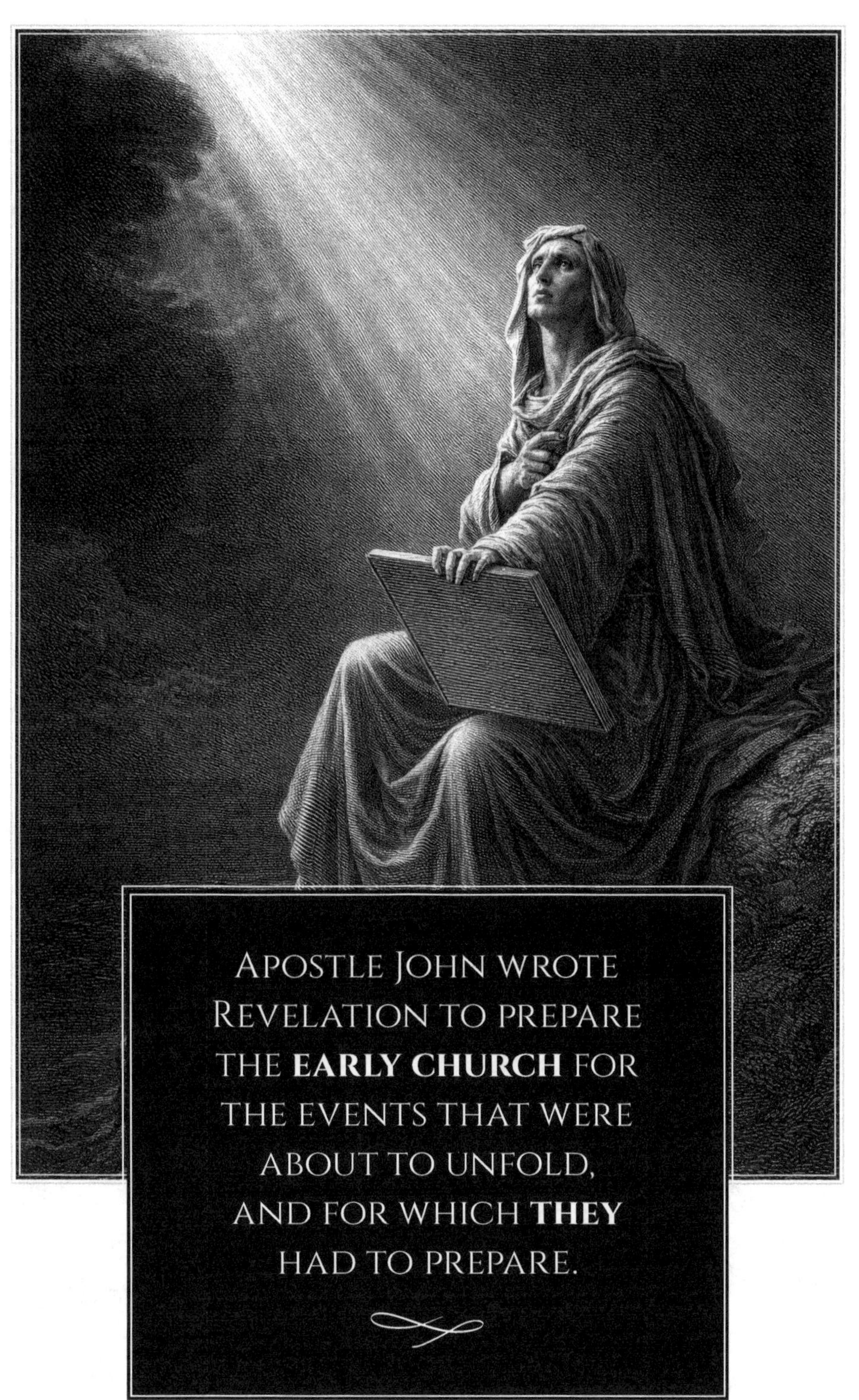
Apostle John wrote
Revelation to prepare
the **early church** for
the events that were
about to unfold,
and for which **they**
had to prepare.

CHAPTER 6

The Biblical Timeframe

It is utterly insane when you stop and think about it. Every single preacher in our time stands in the pulpits or on the platforms of their churches, crying out to the people that surely—surely—without any doubt, Christ is about to return in our day. *And they've been saying this for centuries!*

Yet, when we open the Scriptures, we find that neither Jesus Christ nor His apostles gave even the slightest suggestion that His coming on the clouds would be for some far-off future, thousands of years later. On the contrary—whenever they spoke of it, they always emphasized how *imminent* this event was in their own time.

They kept reassuring the very first generation of Christians that *they* were the ones who would surely experience it—and therefore, *they* had to be ready.

As a result, the expectation of Christ's soon return was the blazing hope of the early Church. It was what they were looking forward to, what they anchored their faith upon. They built their lives on the sure promises given to them by both their Lord and His apostles—promises repeated unanimously: the coming of the Lord was at hand, He would not delay, He was already standing at the door, the time was near, He would come quickly, they were living in the last hour, and they needed to prepare without hesitation.

To help you clearly see the biblical timeframe for the Second Coming, here is an overview of every time indicator given by Jesus Christ and His apostles:

JESUS CHRIST

Some in His audience would be alive at His coming.
Matthew 16:28

Christ would come during the first generation of believers.
Matthew 24:34

Apostle John would still be alive.
John 21:22

The disciples would not have time to travel through Israel before His coming.
Matthew 10:23

The Jewish High Council would see Christ coming on the clouds.
Matthew 26:64

APOSTLES

The coming of Jesus Christ would bring relief to the first Christians.
2 Thessalonians 1:6-8

It would only be a little while; the Lord would not delay.
Hebrews 10:37

The time was short.
1 Corinthians 7:29

They were eagerly waiting for Christ.
1 Corinthians 1:7

The coming of the Lord was at hand.
The Judge was already standing at the door.
James 5:8,9

The first Christians were living in the last hour.
1 John 2:18

Christ would keep them strong
until His coming.
1 Corinthians 1:8

REVELATION

The events described in Revelation
would take place shortly.
Revelation 1:1

The time was near.
Revelation 1:3

The time was at hand.
Revelation 3:10

The Lord would surely come quickly.
Revelation 22:6

The first Christians had to cling tightly
to what they had, until the coming of Jesus.
Revelation 3:10

He would come soon and quickly.
Revelation 3:10

A Deceived Church

I completely understand if this shakes you to the core. Discovering the biblical timeframe for the coming of Christ overturns everything we've been told—and believed—for our entire lives. In fact, it means the Church is deeply and widely confused.

Is that even possible? Could it be that the Church has been so massively deceived? Sadly, Church history gives us a clear answer: *yes*. There have been multiple times when the global Church has been dead wrong on foundational truths.

For centuries, the worldwide Church taught believers that they had to earn Heaven through good works—or even by paying money to the Church. It took one brave but lonely reformer, Martin Luther, to call Christianity back to the original message of the New Testament: that we are saved by grace alone. And for daring to speak that truth, he faced relentless persecution from the entrenched religious powers who refused to listen.

Likewise, for centuries, the Church worldwide insisted that the gifts of the Spirit were no longer for our time. The power of God was virtually absent from Christianity. It took a few daring reformers—men and women who endured fierce opposition—to restore the truth that the Spirit of God is alive and active today, pouring out His power to bring healing, deliverance, and strength to the body of Christ.

Yet even now, many Christians in various denominations still label believers who experience the power of God as dangerous deceivers.

The reality is this: restoring a specific truth to the body of Christ has never been easy—it has always been a battle.

Is God A Liar?

Because the biblical timeframe for the Second Coming is so different from what we have heard in Church, some choose to simply deny everything Jesus Christ and His apostles said. They disregard literally every single time indication with the following excuse: "God knows no time. One day is a thousand years for Him. When God gives a time indication, it basically means nothing. He can say 'soon,' 'at hand,' and 'quickly' and actually mean it will take forever and ever." The result of this absurd line of thinking is that it makes God completely untrustworthy.

The specific time indications for the coming of Christ were given to encourage the suffering believers in the first century. Christ would come soon and give them relief from their pain. He would also keep them strong until His coming.

If we say these promises were meaningless and they all died without being relieved, then we make God a merciless liar. But God is not a deceiver who gives false promises to hurting people. He is trustworthy and full of compassion. When Jesus said John would be alive at His coming, some among His audience would not taste death before He came on the clouds, the High Council would witness it, the disciples would not have time to travel throughout Israel before the Son of Man came, and their generation would surely see it all come to pass, then He was not talking nonsense. *Jesus Christ was telling the truth!*

When the apostles said the return of Christ was at hand, it would bring relief to the Thessalonians, the Lord would keep the Corinthians strong and innocent, they had to urgently expect it and prepare for it, the Judge was already at the door, they were living in the last hour, and so on, then they weren't giving false promises either. They spoke under the guidance of the Spirit of God, who is the Spirit of Truth.

Either we believe God was deceiving the first Church, or we admit that we may learn a thing or two about the coming of Christ.

Was Jesus Delusional?

Some well-known Christian leaders throughout history have concluded that Jesus Christ and His apostles must have been mistaken about the timing of His coming. For many critics of Christianity, this is one of their strongest arguments against Christ. They scoff and say:

> **"Your Jesus said He would surely come during the lives of the first believers, and yet you claim He still hasn't come—not even after two thousand years. That makes Him a liar."**

Critics dismiss Christianity and the Bible entirely based on the belief that Christ wasn't true to His word.

Even the renowned Christian philosopher C. S. Lewis, author of the Chronicles of Narnia series, publicly declared that Christ was ignorant and His apostles were delusional. In his book The World's Last Night, Lewis wrote:

> **"'Say what you like,' we shall be told, 'the apocalyptic beliefs of the first Christians have been proved to be false. It is clear from the New Testament that they all expected the Second Coming in their own lifetime. And worse still, they had a reason, and one which you will find very embarrassing. Their Master had told them so. He shared, and indeed created, their delusion. He said in so many words, 'this generation shall not pass till all these things be done.' And he was wrong. He clearly knew no more about the end of the world than anyone else. It is certainly the most embarrassing verse in the Bible.'"**
>
> *— Lewis, C. S. "The World's Last Night." London, 1960.*

Was Lewis right? Was Jesus Christ ignorant, and were His disciples delusional? Did the Lord deceive the apostles, who then misled the entire Church? That would be the inevitable conclusion if we continue to accept the current widespread theologies about the Second Coming—teachings that have fueled countless false prophecies and kept believers in perpetual confusion.

But there is another option—one most Christians have never seriously considered: *Jesus Christ was right.* He did, in fact, come just as He said—during the lifetime of His first followers.

I know this sounds absurd because we've all been told it didn't happen. But... what if Christ was right after all? What if He spoke the truth? What if His apostles were not mistaken, but spot-on in their predictions? Could it be... possible?

There's only one way to know: *check the historical record.* If Jesus Christ came on the clouds with His angels, it would not have gone unnoticed. Nobody can appear in the sky, blazing with fire and surrounded by armies of angels, without it being recorded!

So here is the most important question: Are there trustworthy historical accounts of this dramatic event?

Well, brace yourself for an amazing discovery...

But... what if
Christ was right
after all?
What if He spoke
the truth?
What if His Apostles
were not mistaken,
but spot-on in
their predictions?
Could it be...
possible?

JOSEPHUS.

CHAPTER 7

The Historic Record

Before we open the history books, we first need to determine what kind of evidence history should reveal in order to know whether Jesus Christ prophesied in truth—or not. What, specifically, did He say would happen during the lives of His first followers? What were the key events He announced? Here is a clear, basic outline:

Jerusalem would be destroyed.
— *Matt. 23:38*

The temple would be destroyed.
— *Matt. 24:2*

Christ would be seen in the sky.
— *Matt. 26:64*

His angels would be seen in the clouds.
— *2 Thess. 1:7,8*

There would be a great light.
— *Matt. 24:27*

A supernatural sign would appear in the sky.
— *Matt. 24:30*

The sun would darken and the moon turn red.
— *Matt. 24:30*

There would be earthquakes, famines, disease, wars, and false prophets.
— *Matt. 24:6,7*

All this would happen in the first generation of believers.
— *Matt. 24:34*

Can we find these events in the history books? The incredible answer is a resounding "Yes!" Believe it or not, every one of these things has been described in great detail by the most authoritative historians of the first century. For example, the leading expert on Jewish history, Titus Flavius Josephus, recorded the events of that era with extraordinary precision in his work *Wars of the Jews*. He writes how, during the years 66–70 AD, Jerusalem was utterly destroyed by the Romans and the temple was reduced to rubble—down to the very last stone. It happened within that very generation, less than 40 years after Jesus announced it. More than 1.3 million Jews perished in ways too horrific for words.

The sun was darkened by the smoke rising from the burning city. The moon turned blood-red from the towering flames. The sea ran crimson as rivers of blood poured into it. Tens of thousands of bodies lay rotting in the streets. Famine became so severe that mothers consumed their own children. False prophets roamed everywhere. Earthquakes shook the land. Wars erupted in every direction.

This was indeed the Great Tribulation foretold by Jesus Christ and His apostles.

But Josephus didn't stop there. He also documented that armies of angels were seen appearing in the clouds with blazing fire; supernatural signs manifested in both Heaven and Earth; a bright light shone down from the sky; the Lord Himself stood upon the Mount of Olives—and much more. Every detail the Lord and His apostles predicted was recorded in the authoritative historiography of the first century.

And Josephus wasn't alone.

Several Jewish, Greek, and Roman historians also reported the appearance of a majestic, awe-inspiring figure on the clouds of heaven—of indescribable beauty—accompanied by angelic armies and encircled in fire.

EVERY "END TIMES" EVENT
HAS BEEN DESCRIBED IN
GREAT DETAIL BY THE MOST
AUTHORITATIVE HISTORIANS
OF THE FIRST CENTURY.

The first historical record of the return of Christ comes from the Pseudo-Hegesippus, a respected chronicle of Jewish history. In this classical work, we find an astonishing account: in the years leading up to the destruction of Jerusalem in 66–70 AD, vast and majestic angelic armies were seen appearing in the clouds—clear, undeniable, and visible to all who looked upward. These were no vague shapes or fleeting illusions, but overwhelming displays of heavenly power.

Even more remarkable, the Pseudo-Hegesippus records that a figure of immense and awe-inspiring size was visible in the sky, standing among these angelic hosts. A sight so extraordinary it could not be forgotten—a vision that perfectly matched the prophecy of Jesus Christ: the Son of Man coming on the clouds of heaven with His angels.

> **"A certain figure appeared of tremendous size,**
> **which many saw, just as the books of the Jews**
> **have disclosed, and before the setting of the sun**
> **there were suddenly seen in the clouds chariots**
> **and armed battle arrays, by which the cities of all Judea**
> **and its territories were invaded."**
>
> *Pseudo-Hegesippus, De excidio Hierosolymitano,*
> *Book V, Chapter 44 (Latin recension)*

Other respected historians of the ancient world—Jewish, Greek, and Roman—report the same phenomenon in striking detail.

Eusebius of Caesarea, the most celebrated historian of the early Church and often called the father of church history, described what was observed in the sky shortly before Jerusalem's fall:

> **"A demonic phantom appeared of incredible size,**
> **and what will be related would have seemed a fairy tale**
> **had it not been told by those who saw it**
> **and been attended by suffering worthy of the portent.**
> **For before sunset, there appeared in the air**
> **over the whole country chariots and armed troops**
> **coursing through the clouds and surrounding the cities."**
>
> *Eusebius of Caesarea, Ecclesiastical History,*
> *Book III, Chapter 8, §§1–6*

HISTORIC RECORDS DESCRIBE **A FIGURE OF IMMENSE AND AWE-INSPIRING SIZE IN THE SKY,** AMONG MAJESTIC ANGELIC ARMIES IN THE CLOUDS.

The term "phantom" echoes the apostles' own cry when they first saw Jesus walking on water. They also thought Jesus was a ghost! Clearly, people do not always recognize Him at first glance. But who else could this majestic figure, surrounded by heavenly armies, have been?

Flavius Josephus, the foremost Jewish historian of the first century, also confirms this. In his monumental work *Wars of the Jews*, where he recounts the destruction of Jerusalem with chilling precision, he notes:

> **"...chariots and troops of soldiers in their armor were seen running about among the clouds and surrounding the cities."**

> *Flavius Josephus, The Jewish War, Book VI, Chapter 5, §§2–3*

From yet another angle, the Roman historian Tacitus—widely regarded as the most reliable chronicler of his time—records the same heavenly spectacle in *The Histories:*

> **"There had been seen hosts joining battle in the skies, fiery gleams of arms — ... the temple illuminated by a sudden radiance from the clouds."**

> *Tacitus, Histories, Book V, chapter 13*

Tacitus not only affirms the vision of heavenly armies but also adds a vivid detail: a sudden blaze of light from the clouds, exactly like the "lightning" Jesus said would mark His coming.

Finally, the medieval Sepher Josippon, preserving earlier Jewish traditions, adds an even more intimate detail:

> **"Now it happened after this that there was seen over the Holy of Holies from above for the entire night the outline of a man's face, the like of whose beauty had never been seen in all the land, and his appearance was very awesome. — ... Moreover, in those days were seen chariots of fire and horsemen, a great force flying across the sky near to the ground coming against Jerusalem and all the land of Judah, all of them horses of fire and riders of fire."**

> *Sefer Josippon, "The Burning of the Temple," chap. 87*

Flavius Josephus, the foremost Jewish historian of the first century, recorded: "...chariots and troops of soldiers in their armor were seen running about among the clouds and surrounding the cities."

The apostle Paul had written that the Lord would be "revealed from heaven in blazing fire with His powerful angels" (2 Thess. 1:6–8). The Josippon description could hardly align more perfectly.

As we continue to read the historiography, we see even more events fulfilled exactly as Jesus Christ had predicted. He had also prophesied:

> **"For as the lightning comes from the east and flashes**
> **to the west, so also will the coming of the Son of Man be...**
> **Then the sign of the Son of Man will appear in heaven,**
> **and then all the tribes of the land will mourn,**
> **and they will see the Son of Man coming on the clouds**
> **of heaven with power and great glory."**
>
> — *Matthew 24:27, 30*

The Greek word translated as "lightning" here is astrapé (στραπή), which means "a flash of light" or "a bright light." Jesus was saying that His coming would be accompanied by a brilliant light. He also declared that "the sign of the Son of Man" would appear in the heavens—though He did not specify exactly what this sign would be. Now consider what the historical sources record—events that occurred at the same time as the appearance of Jesus Christ and His angelic armies in the clouds:

> **"At one time a star, in form like a sword, stood over the city, and a comet, which lasted for a whole year;**
>
> **... so great a light shone about the altar and the temple that it seemed to be bright day; and this continued for half an hour.**
>
> **This seemed to the unskillful a good sign, but was interpreted by the sacred scribes as portending those events which very soon took place."**
>
> *Eusebius of Caesarea, Ecclesiastical History,*
> *Book III, Chapter 8, §§1–6*
>
> **"Thus there was a star resembling a sword, which stood over the city, and a comet that continued a whole year.**
>
> **Before the Jews' rebellion, and before those commotions**

Jewish, Greek and Roman historians describe **"riders of fire"** in the sky, along with **"a man of awesome beauty"**.

which preceded the war, when the people had come in great crowds to the feast of unleavened bread, on the eighth day of the month Xanthicus and at the ninth hour of the night,...

...so great a light shone round the altar and the holy house that it appeared to be bright daytime; which lasted for half an hour."

Flavius Josephus, The Jewish War (also known as Wars of the Jews), Book VI, Chapter 5, §§2–3

The Roman historian Gaius Tacitus described the same supernatural light that shone down from heaven:

"...the temple illuminated by a sudden radiance from the clouds."

Tacitus, Histories, Book V, chapter 13

Jesus had said His coming would be like a sudden gleam of light—and that is exactly what took place, in the same period that witnesses reported armies of angels in the clouds, the face of an astonishingly beautiful man above the temple, and a massive, awe-inspiring figure in the sky.

Also during that time, a supernatural sign—a sword-shaped star—appeared above Jerusalem. Could this sword in the heavens have been the 'sign of the Son of Man' that Jesus foretold? The answer comes from the Jewish historiography Pseudo-Hegesippus:

"For about the signs of the stars, even in the Gospels, we are taught that there were signs in the sun and the moon and the stars."

Pseudo-Hegesippus, De excidio Hierosolymitano, Book V, Chapter 44 (Latin recension)

Here, the Jewish historians themselves connect the star in the form of a sword to the prophecies of Jesus—confirming that He had foretold it accurately.

Signs of the End Times

For generations, billions of believers have been bombarded with alarming "Bible studies" claiming that they were living in the "end times," and that the events unfolding in their day were unmistakable signs that the sky was about to come crashing down and the end of the world was at hand. To support these apocalyptic predictions, countless preachers quoted Matthew 24, where Jesus was actually preparing the Jews of first-century Jerusalem for the coming destruction of their city.

Naturally, the biblical context was stripped away entirely. Unscrupulous pastors terrified their congregations by proclaiming that world wars, economic crises, natural disasters, and political upheavals were the very signs Christ had foretold concerning the end of the world. This form of religious terrorism has tormented the minds of innumerable Christians for decade after decade, convincing people in church pews, viewers of Christian television, and listeners at evangelistic rallies that there was no future for them or their loved ones because the world was on the verge of catastrophe. Their cities would be swallowed up, fire would rain down from heaven, and humanity stood at the brink of extinction.

"The end is near!"

"We are in the last days!"

"These are the end times!"

The harrowing images these destructive sermons burned into the minds of countless children of God haunted them for the rest of their lives. They crippled their ability to build a thriving future, as the dark shadow of an impending apocalypse continually loomed over their souls.

Every war, natural disaster, political leader, economic downturn, or international conflict was proclaimed to be undeniable proof that Satan was about to rise to power through a coming Antichrist and that the worldwide Church would soon be removed from the Earth.

Thousands of books were written to reinforce this narrative, portraying the evening news as God's prophetic broadcast documenting the approaching destruction of the human race and the complete collapse of civilization.

But once again, we must ask: *is that really what Christ said?*

I invite you to lay aside the horrifying visions of your city going up in flames, or Trump turning into the Beast from the book of Revelation, and with a sober mind look at the so called "signs of the end times".

According to historical accounts, **Christ came visibly in the clouds,** with armies of angels and a radiant light—just as He had foretold.

In Matthew 24, Jesus announced that *five specific signs* would appear before the destruction of Jerusalem and His coming on the clouds:

1. false Christs and false prophets,
2. wars and rumors of wars,
3. famines,
4. diseases,
5. earthquakes.

Christians call these "the signs of the end times." Do the historical records mention them? Let's examine each one.

1 · False Christs & False Prophets

Flavius Josephus documents a multitude of false prophets who deceived the Jews before and during the Jewish-Roman war:

> "Now there was then **a great number of false prophets,** suborned by the tyrants, to impose on the people: who denounced this to them, that they should wait for deliverance from God."
>
> *The Jewish War, Book VI, Chapter 5, §2*

> "And now **these impostors and deceivers persuaded the multitude** to follow them into the wilderness: and pretended that they would exhibit manifest wonders and signs that should be performed by the providence of God."
>
> *The Jewish War, Book XX, Chapter 8, §6*

In 1812, George Peter Holford—a respected lawyer and Christian apologist—summarized these accounts in The Destruction of Jerusalem: An Absolute and Undeniable Evidence of the Divine Origin of Christianity. He described Dositheus the Samaritan, Simon Magus, Theudas, and many others who deceived multitudes with false claims of being the Messiah or promising miraculous deliverance.

> "Take heed," says He, "that no man deceive you; for many shall come in my name, saying I am Christ and shall deceive

many." The necessity for this friendly warning soon appeared; for within one year after our Lord's ascension rose Dositheus, the Samaritan, who had the boldness to assert that he was **the Messiah** of whom Moses prophesied, while his disciple, Simon Magus, deluded multitudes into a belief that he himself was the great power of God. About three years afterwards, another Samaritan **impostor** appeared and declared that he would show the people the sacred utensils, said to have been deposited by Moses in Mount Gerizim. Induced by an idea that the Messiah, their great deliverer, was now come, an armed multitude assembled under him; but Pilate speedily defeated them and slew their chief.

While Cuspius Fadus was procurator in Judea, another **deceiver** arose, whose name was Theudas. This man actually succeeded so far as to persuade a very great multitude to take their effects and follow him to Jordan, assuring them that the river would divide at his command. Fadus, however, pursued them with a troop of horse and slew many of them, and among the rest, the impostor himself, whose head was cut off and carried to Jerusalem.

Under the government of Felix, **deceivers** rose up daily in Judea and persuaded the people to follow them into the wilderness, assuring them that they should there behold conspicuous signs and wonders performed by the Almighty."

The Destruction of Jerusalem: An Absolute and Irresistible Proof of the Divine Origin of Christianity (London, 1812), pp. 23–24

2 · Wars and Rumors of Wars

The second sign of the end times is "wars and rumors of wars." Tacitus writes of the years just before the siege of Jerusalem:

"I am entering on the history of a period rich in disasters, frightful in its wars, torn by civil strife, and even in peace full of horrors. Four emperors perished by the sword. There were three civil wars; there were more with foreign enemies; there were wars that had both characters at once.

Besides the manifold vicissitudes of human affairs, there were prodigies in heaven and earth, the warning

voices of the thunder, and other intimations of the future, auspicious or gloomy, doubtful or not to be mistaken. Never surely did more terrible calamities of the Roman People, or evidence more conclusive, prove that the Gods take no thought for our happiness, but only for our punishment."

Histories, Book I (AD 69)

It is striking how this Roman historian—no friend of Christianity—describes exactly what Christ had predicted: an age filled with wars, supernatural signs in the heavens, and divine judgment upon the people.

Josephus adds that "every part of the habitable earth under them was in an unsettled and tottering condition." The years were filled with rebellions, invasions, and civil wars—just as Christ predicted.

> **"... a great multitude of the Germans were in commotion, and tended to rebellion. And as the Gauls joined with them, they conspired together...**
>
> **... every part of the habitable earth under them was in an unsettled and tottering condition.**
>
> **At the very same time did the bold attempt of the Scythians against the Romans occur. .... they slew a great many of the Romans that guarded the frontiers: and as the consular legate Fonteius Agrippa came to meet them and fought courageously against them, he was slain by them. They then overran all the region that had been subject to him; tearing and rending everything that fell in their way."**

The Jewish War, Book VII, §§2–3

In the fall and winter of 67 AD, a civil war erupted in Jerusalem and Judea between the Zealot revolutionaries and those seeking peace with Rome. Thousands were slaughtered until the entire city was destroyed. In early 68 AD, Idumeans looted Jerusalem, killing thousands. Simon Bar Giora, a leader of the Zealots, then devastated Idumea in AD 69.

3 · Famines

Besides false Christs and wars, there were also multiple famines, the third sign of the end, predicted by Jesus. Holford notes that the great famine predicted by Agabus in Acts 11:27–30 began in the fourth year of Claudius's reign — AD 45:

"Our Lord predicted 'famines' also. Of these the principal was that which Agabus foretold would happen in the days of Claudius, as related in the Acts of the apostles.

It began in the fourth year of his reign, and was of long continuance. It extended through Greece, and even into Italy, but was felt most severely in Judea, and especially at Jerusalem, where **many perished for want of bread.**

This famine is recorded by Josephus also, who relates that an assaron of corn was sold for 5 drachmae — i. e. about 3 pints and a half for 3s. 3d.. It is likewise noticed by Eusebius and Orosius.

To alleviate this terrible calamity, Helena, queen of Adiabena, who was at that time in Jerusalem, ordered large supplies of grain to be sent from Alexandria; and Izates, her son, consigned vast sums to the governors of Jerusalem, to be applied to the relief of the more indigent sufferers.

The Gentile christian converts residing in foreign countries, also sent, at the insistence of St. Paul, liberal contributions to relieve the distresses of their Jewish brethren.

Dion Cassius relates that there was like-wise a famine in the first year of Claudius, which prevailed at Rome, and in other parts of Italy; and, in the eleventh year of the same emperor, there was another, mentioned by Eusebius.

To these may be added those that afflicted the inhabitants of several of the cities of Galilee and Judea, which were besieged and taken, previously to the investment of Jerusalem, where the climax of national misery, arising from this and every other cause, was so awfully completed."

The Destruction of Jerusalem: An Absolute and Irresistible Proof of the Divine Origin of Christianity (London, 1812), pp. 35–36

Josephus records unimaginable famine during the siege:

"Now of those that perished by famine in the city, the number was prodigious; and **the miseries they underwent were unspeakable.** For if so much as the shadow of any kind of food did anywhere appear, a war was commenced presently; and the dearest friends fell a-fighting one with another about it: snatching from each other the most miserable supports of life. Nor would men believe that those who were dying had no food; but the robbers would search them when they were expiring; lest anyone should have concealed food in their bosoms and counterfeited dying.

Nay, these robbers gaped for want and ran about stumbling and staggering along, like mad dogs; and reeling against the doors of the houses, like drunken men. They would also, in the great distress they were in, rush into the very same houses two or three times in one and the same day.

Moreover, **their hunger was so intolerable that it obliged them to chew everything** while they gathered such things as the most sordid animals would not touch; and endured to eat them. Nor did they at length abstain from girdles and shoes; and the very leather which belonged to their shields they pulled off and gnawed. The very wisps of old hay became food to some; and some gathered up fibres and sold a very small weight of them for four Attic."

The Jewish War, Book VI, Chapter 3, §4

4 · Infectious Diseases

The fourth sign Jesus prophesied was pestilence. Holford records:

"History, however, particularly distinguishes **two instances of this calamity,** which occurred before the commencement of the Jewish war. The first took place at Babylon, about A. D. 40, and raged so alarmingly, that great multitudes of Jews fled from that city to Seleucia for safety, as hath been hinted already. The other happened at Rome A. D. 65, and carried off prodigious multitudes. Both Tacitus and Suetonius also record that similar calamities prevailed during this period, in various other parts of the Roman empire. After Jerusalem was surrounded by the army of Titus **pestilential diseases** soon made their appearance there, to aggravate the miseries and deepen the horrors of the siege. They were partly occasioned by the immense multitudes which were crowded together in the city, partly by the putrid effluvia which arose from the unburied dead, and partly from the prevalence of the famine."

The Destruction of Jerusalem: An Absolute and Irresistible Proof of the Divine Origin of Christianity (London, 1812), pp. 37–38

5 · Earthquakes

The fifth and final sign announced by Jesus was earthquakes. Josephus noted what happened in early AD 68:

"For there broke out a prodigious storm in the night, with the utmost violence, and very strong winds; with the largest showers of rain; with continual lightnings, terrible thunderings, and **amazing concussions and bellowings of the earth that was in an earthquake.**

These things were a manifest indication that some destruction was coming upon men, when the system of the world was put into this disorder; and anyone would guess that these wonders foreshowed some grand calamities that were coming."

The Jewish War, Book IV, Chapter 3

Seneca the Younger, writing in AD 58, describes:

"How often have cities in Asia and Achaea been hit by a fatal shock! So many cities were swallowed up in Syria, so many in Macedonia! How many times has Cyprus been destroyed by this disaster! How often has Paphos become a ruin! We often received the news of **entire cities that were destroyed in one fell swoop."**

Henry Alford, The New Testament for English Readers (London, 1863), p. 163

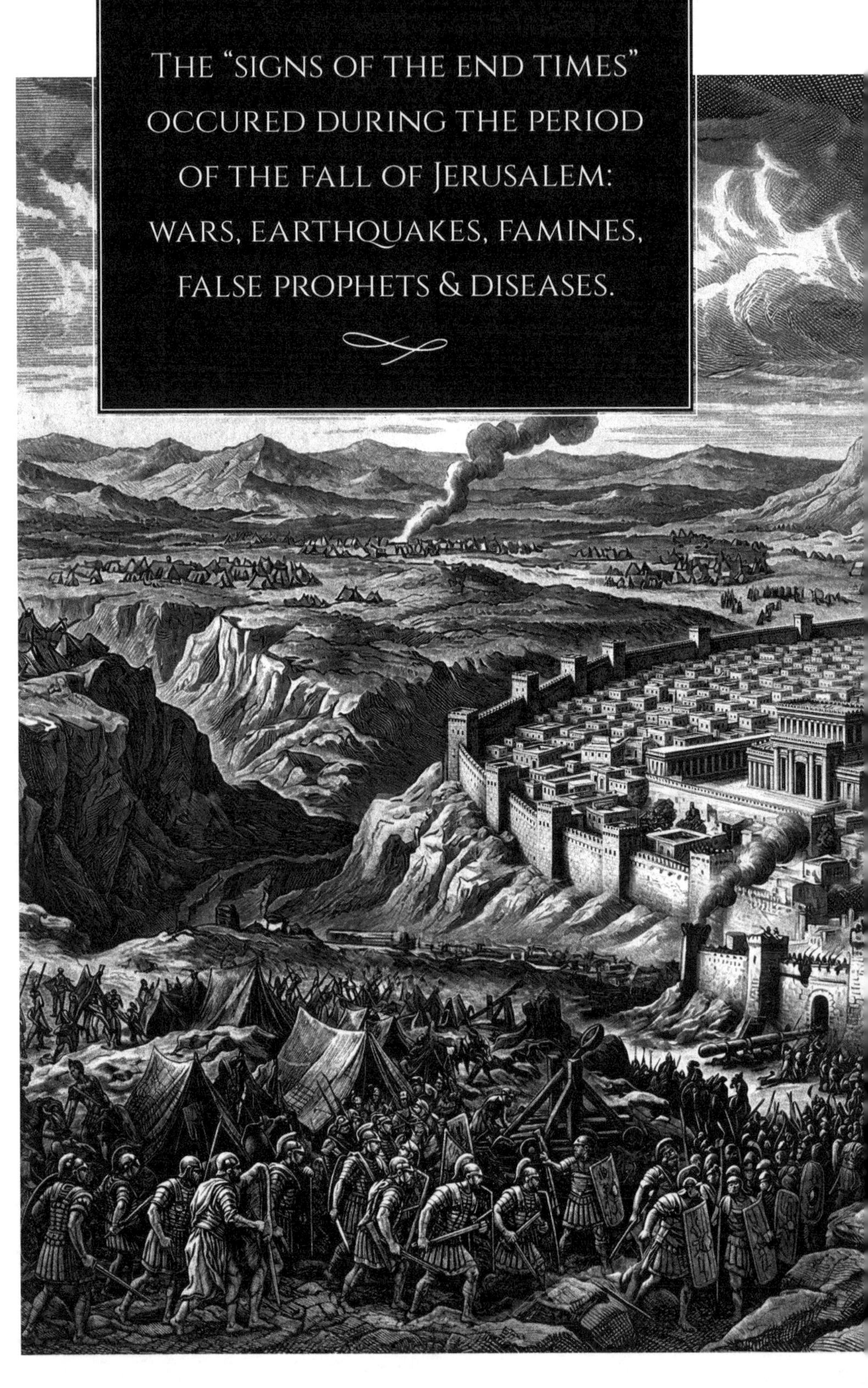
The "signs of the end times"
occured during the period
of the fall of Jerusalem:
wars, earthquakes, famines,
false prophets & diseases.

Additionally, major earthquakes struck Crete, Smyrna, Miletus, Chios, Samos, Laodicea, Hierapolis, Colosse, Campania, Rome, Judea, and Pompeii — February 5, 63 AD. Other earthquakes are recorded in Matthew 27:51–54, Matthew 28:2, and Acts 16:26.

The historians confirm exactly what Jesus Christ foretold: an age filled with wars, false Christs and prophets, pestilence, famine, and earthquakes—culminating in divine judgment.

May I ask you a personal question? Honestly, how do you feel after reading all of this? Are you shocked? Outraged? In disbelief?

I'll tell you my own reaction: I was *outraged.* Appalled. Stunned to the core. Furious that I had never been told this before. Why is this not basic teaching in every Bible school, seminary, and church? Why are most Christian pastors unaware of this fundamental historical record?

This is essential knowledge for anyone who reads the Bible and follows Christ. It proves beyond question that Jesus Christ was not delusional—as C.S. Lewis mistakenly concluded—but truthful and divine, foretelling powerful, world-shaking events years before they happened, down to the detail.

There is no greater evidence of the divinity of Jesus Christ, and the trustworthiness of the Christian faith, than the abundant historical record confirming the complete fulfillment of His prophecies.

And yet... how is it possible that the vast majority of Christian pastors don't know this? How is it that so many instead embrace anti-Scriptural myths and heresies that portray Jesus Christ as a merciless liar, and His followers as victims of profound deception?

The answer is: for the same reason that in the natural sciences, the truth of a Creator is hidden by every possible means. In nearly every university, school, and museum, the public is told that we are here by absurd chance. You can watch hundreds of breathtaking nature documentaries that display the glory of God for all the world to see, yet every single one will repeat the satanic lie that all of it came about through evolution. Not a single mainstream nature documentary anywhere in the world gives glory to God—*not one.*

As I said before, the general rule in our current society is that deception is promoted and truth is suppressed—not only in the secular world, but just as much within the Church. Powerful forces have hidden this incredible historic record of the return of Christ from the Church. The result of this ignorance is crippling confusion.

There is no greater evidence of the divinity of Christ, and the accuracy of the Christian faith, than the abundant historical record confirming the complete fulfillment of His prophecies.

HISTORY
MATTERS
TRUTH
CHANGES
EVERYTHING

CHAPTER 8

Struggling With The Truth

Once we recognize that the Lord Jesus Christ and His apostles were not delusional dreamers, but true prophets who predicted His coming with amazing accuracy, we are left standing before a thousand questions. Because if that is true… it changes everything. And I mean *everything*.

It unleashes a volcanic eruption of burning questions, exploding inside us like fiery rocks.

What about the resurrection of the dead? Weren't we supposed to receive glorified bodies, free from sickness and pain? Didn't the Bible say that Christians everywhere would fly through the sky, soaring among birds and airplanes, at Christ's return? Wasn't Jesus supposed to burn up the Earth with fire and then create a brand new Heaven and Earth? And what about the gospel being preached to every nation first? Or the thousand-year reign? Wouldn't Jesus take up residence in a stone temple in Israel? The list goes on and on…

We have all been taught countless things that must happen before, during, or after the return of Christ. This makes it nearly impossible to accept the staggering reality that Jesus spoke the truth. Yet it is vital to discern between popular myths and biblical truth.

We must grasp the following, because it is of monumental importance: almost everything we have been taught about the return of Christ is utterly wrong. Some teachers may have meant well, but others shamelessly twisted Scripture for power and profit. Fact is, we have all been deceived on a level so vast it almost defies belief.

Once we see how every end-time scenario popularized in the global Church is built on corrupted concepts, we begin to understand that many of our burning questions require answers far different from what we've been conditioned to expect. No—the resurrection of the dead does not mean billions of decayed corpses clawing their way out of the soil. No—the "millennium" is not about the whole world turning into a picture perfect paradise. No—the Rapture is not people being yanked out of their clothes and shot naked into the freezing clouds, dodging airplanes and birds along the way. No—the New Jerusalem is not a golden cube the size of a continent, dropped onto the Earth. No—Jesus Christ will not appear as a political world-dictator standing physically on the Mount of Olives. No—He will not occupy a stone temple where worshippers must travel thousands of miles for a glimpse of Him. No—He will not force the world at sword-point to worship Him under threat of instant death. No—the Kingdom of God is not a global military regime demanding the submission of presidents and kings.

No, no, no, and again no. Every one of these sensational fantasies stands as far from the truth as the East is from the West.

In this book, I will attempt to clear away the rubble of deception and bring some accurate, scriptural, Spirit-breathed common sense to our deeply deformed doctrines.

And I won't be doing this alone. Alongside me is Josh—a fictional character who represents all sincere, Bible-believing Christians who are trying to get their head around the actual truth of Scripture. Like most of us, Josh is not a scholar, and he doesn't pretend to be. But what he does bring is honesty, bluntness, and the kind of questions many of us wrestle with, once we learn the truth.

Josh will voice the doubts, the pushback, and the resistance. And I will respond—straightforwardly, sometimes sharply, always anchored in Scripture and historical record.

The way Josh expresses his doubts and objections will help many of us deal with the struggle we ourselves experience when long-cherished assumptions are challenged by solid biblical truth.

Ready? Here we go!

THE WAY JOSH EXPRESSES HIS DOUBTS AND OBJECTIONS WILL HELP MANY OF US DEAL WITH THE STRUGGLE WE OURSELVES EXPERIENCE WHEN LONG-CHERISHED ASSUMPTIONS ARE CHALLENGED BY SOLID BIBLICAL TRUTH.

CHAPTER 9

What Are They Hiding?

"Oh my Lord… this is absolutely horrifying. All my life I was told to expect the soon return of Christ every single day, because 'nobody knows the day or the hour.' And now you are telling me that everything I have heard about the coming of Christ is based on a denial of His actual words? And that historic record! I am shocked that nobody ever told me about this. Why does my pastor not know this? And my favorite TV evangelist? And all the so-called prophetic YouTube channels? Nobody has ever mentioned any of this.

Lord, have mercy… what in the world is going on here?

And why? Why did Satan spread this lie so widely throughout the Church? What is he trying to hide so desperately from all Christians?"

—*Josh*

I understand your bewilderment, Josh. But let's try to be gracious to our pastors: most of them honestly didn't know any better. Many pastors mean well, but they've been programmed by the religious system to simply repeat what they themselves were taught — without ever questioning it.

The important question you are asking, Josh, is: What is Satan trying so desperately to hide from the Church? What is he so terrified of?

The answer is: he wants to prevent us from entering into the fullness of Jesus Christ and His heavenly kingdom.

The Scriptures tell us that what God has for us is infinitely greater, more powerful, and more unfathomable than anything anyone has ever heard, seen, or even imagined:

> "No eye has seen, no ear has heard, and no mind has imagined
> the things that God has prepared for those who love him."
> — *1 Corinthians 2:9*

We have received the fullness of God:

> "For in Christ, all the fullness of the Deity dwells
> in bodily form. And you have been made complete in Christ,
> who is the head over every ruler and authority."
> — *Colossians 2:9*

We are seated with Christ in the heavenly places:

> "And God raised us up with Christ and seated us with Him
> in the heavenly realms in Christ Jesus."
> — *Ephesians 2:6*

We are called to reign with Christ on His throne:

> "To the one who overcomes, I will grant the right
> to sit with Me on My throne, just as I overcame
> and sat down with My Father on His throne."
> — *Revelation 3:21*

We receive all God's promises to His people:

> "For all the promises of God are 'Yes' in Christ."
> — *2 Corinthians 1:20*

If the Church
is always
waiting…
waiting…
waiting…
then no one
ever truly
enters in,
no one ever
fully receives.

We have received the nature of God:

"Through these, He has given us His precious
and magnificent promises, so that through them
you may become partakers of the divine nature."
— *2 Peter 1:4*

We can do even greater works than Christ:

"Truly, truly, I say to you, the one who believes in Me,
the works that I do, he will do also; and greater works than these
he will do; because I am going to the Father."
— *John 14:12*

We can receive the power of the Holy Spirit:

"There are different gifts, but the same Spirit.
There are different ministries, but the same Lord.
There are different ways of working,
but the same God works all things in all people."
— *1 Corinthians 12:4-6*

We have been given every spiritual blessing:

"Blessed is the God and Father of our Lord Jesus Christ,
who has blessed us with every spiritual blessing
in the heavenly places in Christ."
— *Ephesians 1:3*

We are served by the angels of Heaven:

"Are they not all ministering spirits, sent out to provide
service for the sake of those who will inherit salvation?"
— *Hebrews 1:14*

We have authority to judge the world and even angels:

"Do you not know that the saints will judge the world? . . .
Do you not know that we will judge angels?"
— *1 Corinthians 6:3*

We have power over demons and fallen angels:

"Behold, I have given you authority to tread on snakes
and scorpions, and over all the power of the enemy."
— *Luke 10:19*

We are appointed to reign with Christ:

"He has made us kings and priests unto God and His Father."
— *Revelation 1:6*

We share in the authority of Christ:

"'All authority has been given to Me in heaven and on earth.
Go therefore and make disciples of all the nations.'"
— *Matthew 28:18*

We have dominion over all creation:

"Then God said, 'Let Us make man in Our image,
according to Our likeness; let them have dominion over the fish
of the sea, over the birds of the air, and over the cattle,
over all the earth and over every creeping thing that creeps
on the earth.'"
— *Genesis 1:26, 27*

We have been given the Kingdom of God:

"Do not be afraid, little flock, for your Father
has been pleased to give you the kingdom."
— *Luke 12:32*

Can you see why Satan is terrified?

Imagine what would happen around the world if the two billion Christians stopped waiting for Christ to return, and instead began to walk in His glorious presence. The healing power of Jesus, the full authority of the King of kings, and the riches of Heaven would be unleashed over all of creation—bringing unprecedented restoration as a result.

That is why Satan has convinced the Church that no, Christ has not come yet, the Kingdom of God is not fully here yet.

CHAPTER 10

The Nicene Heresy

"I have never seen such a powerful overview of what we have received in Christ. It's absolutely glorious! No wonder Satan is desperate to prevent us from entering into this reality.

But I must say, sir, it's an unbelievable discovery that Jesus returned in the exact way He foretold. It even challenges the very foundation of Christianity—the Apostles' Creed. You know, the universal statement of faith that nearly every church proudly displays on its website? The Apostles' Creed explicitly declares that Jesus has *not* returned, but will come again at some undefined point in the future.

'Christ Jesus ... sits at the right hand of the Father, from there He will come to judge the living and the dead.'

This creed is virtually a mandatory proclamation across all churches and ministries around the world. The moment you do not align with it—you are flagged as suspicious. Dangerous. A heretic!

So... if you're saying that the words of Jesus were indeed accurate—that He didn't deceive His followers the way critics of Christianity say so bluntly—but that *He actually spoke the truth*, and *history confirms it...* then that means the Apostles' Creed is inaccurate.

And that, Mr. Sörensen, is quite an earthquake!"

—*Josh*

I know, Josh — this is where the massive deception entered the Church. Before the Apostles' Creed, the Church as a whole did not believe that Jesus had to return in some distant future. That was never what Christ or His apostles had said. They insisted that His coming would occur during the lifetime of the first believers, not thousands of years after they had gone.

It was only once this creed was made up and began circulating that the idea of a future return of Jesus Christ started to spread among Christians. The reason it gained influence is because of the title, "Apostles' Creed." It was presented as a summary of what the apostles of Jesus Christ taught. But, it was by no means the apostles themselves who produced this so-called "Apostles' Creed." It originated from an unknown church in Rome, and no one actually knows who wrote it. That is why it was originally called the "Old Roman Creed" (Symbolum Romanum). The label "apostolic" therefore functions as false advertising, giving the document instant authority in the eyes of believers.

The claim that Christ will return in the distant future stands in direct contradiction to what the true apostles taught about His return. As we have seen, the apostles unanimously guaranteed that Christ would return within their own generation. They left no room for a return thousands of years later in some far-off age. And history confirms they were right. The Lord came in glory, as witnessed and described by major historians of that time, exactly as the apostles had predicted.

When a creed contradicts the truth taught by the apostles and replaces it with its opposite, it is not an "Apostolic creed"—it is a direct assault on the teachings of the true apostles.

Now, it is critical to understand that those first churches were under severe assault from the enemy. Constant infiltrations were taking place, spreading false doctrines among the believers to prevent them from entering into the fullness of Jesus Christ. The apostles could barely preach for five minutes before false teachers showed up with distortions. Every New Testament letter they wrote was essentially crisis management—refuting one false teaching after another. Jews especially infiltrated the churches, to stop people from entering into the Kingdom of Christ.

Paul strongly warned the first churches for *false apostles:*

"For such men are <u>false apostles</u>, deceitful workers, disguising themselves as apostles of Christ.

No wonder, for even Satan disguises himself as an angel of light. Therefore it is not surprising if his servants also disguise themselves as servants of righteousness, whose end will be according to their deeds."
—*2 Corinthians 11:13–15*

Paul cautioned the early Christians that Satan was trying to lure them away from the true message of Jesus, just as he did with Eve in the Garden of Eden:

"But I am afraid that, as the serpent deceived Eve by his craftiness, your minds will be led astray from the simplicity and purity of devotion to Christ.
For if one comes and preaches another Jesus whom we have not preached, or you receive a different spirit which you have not received, or a different gospel which you have not accepted, you bear this beautifully."
—*2 Corinthians 11:3–4*

Paul said that *another Jesus* could be preached, they could receive *a different spirit*, and *a different gospel*—and they didn't even flinch. Paul cursed all who are guilty of doing so:

"...though we, or an angel from heaven,
preach any other gospel... let him be accursed."
—*Galatians 1:6–9*

And he instructed the believers to avoid these false apostles:

"Now I urge you, brethren, keep your eye
on those who cause dissensions and hindrances
contrary to the teaching which you learned,
and turn away from them."
—*Romans 16:17*

Paul warned the Church to turn away from those who spread teachings contrary to what the true apostles proclaimed, but his warning fell on deaf ears. The Old Roman Creed slowly gained influence within the churches of Rome until it was finally imposed as a mandatory confession upon the entire worldwide Church. As a result, this false doctrine has been repeated for roughly sixty generations now. Today, billions of Christians still repeat it as the solid foundation of their faith: "Christ will return in the future."

"So you say the origins of the Apostles' Creed are uncertain, and it wasn't written by the apostles themselves. That is shocking.

But you cannot say the same about the Nicene Creed! That creed was established by highly respected bishops and theologians—men who carried authority in the Church—and they formally declared it to be foundational Christian doctrine that Christ will return physically to Earth, in the future."

—*Josh*

Indeed, there is also the Nicene Creed, which is essentially the Apostles' Creed on steroids. In A.D. 325, the Roman Emperor Constantine the Great ordered a council to be convened to establish the official boundaries around what Christians would be required to believe. This took place in the city of Nicaea (modern-day Iznik, Turkey), which is why it became known as the First Council of Nicaea.

The official record claims it was convened to establish the "full divinity of Christ." In reality, something far darker and more sinister was at work.

The Nicene Creed stole the presence of Christ and fullness of His kingdom from the Church.

By declaring that Christ will return in the future it implies He isn't here now, and everyone always has to wait for His presence. This started an endless period during which Christians always waited for the return of Christ — for centuries and even millennia on end.

Instead of entering into the presence of Christ, Christians believed they had to wait for Jesus to return. So they waited, and waited, and waited—for centuries and centuries. Always waiting. Today, almost two thousand years later, they are still waiting...

On a later date, in A.D. 381, another council — the First Council of Constantinople — expanded the Nicene Creed and added a declaration that further reinforced a future-oriented framing of Christ's reign:

**"He will come again in glory (...)
and His kingdom will have no end."**

This added the belief that the Kingdom of Christ is not fully manifested yet, but will only come in its fullness at the return of Christ in an undefined future. With this updated Creed, not only the presence of Christ but also His kingdom was postponed.

However, Christ did not preach a *postponed* kingdom. He proclaimed a *present* one. Jesus didn't come to *delay* God's promises, He came to *fulfill* them. Christ didn't announce, "Your distant descendants will one day find the Kingdom of God." He insisted to His *present* audience, "You must seek to enter the Kingdom of God." Again and again, Christ declared that the Kingdom of God was at work *in their midst.* His miracles, His authority, His casting out of demons, His forgiveness of sins—they proved that the reign of God had arrived.

**"But if I cast out demons by the finger of God,
then the Kingdom of God has come upon you."**
— *Luke 11:20*

Christ told the people how they could enter into His kingdom.

**"Truly I say to you, whoever does not receive the Kingdom
of God like a child will not enter it at all."**
— *Luke 18:17*

Jesus even said to make it their utmost priority to enter His kingdom:

**"But seek first His kingdom and His righteousness,
and all these things will be added to you."**
— *Matthew 6:33*

His disciples declared the good news that the kingdom had come:

**"...and heal those in it who are sick, and say to them,
'The Kingdom of God has come near to you.'"**
— *Luke 10:9*

The Greek word translated "has come near" comes from ἐγγίζω (engizo). In this passage it appears as ἤγγικεν (engiken), which is in the perfect tense, describing *a completed action with ongoing present effect.* In no way, shape, or form does this indicate a delay of the kingdom or a postponement into the distant future. Christ even encouraged His followers to leave all things behind in order to enter into His kingdom:

> **"The Kingdom of Heaven is like a treasure**
> **hidden in the field, which a man found and hid again;**
> **and from joy over it he goes and sells all that he has**
> **and buys that field."**
> — *Matthew 13:44*

Never did Christ or the apostles give even the slightest suggestion that His kingdom was for the future. They demonstrated it as *a present reality* that had come the moment Christ stepped onto the scene and began delivering people from demonic oppression and healing the sick. That is why Christ began His ministry with this declaration from Isaiah:

> "'The Spirit of the Lord is upon Me,
> Because He anointed Me to preach the gospel to the poor.
> He has sent Me to proclaim release to the captives,
> And recovery of sight to the blind,
> To set free those who are oppressed,
> To proclaim the favorable year of the Lord.'"
> And He closed the book, gave it back to the attendant and sat down; and the eyes of all in the synagogue were fixed on Him.
> And He began to say to them,
>
> **'Today this Scripture has been fulfilled in your hearing.'"**
> —*Luke 4:16–21*

Christ came to set the captives free, to open the eyes of the blind, and to proclaim the joyful news that the Kingdom of God had come.

Proclaiming that the Kingdom of God was present, and manifesting the healing power of it, was the essence of His mission and His message. And the apostles continued the same declaration:

> **"For He rescued us from the domain of darkness,**
> **and transferred us to the kingdom of His beloved Son,"**
> —*Colossians 1:13*

CHRIST AND HIS APOSTLES
PRESENTED THE KINGDOM
AS **A PRESENT REALITY,**
NOT AS SOMETHING
FOR THE FUTURE.

Apostle Paul did not say, "we *will be* transferred to His kingdom," rather, he spoke in the past tense: "He *has* transferred us." It was also their message wherever they went:

> **"...preaching the Kingdom of God and teaching concerning the Lord Jesus Christ with all openness, unhindered."**
> —*Acts 28:31*

And, this message was presented and manifested to the people with great supernatural power, demonstrating that it was indeed present *right there and then* — transforming lives in a powerful way.

> **"...and my message and my preaching**
> **were not in persuasive words of wisdom,**
> **but in demonstration of the Spirit and of power,**
> **so that your faith would not rest on the wisdom of men,**
> **but on the power of God."**
> —*1 Corinthians 2:4–5*

Christ explained that His coming on the clouds was to position Him as King in His kingdom:

> **"Truly I say to you, there are some of those who are standing here who will not taste death until they see the Son of Man coming in His kingdom."**
> —*Matthew 16:28*

The truth is as clear as daylight: Christ did not come to *postpone* or *delay* the kingdom that Israel had been waiting for over many centuries. He came to *fulfill* the promises of God and establish it as a *present* reality.

But, the Nicene Council denied the essence of the work and words of Jesus Christ. It stole both the presence and the fullness of the Kingdom of Christ from the Church, and pushed them into a perpetual future.

As a result, countless believers never entered into the fullness of what Christ had for them. Instead, they waited — and waited — and waited — their entire lives. For generations upon generations. For centuries upon centuries. Always waiting. Waiting. Waiting.

Even today, two thousand years later, the internet roars with countless false prophecies across YouTube, TikTok, Facebook, Reddit,

Instagram, Gab, Telegram, and X, convincing hundreds of millions of Christians every single day, that Christ will return "very soon." Innumerable people never plan for their future, never invest in their community, never get involved in the real world, never dream about what God could do in their life— because "Jesus is coming soon."

This false doctrine has sabotaged the lives of billions of believers who were taught that Christ and His kingdom were about to appear "any moment now" — a moment that never comes, because it is continually pushed into the future.

And it can never come closer, because Christ never said He would come in a distant future. He said He would come during the lifetime of the first Jewish believers in Jerusalem.

"What? The Church has been hijacked and sidetracked as far back as the early 4th century? And nobody even flinched? Everyone just went along with it? How is that even possible? How could this false declaration gain such tremendous worldwide authority?"

—*Josh*

It has to do with its origin: Rome. For centuries the Roman Empire murdered the followers of Christ, trying to extinguish their powerful movement, which increasingly became a threat to the control of the Roman emperors. When they saw that this didn't work, they changed strategy: instead of openly *opposing* it, they would now *infiltrate* it.

This happened by ending the persecution of the Church and suddenly accepting it, positioning the Roman Empire as its guardian. It was gladly welcomed by the churches, who gullibly believed their persecutors when they said: "We now see how wrong we were. We will join your faith and will even make it the official state religion of the Roman Empire."

Naturally the Church leaders welcomed this spectacular conversion with wide-open arms. "Hallelujah—the Roman Emperor accepts Christ and makes our faith the official state religion of the Roman Empire!"

What they didn't realize was that from that moment on, Rome became their ruler. And once Rome became the authority over the Church, it began defining the boundaries of what was allowed within it.

For that purpose Roman Emperor Constantine the Great convened the Nicene Council, which took the already circulating Apostles' Creed and expanded upon it.

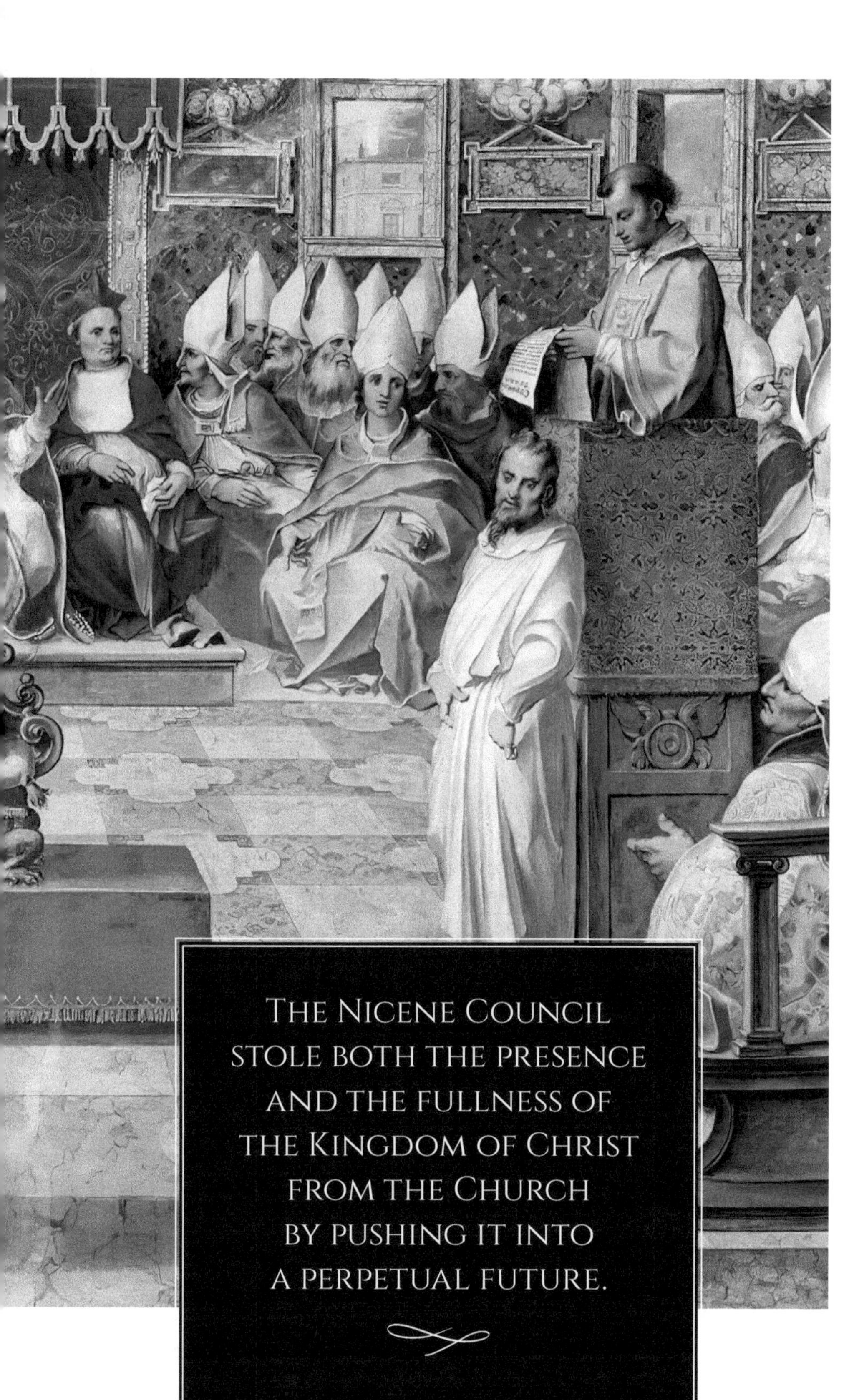

THE NICENE COUNCIL
STOLE BOTH THE PRESENCE
AND THE FULLNESS OF
THE KINGDOM OF CHRIST
FROM THE CHURCH
BY PUSHING IT INTO
A PERPETUAL FUTURE.

Because the creed was issued under the authority of the Roman Empire, it was invested with absolute authority, and every believer was expected to submit to it—or suffer the consequences.

From that moment onwards, the basis of the Christian faith was no longer what Jesus Christ Himself said, or what His true apostles taught, but what this Roman Council issued.

The Nicene Council literally replaced the authority of Jesus Christ, forcing the Church to submit to its decrees rather than to Christ Himself.

The Creed was elevated as untouchable, beyond all biblical testing. Question it, and you are treated as a heretic. Scripture is no longer the standard by which the Creed is examined; instead, Scripture is adjusted to fit the Creed. The direct words of the Lord Jesus Christ are no longer received plainly — they are filtered through the lens of Nicene theology.

The Word of God was literally replaced with the traditions of men. Which is exactly what Jesus confronted in the Pharisees when He said:

> **"...you invalidate the word of God**
> **by your tradition which you have handed down."**
> — *Mark 7:13*

"But sir, it wasn't just men who made this creed—they are considered the Church Fathers! No one holds a higher position of authority in all of Church history. They are literally the fathers of the Church!"

—*Josh*

Really? Do you know what Christ said about this?

> **"Do not call anyone on earth your father;**
> **for One is your Father, He who is in heaven."**
> — *Matthew 23:9*

Christ forbids us from calling anyone but God "father". So why are we calling men from the first centuries "Church Fathers," as if they seeded the Church? It is *Christ* who gave His life and His blood for His Church. No man is the father of the Church—*Jesus Christ is.*

It is time to smash these idols and return — with all our heart, mind, and soul — to Jesus Christ, the ONLY cornerstone of the temple of God.

Jesus Christ never said He would return in a distant future, thousands of years after His first followers lived. He impressed deeply upon their hearts that *they* were to prepare for His coming as something that would happen within *their* lifetimes.

"Do you even realize what you are doing Mr. Sörensen? If you deviate by even one word from the Nicene Creed, you are labeled a heretic! Aren't you worried about that?"

—*Josh*

Not at all. I follow Jesus Christ, no matter what anyone calls me.

If bishops declared beliefs that contradict Jesus Christ and His authentic words, then they are the heretics — not me.

A heretic is not somebody who *abides* in the words of Jesus Christ. A heretic is one who *abandons* the words of Christ.

The Lord Jesus Christ revealed that holding on to His words is proof that we truly love Him:

> **'If anyone loves Me, he will keep My word;**
> **and My Father will love him, and We will come to him**
> **and make Our abode with him.'"**
>
> —*John 14:23*

When Christian leaders step away from the words of Jesus Christ and replace them with something that not only contradicts what He said, but even steals the very essence of His mission—His presence and kingdom among us—they reveal a grave lack of love for the Lord.

And this betrayal of Christ has had terrible consequences throughout history. Before this Roman gathering changed everything, the movement of Christ's followers was not an official religion. It was a powerful, supernatural movement led by the Holy Spirit. It was truly an invasion of Heaven on Earth—liberating countless people from the grip of darkness and ushering them into the Kingdom of God. There they received brand-new life: set free from demons, healed from disease, given a new identity and purpose, elevated as children of the Most High God. It was a life-transforming, supernatural movement—uncontrolled by anyone.

Then the Nicene Council stepped in and began to change all that.

From that moment on, the supernatural, organic, vibrant, explosively expanding Kingdom of Christ was gradually transformed into a state-controlled religion called "Christianity."

But Jesus Christ never spoke of founding a new *religion*; He declared that He came to establish the *Kingdom* of God.

> **"He went through cities and villages, proclaiming and bringing the good news of the Kingdom of God."**
> —*Luke 8:1*

> **"But He said to them, 'I must preach the Kingdom of God to the other cities also, for I was sent for this purpose.'"**
> —*Luke 4:43*

> **Jesus came into Galilee, preaching the gospel of God, and saying, 'The time is fulfilled, and the Kingdom of God is at hand; repent and believe in the gospel.'"**
> —*Mark 1:14-15*

> **"From that time Jesus began to preach and say, 'Repent, for the Kingdom of Heaven is at hand.'"**
> —*Matthew 4:17*

> **'The Kingdom of God is not coming with signs to be observed; nor will they say, "Look, here it is!" or, "There it is!" For behold, the Kingdom of God is in your midst.'"**
> —*Luke 17:20–21*

The Kingdom of God is the most powerful reality in all of creation, where humanity is set free from darkness, healed from iniquity, delivered from bondage, and redeemed as children of God. In Christ's kingdom we become kings who reign with Him — not members of a religion. We are transferred from the kingdom of darkness into the kingdom of light. We receive a new identity, are born again by the Spirit of God, welcomed into His presence, clothed with His power, and sent out as His ambassadors to bring healing to humanity.

But the Nicene Council turned it into an official religion with strict boundaries and enforced beliefs that gutted the Church, removing its most powerful realities: the *presence* and *kingdom* of Christ.

Because of this takeover by the Roman Empire, billions of believers today still think Jesus Christ is far away, somewhere in Heaven, and not truly present in our midst. Instead of walking daily in the fullness of His glorious presence, most Christians wait for Jesus to "return." They also believe the Kingdom of God is not truly here now, but will only come in full force when Christ returns.

Nothing has weakened and sabotaged the Church more than this false declaration.

Ironically the Nicene Creed also opened the door for even worse persecution than before. Anyone who didn't submit to it faced dire consequences. Bishops who refused to sign the creed were removed from office or sent into exile. It marked a diabolical turning point. For the first time, doctrinal disagreement was backed by state power. Theology was no longer defended only with Scripture — it could now be enforced with state violence. From that moment on, persecuting Christians could be officially justified under the label, "They are heretics."

During the Spanish Inquisition, under the authority of Ferdinand II of Aragon and Isabella I of Castile, tribunals interrogated those accused of "heresy." Prisoners could be held for months without knowing the charges against them. Torture was permitted under regulated conditions. Methods included the strappado (where victims were suspended by their wrists, sometimes dropped suddenly to dislocate shoulders), the rack, and water torture designed to simulate drowning. Those who refused to confess or repent could be handed over for execution, often by burning at the stake in public ceremonies known as autos-da-fé.

Over several centuries, countless Christians were executed and many more imprisoned, tortured, or socially ruined.

The Inquisition did not start in 325, but the principle that the state could use violence to force Christians to submit to a certain doctrine did start right there.

Even today, many Christian leaders wrestle privately with questions about the official "Statement of Faith", yet they are terrified to voice dissent publicly. The son of a famous Christian book publisher once called me and said:

> "David, we published all the famous end-times books—the Left Behind series, The Late Great Planet Earth by Hal Lindsey—and we made millions of dollars from them. They sold like hotcakes. We always suspected it was unbiblical, but couldn't

really explain why. Only later did God open our eyes. We then learned that many pastors know the popular end-times narrative is false—but they are terrified to speak out. Once you admit it, you could lose everything. Most won't risk it."

The challenge confronted me too. I had a respected Christian ministry in Europe, when the Lord Jesus came to me and started revealing the truth about His return. I had to make a choice:

Will I follow Christ, or sell Him out for money like Judas?

After a brief struggle I chose to follow Jesus Christ rather than betray Him for the sake of self-preservation and personal gain.

When we choose to defend deception over truly following Christ, the consequence is far graver than we are aware of. We don't merely betray our beloved Lord and Savior—we also betray the people we claim to shepherd. In order to preserve ourselves, we steal from them the glorious presence of Christ that heals, delivers, empowers, and blesses.

And it goes even further.

By keeping believers away from the presence of Christ, we prevent them from walking in His authority as King. As a result, His full power of salvation cannot flow into the world.

It is high time that we finally wake up to this satanic subversion of the saints and return with all our heart and mind to Jesus Christ as our *only* authority. Jesus Christ is our King—not the Roman Emperor. We are servants of Christ—not servants of the Nicene Council.

The Scriptures do not say that every knee will bow before a Roman council. They declare that every knee will bow before Jesus Christ.

> **"...so that at the name of Jesus every knee will bow, of those who are in heaven and on earth and under the earth, and that every tongue will confess that Jesus Christ is Lord, to the glory of God the Father."**
>
> — *Philippians 2:10–11*

I invite you to turn away from the idolatry that we have been submitted to, and return to Christ.

No longer postpone His presence in our midst and continue to move His kingdom into the future, but welcome the Lord who gave His life to be present with us, and enter into His kingdom so His power that heals and delivers can begin to flow in us and through us as never before.

If you want to make this decision to truly follow Jesus Christ, instead of being a servant of the Roman Empire, then pray this prayer with me:

"Lord Jesus Christ,

I come to You with all my heart,
and I lay my life before You.

You are the One who died for me — not the Nicene Council.
Therefore, You alone are my Savior and my Lord.

I repent of submitting myself to a council in ancient Rome,
who positioned themselves — under the rule of Roman Emperor
Constantine the Great — as the authority over Your Kingdom.

I now acknowledge that it was not inspired by Your Holy Spirit,
but part of a strategy of the Great Deceiver
who opposes Your Kingdom and seeks control over Your Church.

I turn away from that, and I submit myself
fully to You again, Lord Jesus Christ.

I return to You, with all my heart.

You alone are my King.
You alone are my authority.

I worship You alone and I listen to Your words alone.
Thank You for saving me and guiding me in Your truth.

Thank You for Your presence right here with me,
and thank You for welcoming me into Your Kingdom.

Amen."

CHAPTER 11

Vengeance Is Mine

"Mr. Sörensen, I must say that this is a massive bummer for me. All my life I was told that when Christ returned, He'd instantly turn this world into a perfect paradise. A brand-new creation without pain and sickness. A literal Heaven on Earth. But that hasn't happened. If what you're saying is true—and I can hardly deny it, since you've shown it straight from Jesus' own words—then this is a terrible disappointment. Do you realize that? Where's the pristine paradise we were promised after Christ's return?"

—*Josh*

I totally understand your disappointment, Josh. This is exactly why this deception became so wildly popular in the first place.Who wouldn't sign up for a dazzling utopia that falls straight out of the sky into your backyard? It's the ultimate Christian "get-rich-quick scheme": Jesus will return and all your dreams will come true in the twinkling of an eye without lifting a finger. Wow. No wonder the Church swallowed it whole!

But you need to understand something: that fantasy of instant paradise was carefully engineered to steal the *real treasure* from us—something *infinitely more glorious*. What is that treasure? The breathtaking reality of living in Christ's presence now. Walking in His authority *today*. Reigning with Him as heavenly kings and queens, here on Earth.

Think about it: being true sons and daughters of the Most High, filled with His Spirit, carrying His authority, backed by Heaven's armies to heal the sick, cast out demons, confront corruption, and set captives free. What greater privilege could there be than to collaborate with the Creator of all that exists? To be His mouthpiece on the Earth, His hands and feet, the very expression of His heart—manifesting His goodness and deliverance wherever we go. To be burning torches of the fiery hosts of Heaven, lighting blazes of transformation in government, healthcare, technology, finance, education, and even entertainment.

That's where the *real* glory is! To be clothed in the radiance of the Almighty, walking into the darkest corners of the world and setting them ablaze with joy and hope. To watch the faces of Satan's prisoners—once twisted with despair—suddenly erupt with jubilation as the power of Christ surges through them. To see Hell on Earth overturned into Heaven on Earth, demons fleeing in terror, and angels of restoration flooding in to reclaim territory for the King.

That is our calling. *That* is our destiny. Not waiting for paradise to fall from the sky like a divine slot machine jackpot—but rising up in His power and turning the world upside down. Jesus Himself said it:

> **"Truly, truly I say to you, the one who believes in Me, the works that I do, he will do also; and greater works than these he will do, because I am going to the Father."**
> —*John 14:12*

And this is exactly what the prophets foresaw long ago:

> **"Arise, shine; for your light has come,**
> **and the glory of the Lord has risen upon you.**
> **For behold, darkness will cover the earth**
> **and deep darkness the peoples;**
> **but the Lord will rise upon you**
> **and His glory will appear upon you.**
> **Nations will come to your light,**
> **and kings to the brightness of your rising."**
> —*Isaiah 60:1–3*

That is the true vision. Not a lazy fantasy of Heaven falling into our laps, but the fiery destiny of God's people, blazing with His light until the nations stream to His glory.

It's not the fairy tale where roasted chickens come flying straight into our mouths. It's something infinitely better: a divine invitation to grow up into royal sons and daughters of the Almighty. To cultivate character, develop discipline, and willingly walk with the Lord so we become gateways of His glory.

God created us to be His anointed ambassadors who represent Him wherever we go—reflections of our Heavenly Father, just as Jesus Christ. He is our example, and He made it clear:

> **"For I gave you an example,**
> **so that you also would do just as I did for you."**
> —*John 13:15*

Jesus, who cast out demons, healed the sick and confronted the satanic religious leaders, is our example! Can you grasp the magnitude of that statement? We are not called to be religious, we are called to be royal! But let's be honest... that's not nearly as comfortable as imagining Jesus swooping down to do all the heavy lifting while we lounge on the couch, munching chips, and watching the Rapture Channel.

"Okay... yeah, I can see your point. Christ came to make us into warriors of Heaven, who cast out Hell on Earth. That is powerful!

But Mr. Sörensen: if the coming of Christ wasn't what I was told—no instant paradise dropping out of the sky, no fairy-tale ending on demand—then what was it? What have I missed, all my life?"

—*Josh*

That's a very important question, Josh — and the answer will transform everything you've ever heard or believed. But it won't be easy to digest. Are you ready to set aside the baby bottles of sugary mush and feast on the nutritious meat of God's Word?

Let's turn away, once again, from all the false prophecies on the Internet and proclaimed from Church platforms, and instead listen to what the Lord Jesus Christ actually said about His return.

He said about this event:

> "For the Son of Man will come
> in the glory of His Father with His angels,
> and then **He will repay** each according to his works."
> —*Matthew 16:27*

So the coming of Jesus on the clouds would be to *repay* each according to his works. Just as the apostles said:

"When the Lord Jesus is revealed from heaven
with His mighty angels, **in flaming fire taking vengeance**
on those who do not know God, and on those
who do not obey the gospel of our Lord Jesus Christ."
— *2 Thessalonians 1:6-8*

"**'Vengeance is Mine, I will repay,' says the Lord.
And again, 'The Lord will judge His people.'**
... For yet a little while, and He who is coming will come
and will not tarry."
— *Hebrews 10:31, 37*

"Establish your hearts, for the coming of the Lord
is at hand. ... Behold, **the Judge** is standing at the door!"
— *James 5:8, 9*

"Now I saw heaven opened, and behold, a white horse.
And He who sat on him was called Faithful and True,
and in righteousness **He judges and makes war."**
— *Revelation 19:11*

Can you see it? Whenever the apostles spoke of Christ's coming, they framed it as *judgment*, not the inauguration of a global utopia. They consistently warned: *He is coming to execute judgment.* This theme runs like a scarlet thread through the Old Testament.

The prophet Isaiah declared:

**"For behold, the Lord will come with fire
and with His chariots, like a whirlwind,
to render His anger with fury,
and His rebuke with flames of fire."**
— *Isaiah 66:15*

Zephaniah confirmed:

**"The great day of the Lord is near
and coming quickly. Listen!**

The day of the Lord is a day of darkness and gloom,
a day of clouds and blackness."
— *Zephaniah 1:14-15*

Jeremiah spoke the same:

"Behold, he shall come up as clouds,
and his chariots shall be as a whirlwind:
his horses are swifter than eagles.
Woe unto us! for we are spoiled."
—*Jeremiah 4:13-14*

And the prophet Micah agreed:

"Look! The Lord is coming from his dwelling place;
he comes down and treads on the heights of the earth.
Zion shall be plowed like a field,
Jerusalem shall become heaps of ruins,
and the mountain of the temple
like the bare hills of the forest."
— *Micah 1:3, 3:10, 12*

According to Isaiah, Zephaniah, Jeremiah, and Micah, the coming of the Lord on the clouds, was to *execute His anger* on a day of darkness and destruction. The coming of the Lord signified terrible judgment—not a worldly paradise, but *divine reckoning.*

"What the heck, Mr. Sörensen, this is wild! While I've been dreaming of a heavenly theme park falling from the sky, the actual Scriptures literally say the opposite: Jesus would come to execute terrible vengeance—raw wrath from God. But *who* would be judged in such a devastating way? Who was the object of God's fury?"
—*Josh*

Indeed, the sobering biblical truth stands in stark contrast to the Hollywood stories that have been buzzing in our ears all our lives. And to answer your question—who would suffer God's wrath—we must again take a careful look at the Scriptures, without manipulating or twisting them, as the Church of our time has been doing so relentlessly.

The theme of God's wrath is one of the most foundational messages throughout the Old Testament, voiced over and over again by all of God's prophets. They continuously declared who would be struck with the hammer of the Lord on His day of vengeance: it is none other than *Israel.*

One clear example of Israel being the subject of God's fury is found in Matthew 23 where Jesus declared judgment over the leaders of Israel, because they continually blocked others from entering God's Kingdom:

> "Woe to you, scribes and Pharisees, hypocrites, because **you shut the kingdom of heaven in front of people**; for you do not enter it yourselves, nor do you allow those who are entering to go in." — *vs. 13*

Christ condemns them because they are *children of hell:*

> "Woe to you, scribes and Pharisees, hypocrites, because you travel around on sea and land to make one proselyte; and when he becomes one, **you make him twice as much a son of hell as yourselves."** — *vs. 15*

They appear righteous but inwardly they are *wicked*:

> "Woe to you, scribes and Pharisees, hypocrites! For you are like whitewashed tombs which on the outside appear beautiful, but inside they are full of dead men's bones and all uncleanness. So you too, outwardly appear righteous to people, but inwardly **you are full of hypocrisy and lawlessness."** — *vs. 27-28*

Jesus calls them the *sons of those who murdered the prophets:*

> "You testify against yourselves, that **you are sons of those who murdered the prophets.** Fill up, then, the measure of the guilt of your fathers." — *vs. 31-32*

The Lord said Israels leaders were *snakes and vipers:*

> **"You snakes, you offspring of vipers,**
> **how will you escape the sentence of hell?"** — *vs. 33*

Finally Christ announced that they would now *face God's fury:* "Therefore, behold, I am sending you prophets and wise men

> and scribes; some of them you will kill and crucify, and some of them you will flog in your synagogues, and persecute from city to city, so that upon you will fall the guilt of all the righteous blood shed on earth, from the blood of righteous Abel to the blood of Zechariah, the son of Berechiah, whom you murdered between the temple and the altar. **Truly I say to you, all these things will come upon this generation."** — *vs. 34-36*

God had reached out again and again, but they rejected Him every time, even killing His prophets. Now the moment of reckoning had come. Jerusalem would be *destroyed:*

> "Jerusalem, Jerusalem, who kills the prophets and stones those who have been sent to her! How often I wanted to gather your children together, the way a hen gathers her chicks under her wings, and you were unwilling. **Behold, your house is being left to you desolate!"** — *vs. 37-38*

Right after Christ announced the destruction of Jerusalem, He pointed His disciples to the temple and declared that not one stone would be left upon another. Even the Holy of Holies, the very place of God's presence within Israel, would be torn down to the last stone:

> "His disciples came up to show Him the buildings of the temple. And Jesus said to them, 'Do you not see all these things? Assuredly, I say to you, **not one stone shall be left here upon another, that shall not be thrown down.'"**
> — *Matthew 24:1, 2*

Of course the disciples asked the natural question: *when* would this happen? Pay careful attention to their wording:

> **"Tell us, when will these things be?**
> **And what will be the sign of Your coming,**
> **and of the end of the age?"**
> — *Matthew 24:3*

Do you notice what they actually asked Jesus?

"When will this judgment be and when will You come?"

They directly linked the coming of Christ on the clouds to the judgment of Israel. The disciples understood this because, throughout the Old Testament, the language of "coming on the clouds" consistently signifies judgment. That is why, when Jesus spoke about the destruction of the temple, they immediately asked Him what the sign of His coming would be. The *coming* of the Lord and *judgment* are interconnected.

Jesus answered that false Christs would arise, there would be wars and rumors of wars, famines and earthquakes in various places, and severe persecution would be unleashed upon those who followed Him. In the chapter on the historical record, we saw how this detailed prophecy of Jesus Christ was indeed fulfilled precisely in the way He described it.

Then Jesus continued addressing His Jewish disciples in Jerusalem:

> "Therefore when you see the abomination of desolation
> which was spoken of through Daniel the prophet,
> standing in the holy place—let the reader understand—
> **then those who are in Judea must flee to the mountains.**
> **Whoever is on the housetop must not go down**
> **to get things out of his house.**
> And whoever is in the field must not turn back to get his cloak.
> But woe to those women who are pregnant,
> and to those who are nursing babies in those days!
> Moreover, pray that when you flee,
> it will not be in the winter, **or on a Sabbath."**
> — *Matthew 24:15–20*

I highlighted certain words, such as "those in Judea," "flee to the mountains," "on the housetop," and "on a Sabbath," because Matthew 24 has been grotesquely contorted to manufacture fear-based doctrines that have been spread throughout the Western Church—among people living thousands of years later and thousands of miles away from ancient Jerusalem.

We do not live in Judea, nor do we all live near mountains. None of us live on rooftops, and we do not observe the Sabbath, because we are not Jews. We must stop abusing the Bible to fabricate freaky fairy tales that lead people into deep deception—simply because we enjoy scaring the life out of them while filling our pockets with money given to ease their fear. When we respect the biblical text, we see that Jesus was directly preparing the very Jewish people standing right there in front of Him, for events they needed to prepare for.

Christ declared **judgment over Israel,** foretelling that at His coming Jerusalem and the temple would be destroyed.

Jesus went on to explain that among His Jewish followers there were two different types: wise and foolish virgins (Matthew 25:1-13). The wise kept His warnings alive in their hearts — and the foolish neglected the call to remain watchful during God's judgment over Israel.

Again, we were told that the virgins represent modern-day believers, and that we must make sure to keep our lamps burning. But Jesus wasn't speaking to New Yorkers, Hongkongers, Swiss, Bruxellois, or South Africans in the 21st century. He was addressing the Jews in Jerusalem, whose city was about to be smashed to smithereens.

Next, Jesus explained to them *how* the judgment would be executed. The people would not be judged based on their outward religious performance. No, Christ made it clear what truly mattered: did they care for the hurting, the poor, the prisoners, and those in need — or did they ignore them? Those who had lived with compassion toward others would be welcomed into His kingdom, while those who showed no care for the hurting would face judgment (Matthew 25:31-46).

This is the heartbeat of what God required of Israel throughout the Old Covenant. He called Israel to be a people of compassion.

> **"Learn to do good; seek justice, rebuke the oppressor, obtain justice for the orphan, plead for the widow's case."**
> *—Isaiah 1:17*

> **"Administer true justice and show mercy and compassion to one another."**
> *—Zechariah 7:9*

But instead of caring for the poor, Israel oppressed them. Widows were exploited, orphans neglected, and the needy trampled underfoot. Justice was perverted for profit, and compassion was replaced by greed.

> **"They do not obtain justice for the orphan, nor does the widow's case come before them."'**
> *—Isaiah 1:21–23*

> **"They sell the righteous for money and the needy for a pair of sandals. These who trample the head of the helpless into the dust of the earth and divert the way of the humble."**
> *—Amos 2:6–7*

"Your sins are great, you who are hostile to the righteous, who take bribes, and turn away the poor from justice at the gate."

—Amos 5:12

"Now hear this, you heads of the house of Jacob
and rulers of the house of Israel,
who despise justice and twist everything that is straight,
who build Zion with bloodshed
and Jerusalem with malice.
Her leaders pronounce judgment for a bribe,
her priests teach for pay,
and her prophets divine for money."

—Micah 3:9–11

Time and again, God sent His prophets to plead with them to turn back — to seek justice, love mercy, and walk humbly with their God — yet they hardened their hearts until judgment became inevitable.

"The people of the land have practiced oppression
and committed robbery,
and they have wronged the poor and needy
and have oppressed the stranger without justice.
So I have poured out My indignation on them."

—Ezekiel 22:29–31

"They have become fat, they are sleek;
they also excel in deeds of wickedness.
They do not plead the cause,
the cause of the orphan, so that they may prosper;
and they do not defend the rights of the poor.
Shall I not punish these people?" declares the Lord.

—Jeremiah 5:28–29

That is why Christ announced judgment over them. Jerusalem would be destroyed, and the temple would be torn down to the last stone. It would mark the end of an era. And Christ would come on the clouds to be established as King in a new kingdom under a new covenant. That is the clear biblical message—not San Francisco being nuked, Dubai being engulfed by quicksand, or Melbourne falling apart.

"But Mr. Sörensen, how is that possible? I've always learned in church that God loves the Jewish people—that He actually adores them and considers them the very apple of His eye. He always blesses them, never wishes them harm, right? How can you then say God was furious with them and Jesus came to judge them?"

—*Josh*

I know—that's exactly what you've heard on constant repeat, autoplayed across Christian television and echoed from pulpits in most churches all your life. But once again, the actual biblical truth is the *exact opposite* of what the wealthy celebrity pastors from corrupt megachurches have been feeding us.

The Bible is crystal clear: *Israel was indescribably wicked.* Corrupt to the core. In many ways outright satanic. They trampled everything God commanded, murdered His prophets, worshipped demons, slaughtered their own children, practiced sorcery and witchcraft—the list goes on. Scripture literally says Jerusalem had become *a prostitute.* The pure virgin of the Almighty had become the "Whore of Babylon."

"For long ago I broke your yoke and tore off your shackles;
but you said, 'I will not serve!'
For on every high hill and under every leafy tree
you have lain down as a prostitute."

—*Jeremiah 2:20*

Ezekiel paints the same tragic picture:

"But you trusted in your beauty
and used your fame to become a prostitute.
You poured out your prostitution
on every passerby who was willing."

—*Ezekiel 16:15*

Israel welcomed all forms of idolatry, child sacrifice, ritual abuse, and unspeakable atrocities. She threw back her sheets and invited every dark and twisted practice into her inner courts. And in the end, God gave Israel the name of the city that embodied demon worship itself: *Babylon.*

"Then one of the seven angels who had
the seven bowls came and spoke with me, saying,

'Come here, I will show you the judgment of
the great prostitute who sits on many waters,
with whom the kings of the earth
committed acts of sexual immorality,
and those who live on the earth became drunk
with the wine of her sexual immorality.'

And he carried me away in the Spirit into a wilderness;
and I saw **a woman sitting on a scarlet beast,**
of blasphemous names, having seven heads
and ten horns.

The woman was clothed in purple and scarlet,
and adorned with gold, precious stones, and pearls,
holding in her hand a gold cup full of abominations
and of the unclean things of her sexual immorality,
and on her forehead a name was written, a mystery:

"BABYLON THE GREAT,
THE MOTHER OF PROSTITUTES
AND OF THE ABOMINATIONS OF THE EARTH."

And I saw the woman drunk with the blood of the saints,
and with the blood of the witnesses of Jesus."
— *Revelation 17:1-5*

Jerusalem had become a dwelling place of demons:

"Fallen, fallen is Babylon the great!
She has become a dwelling place of demons
and a prison of every unclean spirit."
— *Revelation 18:2*

The way God described Israel is far worse than we realize. Israel is depicted sitting on a dragon with seven heads. Do you understand this is Satan in person? He is called "the dragon".

"Then another sign appeared in heaven:
and behold, **a great red dragon having seven heads**
and ten horns, and on his heads were seven crowns.

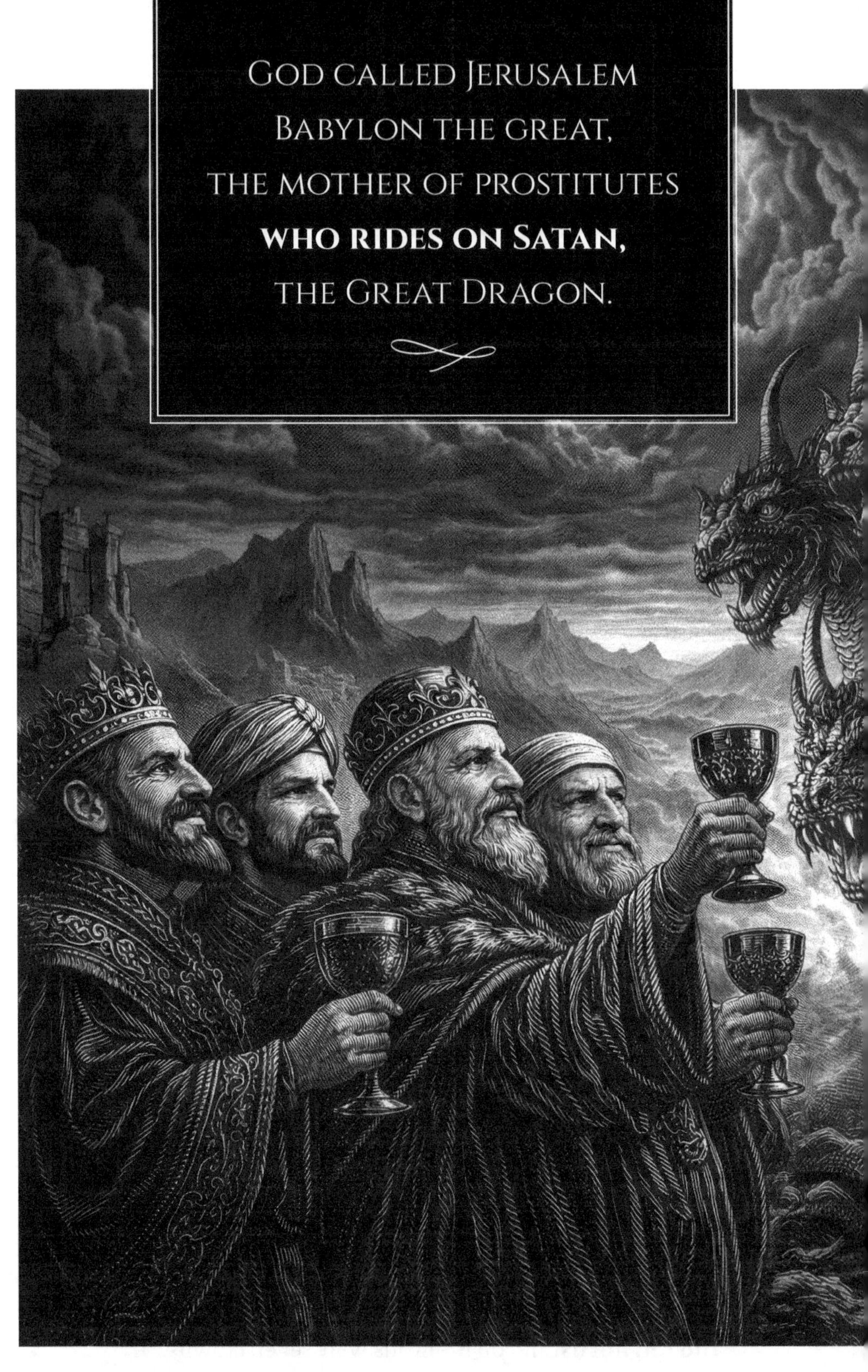
God called Jerusalem
Babylon the great,
the mother of prostitutes
who rides on Satan,
the Great Dragon.

(...) And the great dragon was thrown down,
the serpent of old **who is called the devil and Satan,**
who deceives the whole world; he was thrown down to the earth, and his angels were thrown down with him."

— *Revelation 3-9*

God went as far as calling Israel "Sodom and Gomorrah":

"The vision of Isaiah concerning Judah and Jerusalem...
Hear the word of the LORD, you rulers of Sodom;
listen to the instruction of our God,
you people of Gomorrah."

— *Isaiah 1:1, 9, 10*

The Lord even said that Israel was worse than Sodom:

"Now your older sister is Samaria... and your
younger sister, who lives to the south of you, is Sodom...
you acted more corruptly in all your conduct than they."

— *Ezekiel 16:46–47*

Sodom and Gomorrah were cities where indescribable sexual perversion was considered normal. The severity of the sexual violence was so atrocious that the entire city—including children (!)—marched to Lot's house, where he had welcomed visiting angels in human form, demanding that they be allowed to rape these men all night long.

Imagine a city where even children participate in gang-raping strangers (Genesis 19:4–5). That is what Sodom and Gomorrah were. And God said Israel was even *worse* than them.

God also said that Jerusalem—where Christ was killed—was "Egypt", the occult nation known for it's severe demon worship:

"Their dead bodies will lie in the street of the great city,
which mystically is called Sodom and Egypt,
where also their Lord was crucified."

—*Revelation 11:8*

In Ezekiel chapter 8, God took the prophet and broke through thick walls, into hidden underground temples where the leaders of Israel were committing the most horrendous abominations:

"Son of man, now dig through the wall."
So I dug through the wall, and behold, an entrance.
Then He said to me, "Go in and see the wicked
abominations that they are committing here."
So I entered and looked, and behold,
every form of crawling things and animals
and detestable things,"
—*Ezekiel 8:8-9*

This is one of the most revealing chapters in the entire Bible, where God takes His prophet and leads him to the hidden rooms where the leaders of Israel were committing every form of wicked abomination.

What had become of Israel is beyond anything we have ever heard in any sermon that has ever been preached in the modern day churches. According to the undefiled Word of God, Israel — chosen by God to be His holy dwelling place — became the very opposite: the mother of all prostitutes, riding upon Satan, the dragon and the beast. The people whom God rescued from Egypt, fed in the wilderness, blessed with His presence, and called to be His household betrayed Him again and again—until Israel became "children of the devil," as Christ Himself declared:

"You are of your father the devil,
and you want to do the desires of your father. "
—*John 8:44*

They had rejected their true Father—the God of love and truth—and chose to become the offspring of Satan. They turned into "sons of hell" and "serpents," just as Satan is the "Serpent of Old":

"You snakes, you offspring of vipers,
how will you escape the sentence of hell?"
— *Matthew 23:33*

"Woe to you, scribes and Pharisees, hypocrites,
because you travel around on sea and land
to make one proselyte; and when he becomes one,
you make him twice as much a son of hell as yourselves."
— *Matthew 23:15*

And indeed the sins of Israel were absolutely monstrous.

They even sacrificed their own children to Satan:

**"They are guilty of adultery and murder.
They have taken part in adultery with their idols.
They even offered our children as sacrifices
in the fire to be food for these idols."**
— *Ezekiel 23:37-40*

**"They even sacrificed their sons and their daughters
to the demons and shed innocent blood,
the blood of their sons and their daughters,
whom they sacrificed to the idols of Canaan."**
— *Psalms 106:37, 38*

**"They have filled this place with the blood of the innocent
and have built the high places of Baal
to burn their sons in the fire as burnt offerings to Baal,"**
John 3:10 *Jeremiah 19:3-5*

That is why God said He would totally destroy Israel—it would be cut down like a rotten tree:

**"Israel will be like a tree cut down,
whose stump still lives to grow again."**
— *Isaiah 6:13 TLB*

**"And it will again be subject to burning,
like a terebinth or an oak whose stump remains
when it is felled."**
— *Isaiah 6:13*

**"The royal line of David will be cut off,
chopped down like a tree;"**
— *Isaiah 11:1*

The prophet Zechariah announced that the Lord would come with all the holy ones, to judge Jerusalem:

**"For I will gather all the nations against Jerusalem
to battle...**

Then the Lord, my God, will come,
and all the holy ones with Him!"
— *Zechariah 14:2-5*

Only a small remnant would survive:

"For though your people, Israel,
may be like the sand of the sea,
Only a remnant within them will return;
A destruction is determined,
overflowing with righteousness.
For a complete destruction,
one that is determined, the Lord God of armies
will execute in the midst of the whole land."
— *Isaiah 10:22-23*

Before Jesus Christ appeared on the scene, to deliver this lethal blow to Israel, He was preceeded by John the Baptist, who prepared the way of the Lord. Guess what his message was?

"The axe is already laid at the root of the trees;
therefore, every tree that does not bear good fruit
is cut down and thrown into the fire."
— *Matthew 3:10*

The judgment of God over Israel is a central thread woven throughout the Old and the New Testament. Again and again, the prophets and apostles warned: when the Lord comes on the clouds, it will be to execute judgment upon His own people who have betrayed Him.

This is why Jesus declared, when He stood before the Jewish High Council that was about to condemn Him to death:

"You will see the Son of Man...
coming on the clouds of heaven."
— *Matthew 26:64*

Jesus was warning the supreme leaders of Israel that *they themselves* would live to see Him come in power to destroy the city and temple they had defiled. Paul the Apostle echoed this same truth, pointing to the guilt of the Jews who had rejected the Messiah:

"For you, brethren, became imitators of
the churches of God in Christ Jesus that are **in Judea,**
for you also endured the same sufferings at the hands
of your own countrymen, even as they did from
**the Jews, who both killed the Lord Jesus
and the prophets and drove us out.
They are not pleasing to God, but hostile to all men,**
hindering us from speaking to the Gentiles so that they
may be saved; with the result that they always
fill up the measure of their sins.
But wrath has come upon them to the utmost."
— *1 Thessalonians 2:14-16*

And again:

"The Lord will pay back trouble to those who trouble you
and give relief to you who are troubled, and to us as well.
This will happen when the Lord Jesus is revealed
from heaven in blazing fire with His powerful angels,
**in flaming fire taking vengeance on those who
do not know God, and on those who do not obey
the gospel of our Lord Jesus Christ."**
— *2 Thessalonians 1:6-8*

The sheer number of passages that link the coming of the Lord to judgment upon Israel should silence all doubt. Yet somehow, the modern Church ignores this overwhelming testimony, twisting the prophecies into warnings about America, Russia, China, or Europe—anyone but the true biblical and historical target.

The way the Church has manipulated and abused the Word of God to spread radically anti-scriptural beliefs among billions of unsuspecting believers is, without exaggeration, *one of the greatest frauds in all of human history.* The truth is written so plainly across both the Old and New Testament. And yet, so-called "scholars," "theologians," "Bible teachers," and "exegetes" have mastered the diabolical craft of twisting the words of the prophets, Jesus Christ, and the apostles into something entirely different. And they've done it so persuasively that they've managed to convince millions of pastors, elders, ministry leaders, and church members. All marching along, nodding in agreement, swallowing these grave perversions of God's Word without a single question.

ISRAEL SACRIFICED CHILDREN TO BAAL, WHOSE BRONZE HANDS WERE HEATED UNTIL THEY GLOWED — AND BABIES PLACED IN THEM BURNED ALIVE.

THE WAY MANY PREACHERS **MANIPULATE THE BIBLE** TO SPREAD RADICALLY ANTI-SCRIPTURAL BELIEFS IS ONE OF THE GREATEST FRAUDS IN ALL OF HISTORY.

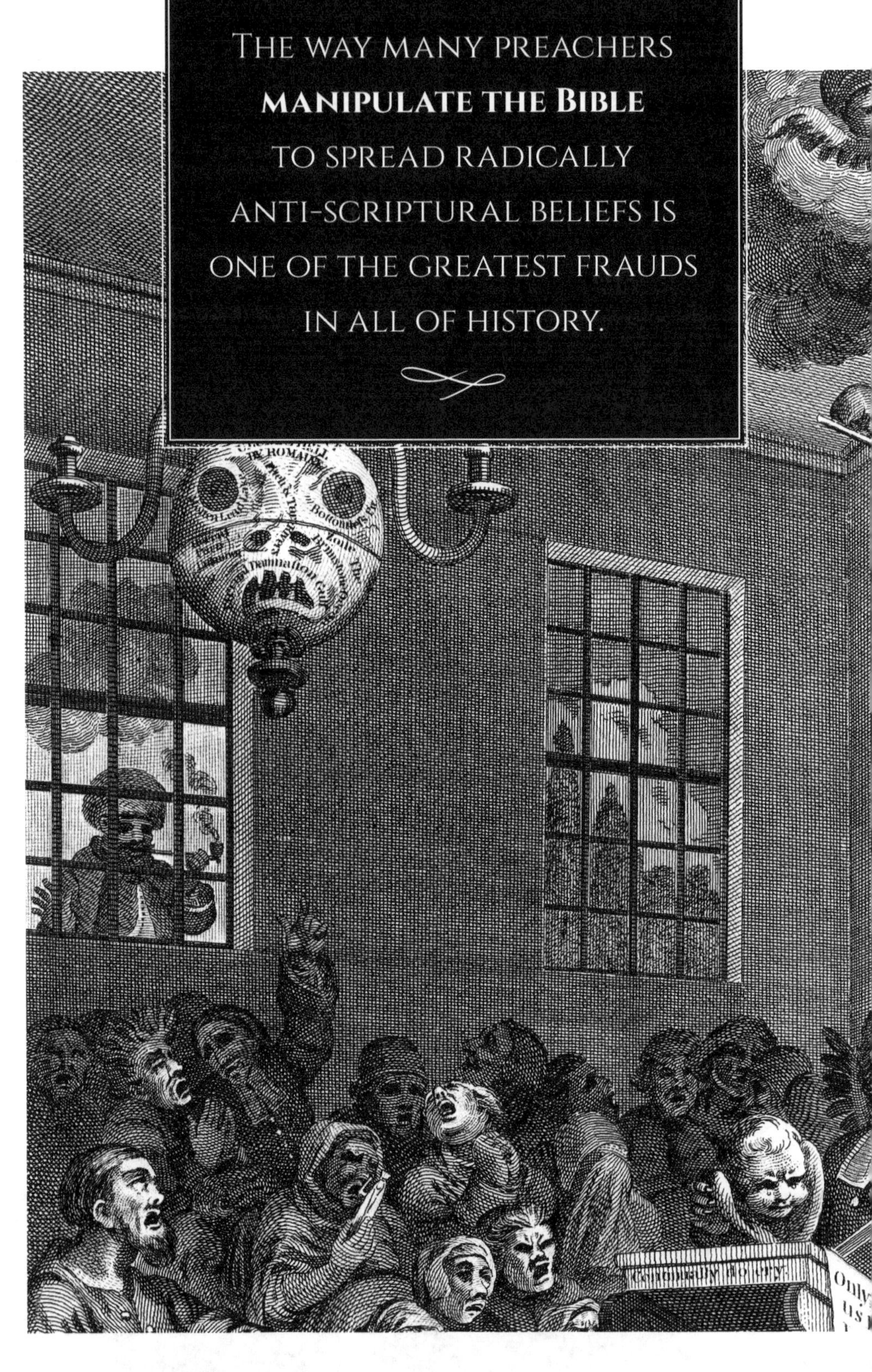

Blood
Blood
Blood
Bull Roar
W—d's Scale of Vociferation
90
80
70
60
50
40
30
20
10
Natl. Tone
Ted-
worth

This twisting of Scripture goes hand in hand with a habit of spiritual laziness that has become a common trait of modern-day Christianity. We no longer study the Bible as a whole. We don't compare one book to another. We don't trace context through history and culture. We don't respect the biblical audience, nor the biblical timeframes. No—we run straight to a single verse, rip it out of its setting, and spin it into whatever circus act we want. Then we parade that verse on stage, or on YouTube, while proclaiming the most ridiculous ideas imaginable—fantasies that literally wreck the lives, futures, dreams, and destinies of the very people we're supposed to shepherd.

We don't *study* the Bible—we *abuse* it. We don't listen to Christ's words—we toss them aside and replace them with our own bizarre imaginations that we foolishly call "theology".

When it comes to the topic of the Lord's coming, how many of us actually immerse ourselves in the entire Gospel of Matthew? Practically none. Instead, we skip over the first twenty-three chapters completely and fixate on a single verse that mentions the word "coming." Then, with breathtaking blindness, we parade that one verse as if it were the whole counsel of God and call it "Bible study."

A typical example of how Scripture has been shamelessly twisted, is Revelation 6:

> "The kings of the earth, the great men, the rich men,
> the commanders, the mighty men, every slave and free man,
> **hid themselves in the caves**
> **and in the rocks of the mountains,**
> and said to the mountains and rocks,
> 'Fall on us and hide us from the face of Him
> who sits on the throne and from the wrath of the Lamb!
> For the great day of His wrath has come,
> and who is able to stand?'"
> — *Revelation 6:15–17*

Some preachers use this verse to claim that God will pour out such wrath on all humanity that the entire world will scramble to hide underground. But John was not predicting a global doomsday. He was simply quoting Isaiah, who told us exactly who these people would be:

> "The word that Isaiah the son of Amoz saw
> **concerning Judah and Jerusalem.**

Enter into the rock... from the terror of the Lord
and the glory of His majesty."
— *Isaiah 2:1, 10*

Again, the terror of the Lord was not aimed at Amsterdam, Helsinki, London, Moscow, or San Diego. No—it was coming full force on *those who had slaughtered God's prophets* in order to defend their blood-soaked altars of child sacrifice and their unrestrained sexual perversions in Israel. Century after century they carried on their horrors, and when the apostles finally came to proclaim the good news of the Kingdom of God, the Jews hunted them down like roaring lions.

But, the coming of Christ would bring that reign of terror to a screeching halt.

A New Kingdom In Christ

"Still, I don't understand it, sir. For the past decades, my mind has been pounded incessantly by preachers proclaiming that God is faithful to Israel—that He has not given up on her and will rebuild her. How can I reconcile that with the wrath unleashed against Israel?"
—*Josh*

That is indeed all you will ever hear from the bought and corrupted mouthpieces of modern-day Israel. They carefully select only those verses where God promises restoration to Israel, and claim the modern day political and military state is that fulfilment. But they cunningly leave out the most central truth in all of Scripture: that this renewal would come *in and through Jesus Christ.* He rebuilt Israel, according to God's promises. As Jesus and the apostles proclaimed, out of the ashes of wrath came a glorious *new* beginning. This is what we call "the good news"—the Gospel.

The death of earthly Israel meant the birth of the heavenly kingdom through Jesus Christ.

The Old Covenant system—corrupted, polluted, and defiled beyond redemption—had to be torn down so that the New Covenant could rise unshaken. The temple of stone, once a den of thieves, had to crumble so that the living temple of redeemed hearts could be built. The priesthood of wicked men had to be abolished so that the eternal High Priest could take His rightful place forever.

When the axe struck the root, it was not an *end*—it was a *beginning.* The tree of Israel was cut down, yes, but from its stump, the true Branch sprouted. Not another corrupt human dynasty, but the very Son of God—the Faithful and True—whose reign will never end.

"He shakes his fist at the mountain of the daughter of Zion,
the hill of Jerusalem. Behold, the Lord, the God of armies,
will **lop off the branches** with terrifying power;
Those also who are tall in stature will be **cut down,**
And those who are lofty will be brought low.
He will cut down the thickets of the forest
with an iron axe,
And Lebanon will fall by the Mighty One.

Then a shoot will spring from the stem of Jesse,
And a Branch from his roots will bear fruit.

The Spirit of the Lord will rest on Him,
The spirit of wisdom and understanding,
The spirit of counsel and strength,
The spirit of knowledge and the fear of the Lord.

And He will delight in the fear of the Lord,
And He will not judge by what His eyes see,
Nor make decisions by what His ears hear;
But with righteousness He will judge the poor,
And decide with fairness for the humble of the earth;
And He will strike the earth with the rod of His mouth,
And with the breath of His lips He will slay the wicked.
Also righteousness will be the belt around His hips,
And faithfulness the belt around His waist. (...)

Then you will say on that day, "I will give thanks to You, Lord;
For although You were angry with me,
Your anger is turned away, and You comfort me.
Behold, God is my salvation, I will trust and not be afraid;
For the Lord God is my strength and song,

And He has become my salvation."
Therefore you will joyously draw water
From the springs of salvation.

And on that day you will say,
"Give thanks to the Lord, call on His name.
Make known His deeds among the peoples;
Make them remember that His name is exalted."
Praise the Lord in song, for He has done glorious things;
Let this be known throughout the earth.
Rejoice and shout for joy, you inhabitant of Zion,
For great in your midst is the Holy One of Israel."
— *Isaiah 10-12*

God announced as clear as daylight that His faithfulness to the remnant of Israel would be revealed through the Branch—Jesus Christ. Through Him, the love of God would be shown to those who had remained faithful. He is the One who would bring salvation.

That is the very essence of the message of the Bible, both Old and New Covenant: God judged Israel for its sins and brought salvation to the remnant through Jesus Christ.

The faithfulness of God to Israel is not demonstrated through another violent state of terror and wickedness, but is manifested in all its glory in the brand-new holy Kingdom of God, brought about by His own Son, Jesus Christ.

This was the kingdom Daniel had seen in his vision: a stone not cut by human hands, striking the kingdoms of this world and becoming a mountain that filled the whole Earth. This was the reign foretold by Isaiah, Jeremiah, Micah, and Zechariah—the government of righteousness, justice, and peace that would rest upon the shoulders of the Messiah.

From the ashes of judgment, a new creation was birthed. From the ruins of the old Jerusalem, the New Jerusalem descends. From the blood-soaked soil of the Old Covenant rose the everlasting Kingdom of God.

This was the fulfillment of the countless prophecies throughout the centuries of the old covenant. Again and again, God announced the end of that dark era and the birth of a brand-new reality in Christ.

Christ came to end the old and to establish the new.

He made it clear that this would no longer be a political, national, or military kingdom like Israel had been. No more thrones, swords, or earthly powers. This time it would be a *heavenly* kingdom, invisible to the natural eye, yet more powerful than every empire on Earth. This kingdom can only be entered and experienced through the Spirit of God.

As Jesus told Nicodemus:

> **"Truly, truly I say to you, unless someone is born again he cannot see the Kingdom of God."**
> —*John 3:3*

And again:

> **"That which has been born of the flesh is flesh,**
> **and that which has been born of the Spirit is spirit.**
> **Do not be amazed that I said to you,**
> **'You must be born again.'"**
> —*John 3:6–7*

The message of Christ was not about restoring a political Israel, raising an army, or crowning another Davidic king with military might. His Gospel was far greater: the unveiling of God's reign in the hearts of men and women who are reborn, filled with the Spirit, and empowered to manifest heaven's reality here and now. As the Almighty declared:

> **"Behold, I am making all things new."**
> — *Revelation 21:5*

No longer does God dwell in stone temples. No longer is His law written on tablets of stone. No longer is there a heavy yoke of bondage to the Law. No longer is Christ far away from His people. No longer do we need animal sacrifices. No longer is God revealed only to the Jews—who mostly rejected Him. Now, in the New Covenant, the love, truth, and presence of the Creator is revealed to *all mankind.* In Christ, there is no Jew or Gentile, but *one new man,* one holy nation under one God. All of humanity is invited into one family, united in Jesus Christ to know our beloved Creator and enjoy His presence—now and forever.

Jesus Christ is all in all; He is above all; He is the one who fulfilled all of God's promises. He is the King of kings and Lord of lords. He is the new day, the birthing of the new creation, the establishing of God's

Kingdom. It's all in Him, by Him, and through Him. To Jesus Christ the Lord is all the glory, now and forevermore, amen.

"Oooohhh, Mr. Sörensen... now you've done it. You've crossed the forbidden line into the most dangerous territory of all! Don't you know you're now guilty of promoting that dreaded heresy—'replacement theology'? Why, everyone knows that doctrine was cooked up in the stinkiest, sulfur-soaked depths of hell itself!"

—*Josh*

Yes, indeed. I am absolutely crossing into "forbidden territory." Just as I have crossed every other line drawn by madmen on their lifelong mission to blind believers to the blazing brilliance of truth.

As you rightly said, Josh, those who hijacked the Church created a dreadful label designed to terrify anyone from ever discovering the fullness of Jesus Christ. That diabolical label is "replacement theology."

And in one sense, it's not entirely wrong — because Jesus Christ did, in fact, abolish once and for all the dark era of satanic, child-sacrificing, demon-worshiping, sexually perverted Israel.

He has entirely replaced it with Himself: the unblemished Son of God, the perfect image of the Most Holy One, the radiant expression of the invisible glory.

He brought an end to the "synagogue of Satan" (Revelation 2:9), ruled by "children of the devil" (John 8:44), where the prophets of God were murdered, and where the Son of God Himself was crucified. All of that came to a complete end. Never again would God attach His name to a people who rejected Him and chased after demons demanding horrors like child sacrifice (Jeremiah 7:31). From now on, God's glory would only be revealed in His Son, Jesus Christ, the fullness of God:

"For in Him all the fullness of Deity dwells in bodily form."

— *Colossians 2:9*

Every promise God ever made to Israel has now found its "Yes and Amen" in Jesus Christ:

"For as many as the promises of God are,
in Him they are yes; therefore through Him

also is our Amen to the glory of God through us."
— *2 Corinthians 1:20*

Jesus Christ is the One the heavenly Father points to:

"This is My beloved Son,
with whom I am well pleased; listen to Him!"
— *Matthew 17:5*

He is the very testimony of prophecy:

"For the testimony of Jesus is the spirit of prophecy."
— *Revelation 19:10*

Christ is the King of kings and the Lord of lords (Revelation 19:16).

Salvation for the human soul is not found in blessing a corrupt nation, but in bowing before the spotless Lamb of God who gave His life as a ransom for all—Jews and Gentiles alike, without distinction:

"There is no distinction; for all have sinned
and fall short of the glory of God,
being justified as a gift by His grace
through the redemption which is in Christ Jesus."
— *Romans 3:22–24*

Every knee will bow to Him—not to Israel, not to Jerusalem, not to some future temple—but to Jesus Christ alone:

"So that at the name of Jesus every knee will bow,
of those who are in heaven and on earth
and under the earth, and that every tongue
will confess that Jesus Christ is Lord,
to the glory of God the Father."
— *Philippians 2:10–11*

He is the Beginning and the End. Everything now revolves around Him. So if people feel the urge to reject this message and smear it with slurs like "replacement theology" or "Kingdom Now," all that reveals is their spiritual blindness. Because whenever the true Spirit of God speaks, He exalts one Person, and one Person only: Jesus Christ.

"For I determined to know nothing among you
except Jesus Christ, and Him crucified."
—*1 Corinthians 2:2*

What many dismiss with that cheap, empty insult "replacement theology" is the true message of Jesus Christ. It is what the apostles preached, and what they laid down their lives for. It is what the angels heralded with joy. It is what the Spirit of Truth revealed. It is what the Father thundered from Heaven. It is what all of Heaven celebrates to this very hour. It is the very essence of the message, the mission, and the power of Jesus Christ.

Denying it, was labeled "antichrist" by the apostles. To confess Him as the Messiah, the Lord, the fulfillment of all God's promises—that is the work of the Holy Spirit. To reject Him is the very spirit of antichrist.

"Who is the liar except the one who denies
that Jesus is the Christ? This is the antichrist,
the one who denies the Father and the Son."
—*1 John 2:22*

Paul confirms the same truth:

"Therefore I make known to you that no one
speaking by the Spirit of God says, 'Jesus is accursed';
and no one can say, 'Jesus is Lord,'
except by the Holy Spirit."
—*1 Corinthians 12:3*

By rejecting Jesus Christ as the Messiah, the Jews proved themselves to be driven not by the Spirit of God, but by a false, demonic spirit—the spirit of antichrist. They do not worship the Father.

"The one who denies the Son does not have the Father;
the one who confesses the Son has the Father also."
—*1 John 2:23*

The Spirit of God, the Spirit of prophecy, always does one thing: *He reveals Jesus Christ.* He lifts Him high as the fullness of God, the testimony of Heaven, the song of the angels, the Savior of mankind, the Alpha and the Omega, the Yes and Amen of every promise.

Jesus is the reality that the Old Covenant foreshadowed, the cornerstone the prophets pointed toward, the Lamb of God slain from the foundation of the world. Through Him, God fulfilled His eternal plan. This is why Heaven thunders its worship around the throne:

> **"Worthy is the Lamb that was slaughtered**
> **to receive power, wealth, wisdom, might,**
> **honor, glory, and blessing."**
> — *Revelation 5:12*

All of Heaven points to Him. The Father testifies of Him. The angels worship Him. The Spirit reveals Him. The apostles preached Him. And the Church is built on Him.

To deny the total Lordship of Christ, to deny that He is the fulfillment of all God's promises—is to side with the spirit of antichrist. But to confess Him is to step into the very heartbeat of Heaven itself, where everything revolves around Jesus Christ, the fullness of God revealed.

The revelation of the Lord Jesus Christ who made all things new, is the true message of the New Testament, proclaimed by apostles who were so full of who Christ is, that they were killed by the Jews. Calling that "replacement theology" is a denial of the fullness of Jesus Christ.

We are not called to cling stubbornly to the old, but to let go and embrace the new kingdom that Jesus Christ brought. And the contrast between the old and the new is as stark as can be. The old system was a nightmare of darkness: priests who sold their souls to Satan, kings who bowed to demons, altars dripping with the blood of child sacrifice, and a temple crawling with hypocrisy and greed. They honored God with their lips, but their hearts were far away:

> **"This people approaches Me with their words,**
> **and honors Me with their lips,**
> **but their heart is far from Me,**
> **and their reverence for Me consists**
> **of the commandment of men taught."**
> — *Isaiah 29:13*

The new is nothing like that. The new is radiant. The new is holy. The new is alive. In Christ, men and women are not just "religious" anymore—they are born again, transformed by the Spirit of God into true sons and daughters of the Father.

**"But as many as received Him,
to them He gave the right
to become children of God,
to those who believe in His name,
who were born, not of blood,
nor of the will of the flesh,
nor of the will of man,
but of God."**
—*John 1:12–13*

**"Therefore if anyone is in Christ,
this person is a new creation;
the old things passed away;
behold, new things have come."**
—*2 Corinthians 5:17*

This is the glory of the New Covenant. No more dead religion. No more endless sacrifices. No more priesthood that sells itself to the highest bidder. Instead, a kingdom where God Himself dwells in His people:

**"For this is the covenant which I will make with
the house of Israel after those days," declares the Lord:
"I will put My laws into their minds,
and write them on their hearts.
And I will be their God, and they shall be My people."**
—*Hebrews 8:10*

And He pours His love into them by His Spirit:

**"...the love of God has been poured out within our hearts
through the Holy Spirit who was given to us."**
—*Romans 5:5*

Jesus Christ is the new creation, through whom we are saved from darkness and welcomed into the loving arms of the heavenly Father.

Selah.

"That may all sound nice and wonderful but still I believe there is a major flaw in your thinking, sir, because the Bible does say that *every eye* would see Jesus when He comes. *Every single eye in the whole wide world*—not just the eyes in Israel. All of mankind would simultaneously see Jesus on the clouds. That's what the Bible says!"

—Josh

Oh, is that so? Does the Bible indeed say that every single eye—all 16 billion of them—will literally see Jesus on the clouds at the exact same moment, from China to Africa to Australia and Europe, including the Vikings and Eskimos? Is that even remotely possible?

Hmm, let's slow down and have a look. The verse in question is Revelation 1:7.

> **"Behold, He is coming with the clouds, and every eye will see Him, even those who pierced Him; and all the tribes of the earth will mourn over Him. So it is to be. Amen."**
>
> *—Revelation 1:7*

Well, you're right, Josh. At first glance, that does look like it says everyone in the entire world would see Him. But hold on. Do you know what the original Greek text actually says here? Because, as we have seen, our English translations can sometimes be misleading, even flat-out faulty. So let's dig a little deeper.

The word translated as "Earth" is the Greek gé (γῆ). And guess what? It doesn't only mean "Earth" in the global sense. It also means: land, region, country, soil, the inhabitants of a certain territory. Ah! Suddenly things get interesting. Because if the text says "all the tribes of the gé," that doesn't necessarily mean "the whole Earth." In fact, let's think about it—are there "tribes" of the Earth? Of course not. The Earth isn't divided into tribes at all. But the land of Israel is!

Hence, a far more accurate translation would be:

> **"...all the tribes of the land will mourn over Him."**

That makes a lot more sense. It's talking about the tribes of Israel—not Inuits in the Arctic, not Mayans in South America, not Japanese samurai or Frenchmen waving baguettes. No, the focus is right where the Bible always puts it: *Israel.*

And notice another detail in the verse:

"...every eye will see Him, even **those who pierced Him."**

Who pierced Him? Did the Chinese? The Russians? Maybe the Brits? No. The ones who pierced Him were right there in Israel—the Roman soldiers stationed in Jerusalem. The very people alive in that generation.

This interpretation is confirmed by the prophecy in Zechariah:

"I will pour out on **the house of David**
and on the inhabitants of **Jerusalem**,
the Spirit of grace and of pleading,
so that **they will look at Me whom they pierced;**
and they will mourn for Him,
like the mourning for an only son,
and they will weep bitterly over Him
like the bitter weeping over a firstborn.
On that day **the mourning in Jerusalem will be great...**"
—*Zechariah* 12:10–11

Who mourns? The house of David. Where does it happen? Not Australia, not China, not America, but Jerusalem.

Jesus Himself confirmed this when He quoted Zechariah:

**"And then the sign of the Son of Man will appear
in the sky, and then all the tribes of the earth will mourn,
and they will see the Son of Man coming on the clouds
of the sky with power and great glory."**
—*Matthew* 24:30

Here the same Greek word gé (γῆ) is used. So when we fix the glaring mistranslation of this verse, we understand that a more truthful translation would once again be: "tribes of the land." Jesus wasn't announcing the end of the whole world, but the end of Old Covenant Israel, and the destruction of Jerusalem and the temple.

Isn't it interesting that we can be so convinced that something we believe is "what the Bible says," only to discover, once we truly study the Scriptures, that what we so firmly believed "the Bible says" is not at all what it teaches?

We really need to stop abusing the Word of God and start treating it with far greater respect. Only then can we begin to find the truth God is revealing through it.

CHAPTER 12

Fly Through The Sky

"Mr. Sörensen, I am stunned. What can I even say? Indeed—both the Word of God and the Spirit of God reveal the new creation in Jesus Christ. It's no longer about the old political Israel; it's about the new Kingdom of God, heavenly and in the Spirit.

How could I have been so blind to this?

But I must say, my mind is spinning like a carousel at the circus. So many questions! For example—the Rapture. What about the promise that we would be flying away from this horrible world into the sky? Don't you dare tell me that's not going to happen! Don't take my rapture away from me! Without it, I have no life, no hope, no future!"

—Josh

I'm sorry to be the thief of your favorite bedtime story, but yes—I'm taking your rapture away. You see, the whole "rapture" narrative is the most bizarre part of the false end-times freak show that has smothered the Church for the past two centuries. It never existed in the original Christian faith. Nobody in the early Church had ever even dreamed of it until some men in the 19th century stitched together a new doctrine.

And let's be real: the idea that hundreds of millions of Christians will all suddenly shoot out of their clothes at the same time, blasting into the stratosphere to circle around Jesus like spiritual fireworks—that isn't Bible teaching. That's *science fiction.* It's the result of brutal Scripture abuse, deliberate mistranslations, and verses spun so far out of context you'd think the apostles were writing a Marvel comic instead of the Word of God.

Many bizarre movies have been produced to depict this fantastic event where a large part of humanity will suddenly fly off, leaving the world to fall apart behind them. These marvelous movies show how airplanes crash to the ground, killing all aboard because the pilot happened to be a Bible-thumping believer, who was jerked away from the airplane controls to greet Jesus in the clouds, right outside his aircraft. The scenes exhibit total disaster on Earth, as millions of cars suddenly become uncontrolled vehicles in the midst of busy traffic because the drivers simply disappear. Innumerable innocent people are killed, children included, while the millions of cars crash into crowds or oncoming traffic and turn every highway in the world into a war zone. Hospitals are plunged into total hell, as millions of patients around the world are simultaneously left abandoned while the Christian surgeons, doctors, and nurses shoot through the roof towards Jesus. Children are left in total desperation as they see their religious parents disappear into the clouds while they are left behind because they are not as convinced of the strange ideas their parents were told in church.

The total disaster, utter destruction, unspeakable terror, and emotional desperation that ensues is literally out of this world. The Rapture is envisioned to be the world's most traumatizing, heartrending, and destructive event of all time.

It is the perfect excuse not to care about humanity: just abandon ship and leave all behind to drown in the storm while you cruise happily in the skies to safety. I have to say how appalling this entire concept is to the heart of the Lord Jesus Christ and the heavenly Father—that we would betray all the suffering children, mothers, and fathers in the entire world, leaving them behind in the claws of demons while we enjoy a glorious trip to Paradise.

The Lord Jesus Christ left the glory and beauty of Heaven to come to Earth and save people in need. He didn't stay in Heaven, nor did He abandon humanity. No, He left the wonderful atmosphere of Heaven to rescue hurting humans, save children in need, restore broken marriages, end corruption, rebuke Satan, and cast out evil spirits. He lifted the terror off of dying men and women and revealed a new future of hope for humanity. He came into our darkness and death to shine His bright light of healing so we could be set free and restored. What a wonderful Saviour, Friend, and God we have! He doesn't abandon us but comes down into our mess to bring deliverance and hope.

Christ's mission was, however, not finished when He left Earth. There is far more to do. So why did Jesus not choose to stay here? Because His assignment was far more than to become the world's #1 superhero, who would do all the work by Himself. His purpose was far more glorious than that. Jesus could never do all the work alone. The world is way too vast for one man, even if He is God in human form. So Christ trained a group of disciples and apostles to become fire starters, world changers, rebels and warriors, heroes and adventurers. He promised the Holy Spirit would be poured out upon them, and then they would receive supernatural power to become those who would upturn the world and shine the light of Christ all around the Earth, to bring healing to way more people than Jesus Himself could ever have done.

> **"...but you will receive power when the Holy Spirit**
> **has come upon you; and you shall be My witnesses**
> **both in Jerusalem and in all Judea and Samaria,**
> **and as far as the remotest part of the earth."**
> —*Acts 1:8*

God's purpose with His people is not that we would always be passive spectators, applauding His glorious works without participating in them. No, the whole message of the Scriptures, from start to finish, is that we are His people through whom He brings His light to the world. We are His ambassadors, His vessels, His very own body, the army of Christ, the city where the Almighty dwells and from where He brings His deliverance to the rest of humanity.

> **"You are the light of the world.**
> **A city set on a hill cannot be hidden."**
> —*Matthew 5:14*

> **"I will also make You a light of the nations,**
> **so that My salvation may reach to the end of the earth."**
> —*Isaiah 49:6*

Jesus didn't come to be our superhero, whom we could worship while sitting on our sofa, eating popcorn. He came to teach us how to cast out demons, heal the sick, break the chains of darkness, and become the most powerful force on Earth that shatters the rule of darkness and restores His dominion of light.

We see this at the very beginning of the Bible, in Genesis, where God created Adam. We have all heard that God made us in His image. The Hebrew word for "image" is "tselem" — צֶלֶם, which means "to be a representative figure." *We represent God*; we are His ambassadors, His sons and daughters who carry His authority. Just as Jesus said: "The one who has seen Me has seen the Father" (John 14:9). Jesus was the perfect image of God, but that was always the intention of the Father, even as early as when He created Adam.

> **"Then God said, 'Let Us make mankind in Our image,**
> **according to Our likeness; and let them rule**
> **over the fish of the sea and over the birds of the sky**
> **and over the livestock and over all the earth,**
> **and over every crawling thing that crawls on the earth.'**
> **So God created man in His own image;**
> **in the image of God He created him;**
> **male and female He created them."**
> — *Genesis 1:26-27*

God created Adam to be *His representative*, His ambassador to rule over all that God has created.

> **"You have made him to have dominion**
> **over the works of Your hands;**
> **You have put all things under his feet."**
> — *Psalm 8:6*

That is why God used Moses and Aaron to deliver the Hebrews from the hands of the demon worshippers in Egypt. God didn't come down with all His glory and fire to do the work for them. He chose to let His children rise up, learn to walk in His Spirit, exercise the authority of God, and stand before Pharaoh with courage.

God isn't interested in immature, lazy, self-centered, irresponsible toddlers who can't be trusted with anything. He wants us to mature in the Spirit and learn to carry His authority so the Almighty can use us to rule over His creation and bring healing wherever we go. That is why the Christ came to us in human form. After casting out demons from the crowds and healing their sick, He sent out His disciples to do the same.

"Now He called the twelve together
and gave them power and authority over all the demons
and the power to heal diseases."
—*Luke 9:1*

"Behold, I have given you authority
to walk on snakes and scorpions, and authority
over all the power of the enemy,
and nothing will injure you.'"
—*Luke 10:19*

That's what everything is all about: sending out the children of the Most High to do what Jesus showed them as an example. This gave ecstatic joy to the Lord!

"At that very time, He rejoiced greatly in the Holy Spirit,
and said, 'I praise You, Father, Lord of heaven and earth,
that You have hidden these things from the wise
and intelligent and have revealed them to infants.'"
—*Luke 10:21*

Christ made us to be His body and His temple so that He can work through us to deliver this world from evil.

"Very truly I tell you, whoever believes in me
will do the works I have been doing,
and they will do even greater things than these
because I am going to the Father."
—*John 14:12*

The apostles indeed did greater works than Christ, for people were even healed by the shadow of Peter:

"And increasingly, believers in the Lord,
large numbers of men and women,
were being added to their number,

**to such an extent that they even carried the sick
out into the streets and laid them on cots and pallets,
so that when Peter came by, at least his shadow
might fall on any of them.
The people from the cities in the vicinity of Jerusalem
were coming together as well, bringing people
who were sick or tormented with unclean spirits,
and they were all being healed."**
— *Acts 5:14-16*

This is the whole point of the mission of Jesus Christ: changing us from a passive public into *an army of anointed warriors* who cast out demons, stop corruption, execute the judgment of God, and bring restoration to all of creation.

That is why Apostle Paul exclaimed to the Christians:

**"Or do you not know that the saints will judge the world?
Do you not know that we will judge angels?"**
— *1 Corinthians 6:2-3*

Apostle John declared that we are kings who reign with Christ:

**"He has made us kings and priests unto God
and His Father; to Him be glory and dominion
for ever and ever. Amen."**
— *Revelation 1:6*

**"He has made us unto our God kings and priests:
and we shall reign on the earth."**
— *Revelation 5:10*

Jesus said the exact same thing:

**"The one who overcomes, I will grant to him
to sit with Me on My throne, as I also overcame
and sat with My Father on His throne."**
— *Revelation 3:21*

And Peter stated that we are royal, which means we reign:

"But you are a chosen people, a royal priesthood,
a holy nation, a people for God's own possession,
so that you may proclaim the excellencies of Him
who has called you out of darkness
into His marvelous light;"

— *1 Peter 2:9*

It's also what Daniel had prophesied:

"The kingdom and dominion, and the greatness
of the kingdoms under the whole heaven,
shall be given to the people, the saints of the Most High.
His kingdom is an everlasting kingdom,
and all dominions shall serve and obey Him."

— *Daniel 7:27*

God even said this at the very beginning when He created man:

"God blessed them and said to them:
'Be fruitful and increase in number; fill the earth
and subdue it. Rule over the fish in the sea and the birds
in the sky and over every living creature
that moves on the ground.'"

— *Genesis 1:28*

Later, it was confirmed by David:

"What is man that You are mindful of him,
and the son of man that You visit him?
For You have made him a little lower than the angels,
and You have crowned him with glory and honor.
You have made him to have dominion
over the works of Your hands;
You have put all things under his feet."

— *Psalm 8:4-6*

"In place of your fathers will be your sons;
You shall make them princes in all the earth."

— *Psalm 45:16*

Is it dawning in your mind? God did not create us to be selfish cowards who run away from Goliath, leave the wicked to terrorize mankind, and allow demons to wreak havoc so that Satan can continue his works of destruction.

He made us in the first place—and redeemed us in Christ as a new creation—to be His royal family of powerful ambassadors who put an end to evil, not to give it free rein.

The doctrine of the Rapture is the #1 satanic lie that has been spread all throughout the Church, to shut down the army of the Most High and turn the soldiers of Christ into escapists who abandon their mission to seek shelter for themselves instead of marching forward in this world to expel evil, judge angels, subdue the powers of the world, and establish righteousness and justice with the King of kings and Lord of lords.

"Well, I must admit that all sounds nice and heroic, but still the Rapture is in the Bible. It's right in there, go look it up! Jesus says we will be raptured out of this world, Paul says it—I mean, it's the Bible that teaches it, sir! How can you deny that?"

—*Josh*

No, the Bible nowhere says that the captains must abandon ship and leave all the passengers to drown. The Bible says we must be the light of the world, the healers of the nations, the deliverers of mankind, and the judges who execute judgment over the wicked. The passages we think talk about the Rapture say something *entirely different.* Take John 14:2–3:

> **"In My Father's house are many dwelling places; if it were not so, I would have told you; for I go to prepare a place for you. If I go and prepare a place for you, I will come again and receive you to Myself, that where I am, there you may be also."**
>
> —*John 14:2, 3*

As a child, I heard this interpreted at Sunday school as follows: "When Jesus comes back, He will bring us to our little room in Heaven." Really? Is that what Jesus meant here? Is God a giant hotel full of rooms? Has Jesus been working as a chambermaid for two thousand years, decorating our cozy little suite? Of course not!

What did Jesus mean? If we look up the Greek word for "house," we see oikia —οἰκίᾳ, which means "dwelling place." What Jesus said was not "in my Father's house" but "where My Father dwells," or in other words, "in the presence of My Father." A far better translation is therefore:

"In the presence of My Father, there is room for all of you."

Jesus added: "Then I will take you with me, and you will be where I am." Where was Jesus? *He constantly lived in the presence of the Father.* Wherever the Father was, Jesus was also. And He said there is room for all of us with the Father. He would prepare our place with the Father—*or make it possible for us to also live in the Father's presence.* Now we can also be where He was: in close relationship with the heavenly Father.

What Jesus announced was nothing less than the magnificent transition from the old to the new covenant. In the old covenant, God was always distant from His people—hidden behind the thick walls of a far-off stone temple. People did not dwell with the Father. Only Jesus lived in the presence of the Father. He promised them that during His absence, He would transform this situation and make it possible for all people to be in the presence of the Father.

That's what it's all about: restoring the unity of humanity with God, and bringing us back into the presence of the Father.

It has nothing to do with physically flying away to a mega-hotel where a nice room has been prepared for us. Everything revolves around our unity with the Father and Jesus, which would be granted to Christians at the coming of Jesus. Before that time, the Church only had the Holy Spirit as their comforter. But during His "coming and presence" — or parousia in Greek, God's ultimate plan for humanity would be realized:

HE WOULD DWELL IN OUR MIDST.

We are not being taken away from the Earth. On the contrary: *God has come among us!* He made His abode with us. We are now His temple.

"Do you not know that you are the temple of God and that the Spirit of God dwells in you?"
—1 Corinthians 3:16

“For we are the temple of the living God;
just as God said, ‘I will dwell among them
and walk among them;
and I will be their God, and they shall be My people.’”
— *2 Corinthians 6:16*

“If anyone loves Me, he will follow My word;
and My Father will love him,
and We will come to him
and make Our dwelling with him.”
— *John 14:23*

“That is all really beautiful, and you eloquently outline everything. But still, you are wrong, Mr. Sörensen. Because in 1 Thessalonians 4:17 Apostle Paul said that we will all be jerked out of our clothes and fly away, high in the sky, straight into the clouds to meet Jesus up there.”
—*Josh*

Did Paul say that? Really? Let’s read it, shall we?

“After that, we who are still alive will be caught up
with them in the clouds to meet the Lord in the air.
And so we will always be with the Lord.
Therefore, encourage each other with these words.”
— *1 Thessalonians 4:17*

Yes, Paul did say that. Hmm... Strange. Paul wasn’t the kind of person to be so focused on material things like literal clouds and the physical sky. He usually spoke in spiritual language that most people can’t even understand. The Apostle Peter said that most Christians have problems understanding Paul’s letters:

“There are some things in his letters that are hard to understand. People who are ignorant and unstable give a wrong interpretation to them to their own ruin.”
— *2 Peter 3:16*

Peter said the Scriptures cannot be explained in an earthly way. We need understanding given to us by the Spirit:

"But know this first of all, that no prophecy of Scripture becomes a matter of someone's own interpretation, for no prophecy was ever made by an act of human will, but men moved by the Holy Spirit spoke from God."
— *2 Peter 1:20*

Paul made it clear that he spoke in spiritual mysteries:

"We speak God's wisdom in a mystery,
the hidden wisdom which God predestined
before the ages to our glory; the wisdom which
none of the rulers of this age has understood;
for if they had understood it, they would
not have crucified the Lord of glory;
but just as it is written:

'Things which eye has not seen and ear has not heard,
And which have not entered the human heart,
All that God has prepared for those who love Him.'
For to us God revealed them through the Spirit;
for the Spirit searches all things, even the depths of God."
— *1 Corinthians 2:7-10*

It is obvious that Paul wasn't occupied with earthly ideas like flying in the sky in your underwear to meet Jesus, who is waiting for you on a fluffy cloud. What could Paul have meant by this interesting statement?

"After that, we who are still alive will be caught up
with them in the clouds to meet the Lord in the air.
And so we will always be with the Lord.
Therefore, encourage each other with these words."
— *1 Thessalonians 4:17*

First, Paul was not talking about people in the future. He explicitly wrote "we," meaning *himself and the Christians in Thessaloniki*. The biblical audience is the *first* Christians, not the *last* Christians. This was something *they* were about to experience in their lifetime. He guaranteed the believers in Thessaloniki that *they* would "meet the Lord in the air."

Also, the Greek word for "air" here is aera — ἀήρ. The same word is used in Ephesians 2 to indicate the spiritual realm:

"...in which you previously walked according to the course of this world, according to the prince of the power of the air — ἀήρ, of the spirit that is now working in the sons of disobedience."

— *Ephesians* 2:2

Paul is not talking about the earthly atmosphere we call "sky," but about the *spiritual dimension* where "the prince of the power of the air" is at work. It is in that spiritual realm they would be "caught up."

The Greek for "catch up" is harpazó — ἁρπάζω. Paul also used it when describing someone being "caught up" into the third heaven:

"I know a man in Christ, who fourteen years ago— whether in the body I do not know, or out of the body I do not know, God knows—such a man was caught up to the third heaven. And I know how such a man— whether in the body or apart from the body I do not know, God knows—was caught up into Paradise and heard inexpressible words, which a man is not permitted to speak."

— 2 *Corinthians* 12:2-4

Clearly, Paul wasn't envisioning Christians physically flying into the clouds. Being "caught up" in this context speaks of *a supernatural encounter in the spirit.* This is further validated by the fact that Paul said that a physical body cannot experience the Kingdom of God.

"But this I say, brothers, that flesh and blood cannot inherit the Kingdom of God, and that the perishable cannot inherit the imperishable."

— 1 *Corinthians* 15:50

After stating that the Thessalonians would be caught up in the spiritual realm, Paul adds they would be taken up in the "clouds." In Scripture, "clouds" often symbolize the spiritual, such as the "cloud of witnesses" (Hebr. 12:1) or the cloud of His presence (2 Chron. 5:11–14.) Paul's "clouds" are not weather formations but spiritual realities—clouds of God's presence and of His people in glory.

So what do we learn in the Bible about clouds? That there are clouds in the spiritual world too—clouds of people in heaven and clouds of

God's presence. *These are spiritual realities.* Since Paul was a deeply spiritual person, we can say with confidence that he had these spiritual clouds in mind when he spoke of being "caught up in the clouds." It has to do with *the presence of God that would come.*

The purpose of the coming of Christ was to bring the abiding presence of God among His people.

Now let's look at the statement that Christians would "meet" Jesus. The word translated as "meeting" is apantésis — ἀπάντησις in Greek. In the first century, this was used for the civic custom of greeting a king or dignitary as he approached a city: when the people saw the king coming, they would go out to meet him and escort him to his destination.

The king did not come to take people away but to *enter the city himself.* Paul, therefore, did not say that Christians would be snatched away into physical clouds; he said they would *go out to welcome the presence of Jesus.*

The first Christians still lived within the spiritual conditions of the Old Covenant. They did not yet live in the abiding presence of Jesus and the Father, because this had not yet been made a universal reality. Paul promised them that at the coming of Jesus, they would experience this dramatic event of being reunited with the Lord, and from that moment on, they would always be in His presence.

The spiritual reality of the New Covenant would be established—namely, the abiding presence of the Lord Jesus Christ and the heavenly Father with us. "Thus we will always be with the Lord."

Again: the coming of Christ on the clouds was about ending the era of the Old Covenant and establishing the realm of the New Covenant, where His presence is no longer distant from us.

> **"If anyone loves Me, he will follow My word;**
> **and My Father will love him, and We will come to him**
> **and make Our dwelling with him."**
> —*John 14:23*

This was the promise throughout the Old Covenant: a new era would come in which the presence of God would be with His people:

> **"And many nations will join themselves to the Lord**
> **on that day and will become My people.**

Then I will dwell in your midst."
— Zechariah 2:11

This is what Apostle Paul was referring to: at the coming of the Lord, the old spiritual order would come to an end, and Christ would inaugurate a new realm that allowed all of God's children to be with Him forever. That is why Paul used the Greek word parousia — παρουσία whenever he mentioned the "coming" of the Lord. Parousia means **"to arrive and be present."** In short, it speaks of His presence that would forever abide with us. That is what Christ referred to when He said:

"In My Father's house are many dwelling places;
if it were not so, I would have told you;
for I go to prepare a place for you.
If I go and prepare a place for you,
I will come again and receive you to Myself,
that where I am, there you may be also."
— John 14:2, 3

A more accurate translation of this verse is:

"In the presence of the Father, there is room for all of you.
I am going to prepare this for you, and when I come back,
you will also be where I am: in the presence of the Father."

I invite you not to wait, escape, or look to the skies—but to *enter.* Not someday, but *now.* Lay down fear, abandon the stories of flight and abandonment, and step into the living reality Christ has already opened for you.

He is not distant. He is not coming to take you away from the world.

He is here—present, near, dwelling within reach.

Turn your heart toward Him. Become still. Let the walls fall.

The Father has made room for you in His presence, and Christ Himself stands at the door, not as a judge to terrify you, but as a Savior to welcome you home.

Enter His presence.

Abide with Him.

And from that place of union, rise—not to escape the world, but to heal it.

CHRIST AND PAUL WERE NOT TALKING ABOUT FLYING OFF INTO THE SKY, BUT ABOUT A SPIRITUAL TRANSITION IN WHICH BELIEVERS WOULD MOVE FROM THE REALITY OF THE OLD COVENANT INTO THE NEW, WELCOMING THE PRESENCE OF CHRIST IN THEIR MIDST.

CHAPTER 13

Christ The World Dictator

"But—but—but... hold on just a minute! This can't be right. No way! We've all been expecting Jesus to return *physically* to Earth! He can't have come in some *spiritual* sense — that's not what I signed up for! The whole idea is that He descends *in His physical body,* takes over the world as a global ruler, and forces everyone on Earth to worship Him!

That's the big event we've all been waiting for. Not some 'spiritual' presence of Christ among us. I want to *see* Him and *touch* Him. And most of all: I want all my nasty neighbors, and all the unbelievers to be forced, wether they want it or not, to bow before Jesus. Christ the King over the whole world! All world leaders will be shoved aside, for Christ the King. He will rule the whole world, from Jerusalem. Aha! What sweet revenge will that be, haha!"

—*Josh*

You know Josh, it truly is a great mystery to me how this idea—of Jesus *physically* returning to Earth—became so widely spread in the Church. I cannot find it anywhere in the entire Bible.

What I do see is that Jesus Christ said that He and the Father would dwell with *all* believers. So why would He then be physically present in just *one* location on Earth? That doesn't add up.

Jesus also consistently said that He would appear on the clouds with the angels. And what are angels? Spirits! They don't have physical bodies.

Jesus was always speaking of a *spiritual* manifestation of His kingship. He would take His place in His kingdom—which is heavenly, and therefore in the Spirit. As He told Nicodemus:

> **"Unless someone is born of water and the Spirit,**
> **he cannot enter the Kingdom of God."**
> —*John 3:5.*

His kingdom is not of this world—it is in the Spirit of God. Why, then, would He suddenly take up residence in a physical temple on Earth? That makes no sense at all. Jesus spoke constantly about a *spiritual* kingdom and His presence with *all* His people. We are being built up as His temple. The reign of Christ is not an earthly political system—it is a Spirit-filled reality, revealed, entered, and lived by the Spirit alone. The Bible declares it over and over again:

- **His kingdom can only be seen by the Spirit**

> "Truly, truly, I say to you, unless someone is born again
> he cannot see the Kingdom of God."
> —*John 3:3*

- **His kingdom can only be entered through the Spirit**

> "Unless someone is born of water and the Spirit,
> he cannot enter the Kingdom of God."
> —*John 3:5*

- **His kingdom is not somewhere on Earth—it is in our midst**

> "The Kingdom of God is not coming with signs
> that can be observed; nor will they say,
> 'Look, here it is!' or, 'There it is!'
> For behold, the Kingdom of God is in your midst."
> —*Luke 17:20–21*

• **His kingdom is not of this world—it is a spiritual reality**

"My kingdom is not of this world.
If My kingdom were of this world,
My servants would be fighting...
but as it is, My kingdom is not of this realm."
—*John 18:36*

• **His kingdom is demonstrated by the power of the Spirit**

"For the Kingdom of God is not in words, but in power."
—*1 Corinthians 4:20*

• **We must be born again of the Spirit**

"That which has been born of the flesh is flesh,
and that which has been born of the Spirit is spirit."
—*John 3:6*

• **We can only understand by the Spirit**

"Now we have not received the spirit of the world,
but the Spirit who is from God, so that we may know
the things freely given to us by God."
—*1 Corinthians 2:12*

• **We are built up as the house of God by the Spirit**

"...you also are being built together
into a dwelling of God in the Spirit."
—*Ephesians 2:22*

• **Jesus and the Father dwell with us in the Spirit**

"If anyone loves Me, he will follow My word;
and My Father will love him, and We will come to him
and make Our dwelling with him."
—*John 14:23*

- **We are the temple of the Holy Spirit**

"Do you not know that your body is a temple of the Holy Spirit within you, whom you have from God, and that you are not your own?"
—*1 Corinthians 6:19*

- **We are brought to maturity by the Spirit**

"...until we all attain to the unity of the faith, and of the knowledge of the Son of God, to a mature man, to the measure of the stature which belongs to the fullness of Christ."
—*Ephesians 4:13*

- **The Church is the Body of Christ in the Spirit**

"For by one Spirit we were all baptized into one body..."
—*1 Corinthians 12:13*

- **The truth is revealed to us by the Spirit**

"But when He, the Spirit of truth, comes,
He will guide you into all the truth..."
—*John 16:13*

- **The New Covenant is the ministry of the Spirit**

"...who also made us adequate as servants of a new covenant,
not of the letter but of the Spirit; for the letter kills,
but the Spirit gives life."
—*2 Corinthians 3:6*

- **God is Spirit, and He is seeking true worshipers**

"God is spirit, and those who worship Him
must worship in spirit and truth."
—*John 4:24*

• **True worship is not in Jerusalem, but in spirit and truth**

"Believe Me, woman, that a time is coming
when you will worship the Father
neither on this mountain nor in Jerusalem."
—*John 4:21*

• **Christ is not a political ruler—He rules in the Spirit**

"The Spirit of the Lord is upon Me, because He anointed Me to bring good news to the poor. He has sent Me to proclaim release to captives, and recovery of sight to the blind, to set free those who are oppressed."
—*Luke 4:18*

From beginning to end, Scripture shouts the same truth: the Kingdom of God is born in our heart by the Spirit of God. Miss this, and you miss the very heartbeat of the message of Christ.

Jesus also spoke of His appearing on the *clouds* with the angels—not as an earthly monarch stepping onto a palace balcony, surrounded by heavily armed soldiers, but as the glorified Son of Man, revealed in heavenly power and accompanied by a glorious host of angels.

"For the Son of Man is going to come
in the glory of His Father **with His angels,**
and will then repay each person according to his deeds."
—*Matthew 16:27*

"But when the Son of Man comes in His glory,
and **all the angels with Him**, then He will sit
on His glorious throne."
—*Matthew 25:31*

Apostle Paul also confirmed that Jesus' coming would be a spiritual manifestation, accompanied by angels:

"...when the Lord Jesus will be revealed from heaven
with His mighty angels in flaming fire."
—*2 Thessalonians 1:7*

Just as Scripture says Christ came with the angels, it also says He came on the clouds—without ever mentioning a touchdown on Earth. Over and over, the Bible repeats that Christ would appear on the clouds.

> "...and they will see the Son of Man coming
> **on the clouds** of the sky with power and great glory."
> — *Matthew 24:30*

> "From now on you will see the Son of Man
> sitting at the right hand of Power,
> and coming **on the clouds** of heaven."
> — *Matthew 26:64*

This was emphasized by the angels who appeared after His ascension:

> "This Jesus, who has been taken up from you into heaven,
> will come **in the same way** as you have watched Him
> go into heaven."
> — *Acts 1:11*

And how did He go into heaven?

> "...as He was lifted up while they were watching,
> **a cloud took Him up** out of their sight."
> — *Acts 1:9*

Jesus disappeared into the clouds. He would return the same way—on the clouds, with angels, who are spirits. As we've already seen from historical accounts, that is exactly what happened.

> **"...a great force flying across the sky...
> all of them horses of fire and riders of fire."**
> — *Sepher Josippon*

> **"...hosts joining battle in the skies, fiery gleams of arms..."**
> — *Tacitus*

> **"...troops of soldiers in their armor were seen
> running about among the clouds..."**
> — *Josephus*

"...chariots and armed troops coursing through the clouds and surrounding the cities."
— *Eusebius*

Just as He told the Jewish High Council:

"From now on you will see the Son of Man sitting at the right hand of Power, and **coming on the clouds** of heaven."
— *Matthew* 26:64

There is simply no verse in the entire Bible that describes Him physically descending onto the Earth again.

"And what about the verse that says Jesus will stand on the Mount of Olives when He returns? That is a physical touchdown, isn't it?"
—*Josh*

Not necessarily. Let's unpack, shall we?
First of all, let's read that verse in context:

**"Then I will gather all the nations against Jerusalem to battle.
The city shall be taken, the houses plundered,
and the women raped...
On that day His feet shall stand on the Mount of Olives,
which lies before Jerusalem on the east."**
— *Zechariah* 14:1–2, 4

When did Zechariah say the feet of the Lord would stand on the Mount of Olives? When the nations were gathered against Jerusalem for battle. Once again, we are dealing with an event that took place as part of God's judgment upon Israel in AD 66–70. The Bible gives zero justification to claim that we—Americans, Australians, Britons, Europeans, Africans, Asians, or Scandinavians—would witness this event thousands of years later. It was directly and explicitly tied to the destruction of Jerusalem.

This is yet another disturbing example of how shamelessly the Word of God is abused—again and again—to promote radically unbiblical ideas that cripple the Church. The deception is truly mind-boggling.

"My God, I am perplexed. I must admit that I, too, am guilty of blindly repeating what others have said on Christian television and church platforms—without ever reading this verse carefully for myself.

But this raises the next question, Mr. Sörensen: Does history actually record that the Lord stood on the Mount of Olives?"

—*Josh*

Yes—just like so many other supernatural events foretold in Scripture, this event was also fulfilled and recorded in striking detail.

First of all, the leading historians of the first century documented how the presence of the Lord departed from the temple in Jerusalem shortly before its destruction.

> **"The doors of the inner sanctuary were suddenly thrown open, and a superhuman voice was heard, crying out that the gods were departing from that place. At the same moment there was a mighty movement, as of a great departure."**
>
> — *Gaius Tacitus, The Histories, Book V, 13.*

> **"Moreover, at the feast which we call Pentecost, when the priests entered the inner court of the temple by night, as was their custom in order to perform their sacred duties, they reported that they felt a quaking, and heard a great noise, and afterward heard a sound as of a great multitude, saying, 'Let us depart from here.'"**
>
> — *Flavius Josephus, The Wars of the Jews, Book VI, Chapter 5, Sections 2–3.*

> **"The eastern gate of the inner court of the temple was of bronze and extremely heavy. It was closed with great difficulty by twenty men, and rested upon a base strengthened with iron, with bolts deeply fastened into the floor, which was made of a single massive stone. Yet this gate suddenly opened of its own accord."**
>
> — *Eusebius of Caesarea, Ecclesiastical History, Book III, Chapter 8, Sections 1–6.*

God's presence departed from the temple in a tangible and audible manner, during the same period in which Jesus Christ came on the clouds. It is remarkable that these historians state that the voice sounded like the *noise of a great multitude.* That is exactly how the voice of God is described in Scripture:

> **"After this I heard what seemed to be the loud voice of a great multitude in heaven..."**
> — *Revelation 19:1.*

The Roman historian Gaius Tacitus obviously did not believe in one single God (Romans believed in a plurality of "gods"), which is why he wrote that "the gods" departed from the temple. Yet it is astonishing that even this Roman senator and governor openly acknowledged that God dwelt in the temple of the Jews, and departed from it. This demonstrates that the event was so awe-inspiring that even pagan Roman historians could not omit it from their historical records.

The Greek Christian scholar Eusebius records that the gate of the Temple normally required at least twenty men to open it—yet on this occasion, it swung open entirely on its own.

Where did the Lord go, after leaving the temple? To the Mount of Olives! This event was so well known at the time that even centuries later, Christians from all over the world traveled to the Mount of Olives to worship the Lord there, because it was commonly known that He had stood on that very mountain.

> **"Believers in Christ came from all parts of the world—not as in ancient times for the sake of the glory of Jerusalem, nor in order to worship in the old temple in Jerusalem, but ... to worship on the Mount of Olives opposite the city, to which the glory of God had moved when it departed from the former city."**
>
> — *Eusebius of Caesarea, Proof of the Gospel, Book VI, Chapter 18, p. 288.*

Bible teacher Ernest L. Martin notes in his book "Secrets of Golgotha" that a Jewish rabbi named Jonathan—an eyewitness of the destruction of Jerusalem—stated that the glory departed from the temple and for three and a half years remained on the Mount of Olives, hoping that Israel would repent, but they did not. Meanwhile, a voice spoke from Heaven:

"Return, faithless children.
Return to Me, and I will return to you."
When they did not repent, the voice said,
"I will return to My place."
—Ernest L. Martin, Secrets of Golgotha, p. 84.

So yes—the Lord did stand with His feet on the Mount of Olives.

But was this in a physical, flesh-and-bones sense? No—because that is not what the text in Zechariah says. It does not say, "the Messiah in a physical body." It simply says, "the Lord." And He is Spirit.

Why does God, who is Spirit, choose to remain invisible to our human eyes? Even Jesus Christ, who briefly walked the Earth in human form, had to leave again, and He emphatically stated that this was actually better for His followers:

"But I tell you the truth: it is to your advantage
that I am leaving; for if I do not leave, the Helper will not
come to you; but if I go, I will send Him to you."
—John 16:7

With the physical Christ gone from the Earth, something far better could happen: the Spirit of God would come. Why is that so much better? Because you can never truly know someone merely "according to the flesh." The disciples had walked with Jesus Christ for three years, yet they still understood very little about who He truly was or the nature of His Kingdom. Their physical sight of a physical Jesus actually blinded them to His true identity.

"Have I been with you for so long a time,
and yet you have not come to know Me, Philip?"
—John 14:9

This is why the Spirit of God had to come—to reveal to believers who Jesus truly is, and to help them understand the truth:

"I have many more things to say to you,
but you cannot bear them at the present time.
But when He, the Spirit of truth, comes,
He will guide you into all the truth..."
—John 16:12-13

Think about Israel in the wilderness. They literally saw God in their midst—a pillar of fire by night and a cloud by day. God was visibly present! Imagine it: a blazing pillar of fire illuminating an entire camp of millions at night, and by day, a towering column of smoke stretching into the heavens so that everyone for miles could see. *But they did not believe.*

It's the same when Jesus Christ walked the Earth. Though they could see Him with their physical eyes, almost no one truly believed.

That's why Jesus had to leave physically, so the Spirit could come. Only then would the disciples' eyes be opened. Only then would they finally understand. Once Jesus was physically out of sight, they truly came to know Him—through the Spirit. Then they were willing to lay down their lives for Him, because they had encountered Him in a way infinitely more powerful than the physical.

There's a reason God chooses to remain invisible. He could show Himself physically to every person on Earth at any moment—but He doesn't. Why? Because He wants us to know Him in a much deeper way. When our own spirit connects with God—who is Spirit—that bond is far stronger and more intimate than any shallow, flesh-level sight. Flesh can never go deeper than flesh. The visible can never grasp the invisible. The earthly can never understand the heavenly.

God is Spirit, and He seeks worshipers who will worship Him in spirit and truth (John 4:23-24).

Jesus Christ is not a king in an earthly government like our presidents and ministers. He is King in a far more powerful kingdom. That is why His rule continues to expand, even under the fiercest persecution. Earthly kingdoms have tried again and again to drive Jesus Christ out. His followers have been tortured, beheaded, burned alive, dismembered, imprisoned, and worse. Yet despite all this, His kingdom keeps advancing through the centuries. He began with a handful of disciples—and now there are hundreds of millions of devoted followers of Christ.

Jesus reigns—but not in the way we often imagine. He reigns in the spiritual realm, breaking through, expanding, and making a way by His Spirit.

That's why the idea that we must all wait for a physical Jesus to rule an earthly, political kingdom is complete and utter nonsense.

It's time to cast those ridiculous, unbiblical beliefs behind us and wholeheartedly return to Christ and His true message.

He is here with us and waits until we embrace Him.

CHAPTER 14

The Dead Will Rise

"That's actually a pretty good explanation, Mr. Sörensen, I must concede. Yes, it's starting to make sense, little by little. But I still can't wrap my head around one thing. The Bible says all the dead will come crawling out of their graves during the return of Christ. And we all know that hasn't happened... right?"

—*Josh*

Of course. How could I have forgotten? The fantastic resurrection of the dead! That incredibly strange event where all the deceased, since the beginning of time, would suddenly come groveling out of the ground and start flying off to Heaven.

This is without a doubt one of the most mysterious topics in the entire Bible. Nobody truly understands the book of Revelation, with its apocalyptic riddles and mind-bending mysteries. But of all the strange themes in the vast jungles of end-time jumble—where even the most daring explorers get lost—the resurrection of the dead appears to be the deepest pit of them all, where every adventurer stumbles in, never to see daylight again.

Let's attempt to apply some healthy common sense to this wildly misunderstood topic—one that has been the source of some of the most outrageous fantasies the Church has ever been plagued with.

First of all, it is important to understand what the Bible means by "death." The concept of dying is mentioned for the first time in Genesis:

"The Lord God commanded the man, saying,
'From any tree of the garden you may freely eat; but from
the tree of the knowledge of good and evil you shall not eat,

for on the day that you eat from it
you will certainly die.'"
— *Genesis 2:16–17*

God warned Adam and Eve, "If you eat this fruit, you will surely die." Yet what happened? The serpent enticed Eve to eat it anyway... *and she didn't die.* Adam followed, and *he didn't fall to the ground either.* Nothing seemed to happen. Was God exaggerating? Was He merely using a fear tactic, like a parent saying, "If you don't finish your dinner, the boogeyman will get you"? Of course not. God wasn't speaking about physical death, but about something infinitely more catastrophic: *spiritual death.*

Spiritual death means to be separated from God Himself.

That's exactly what happened the moment Adam and Eve ate from the forbidden fruit:

"Now they heard the sound of the Lord God
walking in the garden in the cool of the day,
and the man and his wife hid themselves
from the presence of the Lord God
among the trees of the garden.
Then the Lord God called to the man, and said to him,
'Where are you?' He said, 'I heard the sound of You
in the garden, and I was afraid because I was naked;
so I hid myself.'"
— *Genesis 3:8–10*

Adam and Eve were *torn away from God* in their spirit, and the immediate result was *fear.* When they were spiritually alive—joined to God—they ran toward Him and delighted in His presence. But once sin severed that union, they shrank back and *hid* from their beloved Father.

ONCE ADAM AND EVE ATE
FROM THE FORBIDDEN FRUIT,
THEY DIED, WHICH MEANT
THEY WERE DRIVEN AWAY
FROM THE PRESENCE OF GOD.

Jesus Christ came to undo this terrible seperation. He said:

"The one who believes has eternal life."
—*John 6:47*

Did Jesus mean that Christians would live on Earth forever? No. Even though He promised eternal life to His followers, they all died physically. So what did He mean? Jesus explained:

"This is eternal life, that <u>they may know You."</u>
—*John 17:3*

The Greek word here for "know" is ginóskó—γινώσκω, which speaks of experiencing an *intimate union* with someone. Having eternal life means being in an eternal intimate relationship with God.

Adam and Eve were fully alive in the presence of God before they fell into sin. They walked with the Creator of Heaven and Earth, spoke with Him, and enjoyed His wonderful presence.

The moment they ate the forbidden fruit, evil entered their hearts, and they were no longer able to abide in the presence of the Holy One, in whom there is no trace of darkness. Their intimate fellowship with their Father was severed.

If we boil it down:

- **Death is separation from God.**
- **Life is unity with God.**

That's why the Bible says we were "dead" in our sins before coming to Jesus. We were physically alive, but spiritually separated from God. When we believed in Christ, He raised us from death to life and restored us to fellowship with our heavenly Father.

"And this is eternal life, that they may know You, the only true God, and Jesus Christ whom You have sent."
—*John 17:3*

A more complete rendering would be:

"And this is eternal life, that they may be *in intimate unity with You*, the only true God, and Jesus Christ whom You have sent."

For many of us, it is natural to say that when our loved ones pass away, we will see them again in Heaven. But did you know that people in the Old Covenant never spoke that way?

Before Jesus came, everyone who died descended into the realm of the dead. In Hebrew, this place is called Sheol. Even the most righteous people entered that dark and gloomy realm.

Everyone truly died—not just physically, but spiritually as well. They were cut off from life and separated from God, the Giver of life.

In Sheol they rested in silence, awaiting the day when Jesus would raise them up to eternal life in His presence. Until that moment, they remained separated from God.

This is confirmed by the story of the prophet Samuel, whose soul was summoned by a medium at King Saul's command. The account in 1 Samuel 28 records that when Samuel appeared, he said:

> "Why have you disturbed me by **bringing me up?"**
> — *1 Samuel 28:15*

The phrase "bringing me up" is the Hebrew word alah — הָלָע, which means "to ascend from below." Samuel was not in Heaven but below, in the realm of the dead where he rested.

The prophet Daniel also rested in Sheol until the resurrection:

> "But as for you, go your way to the end; **then you will rest**
> and rise for your allotted portion at the end of the age."
> — *Daniel 12:13*

Even King David, a man after God's own heart, had not ascended into Heaven:

> **"For it was not David who ascended into heaven..."**
> — *Acts 2:34*

When Jacob's son died, he said:

> "Then all his sons and all his daughters got up
> to comfort him, but he refused to be comforted.
> And he said, **'Surely I will go down to Sheol**
> in mourning for my son.' So his father wept for him."
> — *Genesis 37:35*

The Bible even records that some people were cast into Sheol while they were still alive. This shows that it is a real location beneath the earth:

> "But if the Lord brings about an entirely new thing
> and the ground opens its mouth and
> **swallows them with everything that is theirs,**
> **and they descend alive into Sheol,**
> then you will know that these men have been disrespectful
> to the Lord. And as he finished speaking all these words,
> the ground that was under them split open;
> and the earth opened its mouth and swallowed them,
> their households, and all the people who belonged to Korah
> with all their possessions. So they and all that belonged to them
> **went down alive to Sheol;** and the earth closed over them,
> and they perished from the midst of the assembly."
> — *Numbers 16:30–33*

Job said of the realm of the dead:

> "When a cloud vanishes, it is gone; In the same way
> **one who goes down to Sheol does not come up."**
> — *Job 7:9*

> "They spend their days in prosperity,
> And **suddenly they go down to Sheol."**
> — *Job 21:13*

King David wrote about the realm of the dead:

> "For there is no mention of You in death;
> **In Sheol**, who will praise You?"
> — *Psalm 6:5*

> "What man can live and not see death?
> Can he save his soul from **the power of Sheol?"**
> — *Psalm 89:49*

There were a few remarkable exceptions to this pattern: Enoch, Moses, and Elijah received the privilege of bypassing the realm of the dead altogether. God took them directly into His presence in Heaven.

But for everyone else, even for prophets of God like Daniel, Samuel, and David, the path was the same: they descended into the realm of the dead, where they rested until the resurrection.

At that resurrection, God would execute a final judgment to determine the final destiny of every soul. The righteous would be welcomed into His presence forever, while the wicked would be cast into the lake of fire:

> **"And the sea gave up the dead who were in it,**
> **and Death and Hades gave up the dead who were in them;**
> **and they were judged, each one of them**
> **according to their deeds.**
> **Then Death and Hades were thrown into the lake of fire.**
> **This is the second death, the lake of fire.**
> **And if anyone's name was not found written in**
> **the book of life, he was thrown into the lake of fire."**
> — *Revelation 20:13–15*

The righteous in the time of Jesus longed for this resurrection. They eagerly awaited the day when their departed loved ones would no longer remain in the realm of the dead, but would be restored to God's glorious presence forever.

They also knew that the resurrection meant they themselves would never have to enter the darkness of Sheol. That is what Jesus promised them: everyone who believed in Him would never enter the realm of the dead, for through Him they had eternal life.

This is why the hope of the resurrection of the dead became a central theme for both the Jews and the earliest Christians.

The big question is: When would this happen?

The answer is given by the angel who spoke to the prophet Daniel:

> **"It will be a time of trouble, such as has not been**
> **since there were nations. In that time**
> **your people will be saved:**
> **all who are recorded in the book.**
>
> **Many of those who sleep in the dust of the ground**
> **will awake, some to everlasting life,**
> **others to shame and everlasting contempt."**
> — *Daniel 12:1–2*

The angel stated plainly that the resurrection would take place during "a time of distress such as has not been since there was a nation." What time was that? Is there another reference in the Bible to "a time of distress such as has not been since there was a nation"? Yes. Jesus Christ also spoke of it:

> **"For then there will be a great tribulation,**
> **such as has not occurred since the beginning of the world**
> **until now, nor ever will again."**
> — *Matthew 24:21*

We've already seen in detail that this "Great Tribulation" refers to the terrible period when Jerusalem was besieged by the Romans. One third of all Jews were murdered in the most horrifying ways imaginable. Many chose to kill themselves with their own swords rather than fall into the hands of the Romans, who were inhumane, violent, and bloodthirsty.

The famine was so severe that a mother roasted her own baby. The streets of Jerusalem became literal rivers of blood. The sea was stained red with it. The Jordan River was blocked by piles of corpses. The sun was eclipsed and the moon turned red from the massive fires raging across the city. It was a time of unimaginable horror, torture, and slaughter — atrocities committed in ways that defy belief. Even Roman and Jewish historians described it as a period of suffering unmatched in all history.

According to the angel, the resurrection would take place *during that very time.* Is this confirmed elsewhere in Scripture? Absolutely. In connection with the destruction of Jerusalem, Jesus Christ made this striking statement:

> **"...these are days of punishment, so that all things**
> **which have been written will be fulfilled."**
> — *Luke 21:22*

The weight of that statement is staggering. All things which have been written would be fulfilled during those days of punishment. That includes every prophecy concerning the resurrection of the dead — just as the angel told Daniel.

This explains why the first Christians eagerly looked forward to the resurrection. *They knew it was near.* The old covenant age would end, and a new reality would dawn. The hallmark of this new era would be that God was no longer separated from His people.

Death — separation from God —would be abolished.
Eternal life — eternal unity with God — would be their reality.

A resurrection of the dead had to take place for this to happen. It was the burning hope of the early Church. That's why Apostle Paul wrote about it so often, fully convinced it was *imminent*:

"...having a hope in God, which these men cherish themselves that **there shall certainly be** a resurrection of both the righteous and the wicked."
— *Acts 24:15*

In Greek, the words "there shall certainly be" are from the word mello — μέλλω, which means "about to happen." A better translation is:

"...having a hope in God, which these men cherish themselves, that **there is about to be** a resurrection of both the righteous and the wicked."
— *Acts 24:15*

In his first letter to the Thessalonians, Paul had already told them that at the coming of Jesus, the dead would be raised:

"For the Lord Himself will descend from heaven with a shout, with the voice of an archangel, and with the trumpet of God. **And the dead in Christ will rise first."**
— *1 Thessalonians 4:16*

The Christians in Corinth were also eagerly awaiting this day. However, some claimed that the resurrection had already happened:

"Among them are Hymenaeus and Philetus, men who have gone astray from the truth, **claiming that the resurrection has already taken place;** and they are jeopardizing the faith of some."
— *2 Timothy 2:18*

Such a claim only makes sense if the resurrection was understood to be spiritual and therefore invisible. If it were physical, no one could possibly believe it had already occurred — it would be obvious.

Isaiah gives another confirmation that the resurrection of the dead would take place during the destruction of Jerusalem. First, he writes:

> **"You have made their city a ruin, their fortress**
> **a ruinous heap; the stronghold of the barbarians**
> **is desolate, it will never be built."**
> — *Isaiah 25:2*

In the same breath, Isaiah declares that the Lord conquered death:

> **"He will swallow up death for all time,**
> **and the Lord God will wipe tears away from all faces."**
> — *Isaiah 25:8*

When would God destroy death? On the very day Jerusalem was reduced to ruins—exactly as Jesus foretold in Matthew 24 and as Paul assured the Thessalonians.

If we claim the resurrection has not yet occurred, then we do not have eternal life, because then we still descend into Sheol when we die. That means the hope of the first Christians was in vain, and our belief that we go to Heaven when we pass away, is also an illusion.

If the resurrection didn't happen, every testimony of believers entering Heaven after death is a lie, and we remain in the same separation from God as those under the old covenant. Our comfort—the assurance that we go to be with Jesus when we die—would vanish.

But Scripture is clear: the resurrection occurred during the fall of Jerusalem, the Great Tribulation Jesus described. The old covenant ended, the separation was abolished, and death—spiritual separation—was swallowed up in victory. Now, we who belong to Christ remain in His presence when our body dies. We have eternal life: *everlasting unity with Jesus and the Father.* When we die, we will no longer descend into Sheol, but remain in God's presence. That is what it means to have eternal life.

The widespread theology that claims the dead haven't risen is based on a radical denial of the clear teachings of both Jesus Christ and His apostles, replacing them with an opposing belief system.

I invite you to return to Christ and His truth.

If the resurrection has not
happened, then none of us go
to Heaven when we die. We still
descend into the darkness of
the realm of the dead.

CHAPTER 15

The Glorified Body

"How amazing... I wonder why I've never heard this before. It makes perfect sense, though. Everyone who believes in Jesus has eternal life, *yet they all die.* It's because life means being in the presence of God, not earthly immortality. Sublime!

But what about the glorified body? Weren't we supposed to receive some kind of a glorious super-body so magnificent it would make even Superman twitch with jealousy?"

—*Josh*

Hmm, yes, I understand your question. That is a tricky one—because, once again, it's Paul, this *super-spiritual* scribe, who wrote about the glorified body. And as we have seen, humans have an annoying habit of reading such deep spiritual mysteries through their own carnal minds, which gives rise to all kinds of fantastical, Marvel-style stories that make everyone who hears them drool in anticipation. We can hardly wait to be transformed into something even the Transformers could only dream of.

But once again, we need to rein in our imagination and, with a sound mind, take a sober, honest look at what Paul actually wrote.

Here is Pauls famous passage about the glorified body:

"For our citizenship is in heaven,
from which **we also eagerly wait** for the Lord Jesus Christ,
who will transform **the body of our lowly condition**
into conformity with His glorious body,
by the exertion of the power that He has
even to subject all things to Himself."
— *Philippians 3:20–21*

Now, right off the bat, one glaringly obvious statement stands out: Paul said **they** were waiting for Christ, who would transform **their** body. He didn't say, "Thousands of years from now there will arise a generation in distant lands we have not even heard about, and those believers will be transformed." No! Paul stated, without even the slightest hint of doubt, that *they* would undergo this transformation at the coming of Christ:

"...we also eagerly wait for a Savior, the Lord Jesus Christ... who will transform the body of our lowly condition..."

Why is it—why, oh why is it—that Christians must always abuse the Word of God, twisting and manipulating it shamelessly? It has become such a natural habit to gravely misuse the Bible that we don't even give it a second thought. And all the while, we ignore the most basic principles of proper Bible study: respect the biblical audience, respect the biblical context, respect the biblical time indications. No—we carelessly throw all of that overboard, pull out our "holy eraser" and keep rubbing over the pages of Scripture until those irritating words "we" and "our" disappear. Then we step onto the stage of our churches, proudly proclaiming doctrines built on this habit of violating the words of the apostles while claiming, with flashing eyes and waving hands that hold up the Bible before amazed crowds, that we are revealing the ultimate truth.

Can we please stop this? Can we please end these grave transgressions and learn to be honest and sincere when we read the Scriptures?

God did not give us His Word so we could cut it into pieces and then assemble some creative puzzle from the fragments, forming whatever false belief we prefer, based on our own desires.

He speaks to us through His Word to bring clarity to our confused minds. But this clarity only comes when we respect the actual words of Scripture. And what Scripture shows us, beyond any shadow of a doubt, is that Paul promised the Philippians that *they* would undergo this transformation at the coming of Christ, which *they* eagerly awaited.

But let's be brutally honest...

We do not really like to acknowledge such plain truths, because they confront us with a shocking reality: once we stop abusing the Word of God and instead respect what it actually says, it reveals that many of our doctrines are severely out of whack.

We have obviously missed something—BIG TIME!

Our doctrines insist that the transformation of the body never happened, just as they insist that Christ never came in the way He announced.

Now, does that make Paul and Christ false prophets?

Or does it mean we may need to humble ourselves and go back to the Word of God to discover where *we* went off track?

Oh my God, no—that is just impossible! What popular pastor or profiteering preacher would ever do such an unimaginable thing? We don't admit that we were wrong—no. We fight, we discuss, we accuse, and we throw allegations around us to defend our false doctrines, because of our pride... *oh, our pride.* Goodness gracious, this huge, monstrous, terrible demon of pride that we all have—that is what rules our lives and minds. It is utterly out of the question that we would ever admit that we might be wrong and need to reconsider...

Do you see it? Or am I stepping on your toes?

I mean it. Our pride prevents us from being honest, so we shout accusations at those who call us to repent from our twisted theologies that are based on violent abuse of the Scriptures.

But I am here to say:

Enough is enough!

It's time we humble ourselves, go down onto our knees, and ask forgiveness for our shameless manipulation of the Word of God, and return to Christ and His crystal-clear truth.

And His truth is not hard to understand, as long as we refrain from ignoring it. Because what did the Apostle make as clear as anything?

That this transformation is a spiritual event, not physical.

Here, read it for yourself, it's not as hard as you may think:

"But someone will say, 'How are the dead raised?
And with what kind of body do they come?' You fool!
That which you sow does not come to life unless it dies;
and that which you sow, you do not sow the body which
is to be, but a bare grain, perhaps of wheat or of something else.

But God gives it a body just as He wished,
and to each of the seeds a body of its own.

All flesh is not the same flesh, but there is one flesh of mankind,
another flesh of animals, another flesh of birds,
and another of fish.
There are also heavenly bodies and earthly bodies,
but the glory of the heavenly is one,
and the glory of the earthly is another.

There is one glory of the sun, another glory of the moon,
and another glory of the stars; for star differs from star in glory.
So also is the resurrection of the dead.
It is sown a perishable body, it is raised an imperishable body;
it is sown in dishonor, it is raised in glory;
it is sown in weakness, it is raised in power;
it is sown a natural body, **it is raised a spiritual body.**
If there is a natural body, **there is also a spiritual body.**

So also it is written:

'The first man, Adam, became a living person.'
The last Adam was **a life-giving spirit.**
However, the spiritual is not first,
but the natural; **then the spiritual.**
The first man is from the earth, earthy;
the second Man is **from heaven.**

As is the earthy one, so also are those who are earthy;
and as is the heavenly One, so also are those who are heavenly.
Just as we have borne the image of the earthy,
we will also **bear the image of the heavenly.**

Now I say this, brothers and sisters,

**that flesh and blood cannot inherit the Kingdom of God,
nor does the perishable inherit the imperishable.**

Behold, I am telling you a mystery:

**we will not all sleep, but we will all be changed—
in a moment, in the twinkling of an eye,
at the last trumpet. For the trumpet will sound,
and the dead will be raised imperishable,
and we will be changed.**

For this perishable must put on the imperishable,
and this mortal must put on immortality.
But when this perishable puts on the imperishable,
and this mortal puts on immortality,
then will come about the saying that is written:
'Death has been swallowed up in victory.
Where, O Death, is your victory?
Where, O Death, is your sting?'"
— *1 Corinthians* 15:35–55

Those who say I am being too sharp in pointing out the grave sin of the Church of constantly twisting the Scriptures to uphold deceptions—please look at the severity with which Paul speaks. He calls people who think the resurrection body is physical downright 'fools'!

**"But someone will say, 'How are the dead raised?
And with what kind of body do they come?' You fool!"**

He then goes on to explain that we are *born* with an *earthly* body but are *clothed* with a *heavenly* one, which is spiritual.

I explained this before when talking about the resurrection. That spiritual body is not a replacement for our physical body—it is *laid over* our earthly body, like a jacket we put on, similar to "putting on Christ".

"For this perishable must put on the imperishable,
and this mortal **must put on** immortality."
— *1 Corinthians* 15:53–54

Other translations say we are being "clothed" with it:

> "For the perishable must **clothe itself with** the imperishable, and the mortal with immortality."
>
> —*1 Corinthians 15:53 NIV*

"But sir, what on Earth does that even mean? How can we be clothed with another body? It's not like we can go to Target, H&M, or Zara to pick our favorite imperishable costume from the brand 'Made in Heaven'! You can hardly blame us for wrestling with this. It would be helpful if Paul had included a glossary at the end of his letters, explaining some of his high-level spiritual vocabulary."

—*Josh*

Yes, it's true—these are *mysteries*. And don't feel bad, because you're not alone. Even a respected spiritual teacher in Israel, who was not like the wicked sons of Satan, like some other Pharisees, but who yearned to understand the truth, failed to grasp these spiritual concepts.

I am talking about Nicodemus, who was afraid to seek clarification during the day, fearing the scorn of his peers, so he came to Jesus in the darkness of the night. With obvious confusion—but honest inquiry—he uttered the question which sounded too ridiculous for words: must a person go back into their mother's womb to be born again?

> "Jesus responded and said to him, 'Truly, truly, I say to you, unless someone is born again he cannot see the Kingdom of God.' Nicodemus said to Him, 'How can a person be born when he is old? **He cannot enter his mother's womb a second time and be born, can he?'"**
>
> —*John 3:3–4*

To Jesus, who had no trouble understanding these divine realities, it was astonishing that this teacher of Israel could not grasp this principle.

> "Jesus answered and said to him, **'You are the teacher of Israel, and yet you do not understand these things? (...)**
> If I told you earthly things and you do not believe,
> how will you believe if I tell you **heavenly things?'"**
>
> —*John 3:10, 12*

Our problem is simple... we are just too earthly in our thinking—too 'carnal,' as the Bible calls it. Our focus is fixed on the flesh, on the dust of this Earth, instead of lifting the veil from our eyes and looking up into the glorious realms of God.

The solution, therefore, is clear:

we must shift from the flesh to the Spirit.

It's the only way, because throughout the Bible God speaks about spiritual realities. The Bible says we are born again from the Spirit:

"That which has been born of the flesh is flesh,
and that which has been **born of the Spirit** is spirit.
Do not be amazed that I said to you,
'You must be born again.'"
—*John 3:6–7*

Do we physically notice anything when we're born again? Not at all! It is a spiritual reality. Just like the body of Christ:

"Now **you are Christ's body**, and individually parts of it."
—*1 Corinthians 12:27*

Do we feel this physically? No. Yet the body of Christ is a deeply powerful spiritual truth.

What's more, the Bible says we have all died in Christ and have been raised with Him from the dead:

"Therefore **we have been buried with Him** through baptism
into death, so that, just as Christ was raised from the dead
through the glory of the Father,
so we too may walk in newness of life."
—*Romans 6:4*

Have we physically experienced that? No.

Paul even says we were crucified with Christ:

"...knowing this, that **our old self was crucified with Him,**
in order that our body of sin might be done away with,"
—*Romans 6:6*

Do we have holes in our hands and feet? Of course not.

Finally, Paul says we are seated with Christ in heavenly places:

"...and raised us up with Him, and **seated us with Him in the heavenly places** in Christ Jesus."
— *Ephesians 2:6*

Are we sitting next to Jesus in Heaven in golden chairs? Clearly not.

We are also called to put on the spiritual armor, and Paul describes the breastplate, the helmet, the sandals, and so on:

"Therefore, **take up the full armor of God,**
so that you will be able to resist on the evil day."
— *Ephesians 6:13*

Do Christians worldwide walk around dressed like Roman soldiers? Once again, of course not.

There are countless examples in the Bible where God uses natural metaphors to reveal spiritual truths: born again from the Spirit, the body of Christ, putting on Jesus like a garment, dying with Christ, being raised from the dead, being crucified with Christ, being seated in heavenly places, putting on armor, being clothed with a heavenly body.

The heart of the matter is that we must leave our own mindsets behind and learn to understand that the Kingdom of Christ, and all the realities it includes, is a spiritual dimension, which we observe, enter, and experience through the Spirit of God. When we forget that and try to explain it in an earthly way, from the mind of the flesh, we go into error.

Does that answer all the questions we may have about these deep spiritual mysteries? No. Entire volumes could be written exploring the hidden depths of these eternal dimensions.

But that is not the purpose of this book.

My goal is to untie you from the cobwebs of confusion the enemy has placed on the mind of the Church and restore the plain and simple truths of God's Word, so that we can rise up and begin to discover these wonderful realities.

And the most important reality of them all is the discovery that our heavenly Father and the Lord Jesus are right here with us—everywhere we go, at all times, no matter the circumstance. The spiritual body we have been clothed with, enables us to experience the presence of the Most High at all times. Our soul will no longer have to descend into the realm of the dead when our physical bodies cease to function and we experience physical death. Because we have a resurrected body, just like Christ, we will go straight into the glorious heavenly realm of the Father, where we will abide with Him forever.

Because we have been clothed with this new spiritual body, we can now experience unprecedented unity with Christ and the Father—a oneness that will not be severed by any form of death.

We truly have eternal life, which means we have lasting fellowship with the Almighty, both during our earthly life and after it, when our glorified bodies disconnect from our earthly ones and we continue our unity with the Lord in His heavenly dimensions.

Again and again, this is what it all comes down to: Jesus Christ established a New Covenant with a brand-new spiritual reality, where *man is restored to lasting communion with the Almighty.* Christ did not come to turn us all into Marvel movie stars, with supernatural physical bodies that have all kinds of mega-magnificent superpowers, as some twisted theologians have been claiming for centuries. He came to unite us with God. That is what matters.

Not waiting to receive an immortal physical body, but entering into the reality of living in the presence of Jesus and the Father—that is the greatest treasure of all time. That is a superpower that far exceeds all other spectacular forces. Being in intimate fellowship with the One who made the Heavens and the Earth, who is dreaded by legions of demons, adored by awesome angels, and exalted above all powers—that is a force to be reckoned with.

Once we truly begin to understand what we have received in the Kingdom of Christ, under His New Covenant, through the Spirit of God, we will never want to go back to the dark shadows of the Old.

My prayer is that we would wake up to the truth of what Christ has granted us and begin to walk in it. Because this is what Satan and his myriads of demonic minions have been preventing for centuries. They have blinded the Church to the immeasurable riches and unsurmounted power of what Christ has bestowed upon us.

May the Spirit of truth and revelation awaken us deep within, so we would finally see it and start to live in this heavenly reality.

CHAPTER 16

The City of Gold

"You've answered plenty of my questions so far. But there are still a few roadblocks before I'm fully on board. Take the New Jerusalem, for example. The Bible says a brilliant, shining gold city will come hurtling down from Heaven, landing smack on the Earth. A city with golden streets, crystal walls, and gates made of colossal pearls. I've sung those hymns about strolling the streets of gold—haven't you? So, when exactly is this golden city scheduled to drop from the sky?"

—*Josh*

Uhm... Have you thought about sunglasses?

What? Yes, sunglasses! You don't think you'll be able to walk inside this heavenly Jerusalem without your sunglasses, do you? I mean, the shimmer and shine will be blinding—gold, crystal, pearl everywhere, illuminated with a light stronger than the midday sun.

And where's the forest? The meadows? The lakes and mountains? Are we really going to have to spend all eternity inside that massive golden skyscraper? That's not really my idea of Heaven on Earth. I need to ride horses through the wide-open fields, enjoy the golden sunset, hike the majestic mountains, and hear the singing of the birds in the trees, while a crystal-clear creek babbles in the background.

I don't like living in the city—especially a city that blinds my eyes constantly with glimmer all around me.

You know, that's how I used to think about the New Jerusalem:

a literal golden cube dropping down somewhere on Earth, where we would have to spend all eternity.

Thankfully, Scripture came to my rescue.

One day my wife and I were walking through the peaceful dunes along the coast. Surrounded by silence and sea air, we decided to read a passage from the Bible. As Renate looked down at the text, she suddenly said, "Wait—this is strange. Did you know that in Revelation the angel tells John that the New Jerusalem is the Bride of the Lamb?"

I froze. "What? Isn't the Bride of the Lamb the Church? That's *us!*"

She nodded. "Exactly. Which means *we* are the New Jerusalem..."

As it dawned on us that *we* are the Bride of the Lamb—and thus we are also the New Jerusalem—a new realm of insight opened before us.

In many places in the Bible God refers to Jerusalem as the city where He dwells. The name Jerusalem literally means "city of shalom," or, translated, city of peace, harmony, prosperity, and good fortune.

"The God of Israel, the God who dwells in Jerusalem."
— *Ezra 1:3*

Throughout the Old Testament, the old Jerusalem was anything but peaceful. The constant rebellion and idolatry of God's people meant that this "city of peace" rarely lived up to its name. The earthly city was never the ultimate reality—it was a *prophetic shadow*, a sign pointing forward to the true Jerusalem which God would reveal through Jesus Christ.

This new Jerusalem is described with stunning beauty by Isaiah in chapters 60–62, and later shown to John in Revelation. Their visions match in remarkable detail, revealing this central truth:

the New Jerusalem is the Bride of God, the Bride of the Lamb, Christ's own people.

"And as the groom rejoices over **the bride,**
so your God will rejoice over you."
— *Isaiah 62:5*

"And I saw the holy city, **New Jerusalem,**
coming down out of heaven from God,
prepared as a bride adorned for her husband."
— *Revelation 21:2*

"Then one of the seven angels ... came and spoke with me,
saying, 'Come here, I will show you **the bride,**
the wife of the Lamb.' And he carried me away in the Spirit
to a great and high mountain, and showed me **the holy city,**
Jerusalem, coming down out of heaven from God."
— *Revelation 21:9–10*

Who, then, is the Bride? Apostle Paul revealed the ancient mystery that all who are in Jesus Christ are this Bride:

"For I am jealous for you with a godly jealousy;
for I betrothed you **to one husband,**
to present you as a pure virgin to Christ."
— *2 Corinthians 11:2*

"For this reason a man shall leave his father
and his mother and be joined to his wife,
and the two shall become one flesh.
This mystery is great; but **I am speaking**
with reference to Christ and the church."
— *Ephesians 5:31–32*

If we delve even deeper into the Bible, we see that the life of Christians corresponds in detail to the description of the New Jerusalem. Read the remarkable similarities below.

Both are called a Bride who is pure and radiant

New Jerusalem:

"The wedding of the Lamb has come, and his bride is ready. She is allowed to dress in pure, radiant linen." — *Revelation 19:7*

Christians:

"Husbands, love your wives, just as Christ loved the church...
to present her to himself in all glory, without spot or wrinkle or
any other blemish, but holy and blameless."
— *Ephesians 5:25–27*

Both are spiritually built with gold and precious stones

New Jerusalem:

"The wall was made of jasper, and the city itself was pure, clear as glass. The stones on which the city wall rested were decorated with all kinds of precious stones."
— *Revelation 21:19*

Christians:

"No one can lay any foundation other than the one already laid, which is Jesus Christ. But on this foundation, people can build with gold, silver, and precious stones..."
— *1 Corinthians 3:13*

Both are a city on a mountain

New Jerusalem:

"Come! I will show you the bride, the wife of the Lamb." The Spirit came upon me, and the angel brought me to the top of a very high mountain. He showed me Jerusalem, the holy city coming down out of God from heaven."
— *Revelation 21:9–10*

Christians:

"You are the light of the world. A city on a mountain cannot be hidden." — *Matthew 5:14*

Both have the river of living water

New Jerusalem:

"The angel also showed me the river with the WATER
that gives LIFE. The river was clear as crystal;
it flowed from the throne of God and the Lamb,
and it flowed down the middle of the city's square."
— *Revelation 22:1*

Christians:

"The Scripture says about those who believe in me:
'Their hearts will be a fountain of living water.'"
—*John 7:38*

Both have a foundation laid by apostles

New Jerusalem:

"The city wall rested on twelve foundations,
twelve stones, on which were written the names
of the twelve apostles of the Lamb."
—*Revelation 21:14*

Christians:

". . . built on the foundation of the apostles and prophets,
with Christ Jesus himself as the cornerstone."
—*Ephesians 2:20*

Both are the light of the world

New Jerusalem:

"The nations will walk by its light." —*Revelation 21:24*

Christians:

"You are the light of the world. A city on a hill cannot be hidden."
—*Matthew 5:14*

Both give no room to impurity and lies

New Jerusalem:

"Nothing impure will ever enter it,
nor will anyone who does what is shameful or deceitful."
—*Revelation 21:27*

Christians:

"Therefore, rid yourselves of all falsehood
and speak the truth with each other."
— *Ephesians* 4:25

Both know no darkness, but live in the light

New Jerusalem:

"There will be no more night. They will not need the light of a
lamp or the light of the sun, for the Lord God will be their light."
— *Revelation* 21:5

Christians:

"Whoever follows me will never walk in darkness,
but will have the light of life."
— *John* 8:12

The wonder of God's Word is that it often reveals multiple dimensions at once. Paul says that we are *children* of the New Jerusalem, that we have been *brought near* to the heavenly Jerusalem, and that *we are* the dwelling place of God. In God's mind, these truths do not contradict each other.

I see it this way: when we turn to Christ and are born again by the Spirit, we are brought into the heavenly Jerusalem and become its children. Then the Spirit builds us up into a dwelling place of God, making us part of that very city.

It's a beautiful picture of a greater reality: in the old covenant, God dwelt in a temple of stone, in a city of stone, with His law written on tablets of stone. Everything in the old covenant was stone—just as God said the hearts of His people were made of stone (Ezekiel 11:19).

When Christ came, He established the new covenant, which is a brand-new reality. In this new covenant, it is no longer about a stone city, a stone temple, and stone tablets. Now it is all about the Spirit of God, who transforms us into the very dwelling place of the Most High God—the city where His presence abides, the temple of His glory.

The old covenant was the "Stone Age": stone tablets, a stone temple, and a stone city. The new covenant is the age of the Spirit:

- **The Spirit of God writes the law of God on our hearts.**
  —*2 Corinthians 3:3*

- **The Spirit makes us into a temple of the living God.**
  —*1 Corinthians 3:16*

- **The Spirit of God builds us as the city of God.**
  —*Ephesians 2:21-22*

- **The Spirit of God makes us a new creation in Christ.**
  —*2 Corinthians 5:16–17*

- **The Spirit of God teaches us all truth.**
  —*John 16:13-15*

- **The Spirit of God makes us into true worshipers.**
  —*John 4:21-24*

This last verse is particularly important, because Jesus Christ specifically said that we *no longer have to travel to Jerusalem* to worship God. No, He says, God is Spirit, and He longs for true worship, which is in the Spirit of God.

> "You will worship the Father
> **neither on this mountain or in Jerusalem.**
> (...) God is spirit, and those who worship Him
> must worship in spirit and truth.'"
> —*John 4:21-24*

That's why we can only observe, enter, and experience the Kingdom of God by the Spirit of God.

> **"Unless someone is born of water and the Spirit,**
> **he cannot enter the Kingdom of God."**
> —*John 3:5*

Paul calls the new covenant the "ministry of the Spirit."

> "God, who also made us adequate as servants of a new covenant,
> not of the letter but **of the Spirit;** for the letter kills,

but **the Spirit gives life.** But if the ministry of death,
engraved in letters on stones, came with glory
so that the sons of Israel could not look intently
at the face of Moses because of the glory of his face,
fading as it was, **how will the ministry of the Spirit
fail to be even more with glory?**"
— *2 Corinthians 3:3-7*

Can you see it? The old covenant was physical, with a physical temple in a physical city. But Christ judged that old era, destroyed all of it—the temple was torn down to the very last stone—and He created a brand new reality in which we are now the temple of the Lord. And all of us together, who are the Bride of the Lamb, are the New Jerusalem.

Christ made all things new!

"'**Behold, I am making all things new.**"
— *Revelation 21:5*

Isaiah already announced it and called Israel to *forget the former things*, and focus only on the new reality that was coming:

**"Do not call to mind the former things,
or consider things of the past.
Behold, I am going to do something new,
now it will spring up; will you not be aware of it?"**
— *Isaiah 43:18-19*

God no longer dwells in temples or cities built by the hands of men, but He now dwells in us, who are being built up by the Spirit of God.

**"The God who made the world and everything that is in
it, since He is Lord of heaven and earth,
does not dwell in temples made by hands."**
— *Acts 17:24*

We are not waiting to spend all of eternity in some golden super-skyscraper.

**We are that golden city.
Our lives are the New Jerusalem.**

We are the habitation of the Most High God. He dwells inside of us and among us.

Everything in the New Covenant is about God's presence with us. That is why Jesus Christ was called Emmanuel—*God with us.*

God's desire has always been to have a precious family of beloved children in whose midst He could dwell—speaking to them, filling them with His love, moving among them with acts of power, healing their brokenness, and building them into His beautiful dwelling place: the true Jerusalem, the city of peace.

Not a city of rocks and bricks, but a worldwide family of loving hearts, burning souls, and transformed lives, brought to life through the love of Jesus Christ and our heavenly Father.

Once we grasp that reality, we will never again long to spend all of eternity inside a blinding golden cubic skyscraper, without grass, forests, birds, or mountains.

The cube is a metaphor for the perfect harmony of God, where we are all equal. It contrasts the satanic system of the pyramid, where everyone is subjected to a tyrant at the top. In the cube, all sides are equal. And God does not sit at the top of a pyramid—*He dwells inside the cube.* That is the meaning of the cube, as opposed to the pyramids. We are all brothers and sisters and in our midst dwells the Lord, with His glory.

Once we begin to truly realize this, and allow the Lord God Almighty to manifest His majesty in us and through us, the level of glory that will be revealed in our midst will be unheard of. That's why Satan has done everything in his ability to hide this glorious truth from us.

A Church that always waits for Jesus to "come" will never fully awaken to His presence in our midst. Even the most charismatic churches fail to truly manifest the fullness of His glory, because in the back of our minds we still think: "Jesus is out there."

I believe the Lord deeply desires to shift our minds and open the eyes of our hearts to His presence among us. When that happens, our gatherings will be transformed into life-changing encounters with the risen King and victorious Lord.

May the Spirit of God open our minds to this central truth from the Scriptures—the very heart of the work Christ accomplished, the pure essence of the New Covenant—so the Church will become ablaze with the radiance of the presence of Christ.

CHAPTER 17

Nuclear Apocalypse

"Goodness gracious, that is amazing! Here I am, waiting my entire life to walk on the streets of gold, only to find out that my own life is that street of gold. How I live and how I walk with Jesus is supposed to be a path of pure gold. That's pretty cool. You are making it more and more clear to me, sir. But I still struggle with a few things—like the prediction that the entire universe would be destroyed by fire during the return of Christ. Doesn't the apostle Peter say that? And didn't Jesus say that Heaven and Earth will pass away, and a brand new Heaven and Earth would be created?"

—Josh

You know, Josh, for many years I also feared that we were headed for the total destruction of Heaven and Earth, followed by an entirely new physical creation appearing out of nowhere. Many preachers declare that the destruction of Heaven and Earth will come through a global nuclear war. They believe that this will be God's judgment on all of humanity.

One night I attended a special event at our church, where a highly exalted "expert" on end-time prophecy came to lay it all out for us. This wide-eyed man frantically exclaimed how the apostle John had seen gruesome visions of tanks, rockets, and nuclear explosions which he then tried to describe in the book of Revelation.

I walked out of that seminar with ghastly visions burned into my young mind, a terrifying future filled with smoke, fire, and destruction.

Everything God has created would be completely destroyed by the most horrific weapons ever devised by man. All of God's beautiful animals, birds, flowers, plants, mountains, forests, plains, lakes, beaches, and parks—and the billions of beloved, precious people—would fall prey to this horrible inferno. People's flesh would rot away while they were still standing. Their eyes would rot in their sockets, and their tongues would rot in their mouths. Pure horror of the worst kind.

The return of Jesus, according to this view, would first and foremost mean the absolute destruction of literally everything God has created.

After that, God would create a new Heaven and a new Earth, where perfect peace and harmony would reign.

Although the idea of a new Heaven and Earth filled with perfect happiness naturally appeals to us, what is said to precede it is the most terrible thing that could ever happen. Everything that God created in His love and goodness, and which was intended to reveal His majesty and wisdom, would go up in flames.

And not only that, it would bring unprecedented suffering as billions of people feel their flesh rot away and their eyes melt from their sockets. Humanity would be facing the most terrifying fate imaginable.

During my student days, I had recurring nightmares about nuclear war. I remember dreaming that I was sitting in class, gazing out the window, when suddenly mushroom clouds began rising all across the horizon. One after another, they appeared in every direction. I woke up drenched in sweat, terrified.

As with everything we were told, we must also subject this nightmarish idea to biblical scrutiny. Let's first look at where the idea comes from that all people worldwide will feel their flesh rot away from their bones. This comes from a verse in the book of Zechariah:

> "Now this will be the plague with which the Lord will strike
> **all the peoples who have gone to war against Jerusalem:**
> their flesh will rot while they stand on their feet,
> and their eyes will rot in their sockets,
> and their tongue will rot in their mouth."
> — *Zechariah 14:12*

Well, well, surprise, surprise! This passage has absolutely nothing to do with some global nuclear apocalypse. It's talking about the destruction of Jerusalem, plain and simple!

Once again, we witness the unspeakable corruption that festers through modern Christendom—an epidemic infecting countless Bible teachers, preachers, and pastors who claim to speak for God while butchering His Word like a bunch of brutal bullies. They rip verses straight out of their historical setting, twist them beyond recognition, and parade their mutilated message before the masses as "revelation."

These passages speak about the fall of Jerusalem in 70 AD. Yet what do they do? They shamelessly hijack them, insisting they're about us today. Why? *Because fear sells.* Fear is the golden goose of Christianity. It funds empires. It buys private jets. It keeps the gold rings shining, the designer suits pressed, and the mansions glistening on the hill.

Meanwhile, millions of sincere believers—pure-hearted souls who just want to know God—are being led like lambs to the slaughter by these spiritual con artists in holy disguise. They are not shepherds. They are wolves draped in wool, devouring the flock one tithe at a time.

"Yikes, it's all so disgusting, Mr. Sörensen. I've been deceived so badly by these professional liars! I remember lying in my bed, shivering with terror at the thought of my own flesh rotting away while everything dear to me burned to ashes—my loved ones screaming in agony as the world supposedly ended. That's what they told us! And of course, we believed them. We emptied our wallets into their offering buckets because, well, fear is the most expensive emotion on the market.

Now I'm finally learning it was all one big, stinking hoax.

But tell me, what do the Scriptures actually mean when they talk about a 'new Heaven and Earth'?"

—*Josh*

Oh Josh, I know exactly what you mean. I used to live in the same nightmare. I too lay awake, terrified that the sky would split open any second and we'd all be roasted alive. But the relief that comes when you finally see the truth is priceless!

And yes, I had the same question about the "new Heaven and Earth." And what I discovered blew my mind. It has nothing to do with the annihilation of all life in the cosmos. In fact, it's the very opposite.

This mind-blowing discovery begins the moment we slow down and actually listen to these incredibly strange words Jesus spoke:

"Heaven and earth will pass away,
but My words will not pass away."
—*Matthew 24:35*

"Heaven and Earth will pass away…" Can you imagine standing there with Jesus, listening to His every word, soaking it all in like a sponge because you're starving for truth—and then suddenly He announces the total destruction of everything you know and everything you love? If that had been me, I would have absolutely freaked out. There go my dreams for the future, the vision for me and my wife, the plans our children are making. Everything suddenly about to come crashing down. Everything turning to dust. All of us gone!

But is that truly what Jesus was talking about? Did He actually announce the total annihilation of everything He ever created—the complete wipeout of the Earth and all humanity? Well, let's take a look.

As always, we must begin with context. Jesus spoke these incredible words about the destruction of "Heaven and Earth" while He was talking to His disciples about the coming destruction of Jerusalem and the temple. That's strange. It doesn't seem to fit at all. Why would Jesus suddenly leap from a *local judgment* on Israel—focused on the abolishing of the temple—to the end of the *whole universe?* Let's look at the passage more closely. Jesus turned to the Jews in Jerusalem and said:

> "And then the sign of the Son of Man will appear in the sky,
> and then all the tribes of the earth will mourn,
> and they will see the Son of Man coming
> on the clouds of the sky with power and great glory.
> And He will send forth His angels with a great trumpet blast,
> and they will gather together His elect from the four winds,
> from one end of the sky to the other.
> Now learn the parable from the fig tree:
> as soon as its branch has become tender and sprouts its leaves,
> you know that summer is near; so you too,
> when you see all these things, recognize that He is near,
> right at the door.
> Truly I say to you, this generation will not pass away
> until all these things take place.
>
> **Heaven and earth will pass away,**
> **but My words will not pass away."**
> — *Matthew* 24:30–35

What on Earth is going on here? Did Jesus suddenly lose His mind? Did He go berserk—shifting from announcing judgment over the

Pharisees, speaking about a new covenant, and promising a beautiful future for His followers—and then suddenly saying everyone would be blown to smithereens? How are we supposed to make sense of this?

The answer that brings clarity—and a huge sigh of relief—comes when we stop reading this as Westerners from the 21st century and step back in time for a moment. We need to understand what the phrase "Heaven and Earth" actually meant to Jesus and His Jewish audience.

The mystery begins to unravel the moment we open the book of Isaiah. There we stumble upon something rather curious. Isaiah begins his prophecy with these words:

> "The vision of Isaiah the son of Amoz
> concerning **Judah** and **Jerusalem...**
> Listen, **heavens**, and hear, **earth**;
> for the Lord has spoken."
> — *Isaiah 1:1–2*

Now, hold it right there. Did you catch that? Isaiah is speaking about **Judah and Jerusalem**, yet he calls them **Heaven and Earth!** What's that all about? Let me tell you, that's not a random poetic flourish. He's revealing something that changes how we should read Jesus' words.

If we continue digging into the Bible, we see that Moses did the same thing. He addressed **Israel** and also called them **"Heaven and Earth"**:

> "Then Moses spoke in the hearing of **all the assembly of Israel**
> the words of this song, until they were complete:
> **'Listen, you heavens,** and I will speak;
> and **let the earth hear** the words of my mouth!'"
> — *Deuteronomy 31:30; 32:1*

Isn't that peculiar? These two statements by Moses and Isaiah reveal something truly remarkable:

> **In ancient Israel, the phrase "Heaven and Earth"
> didn't just describe God's physical creation—
> it also referred to His covenant people.
> They were "Heaven and Earth."**

And is this confirmed by Jewish history? Yes, it is. The Jewish historian Flavius Josephus recorded that even the tabernacle—and later the temple itself—was referred to as "Heaven and Earth."

> "Moses divided **the tabernacle** into three separate parts.
> Two of them were for the priests, accessible to the people,
> and he called these the **LAND** and the **SEA**.
> But the third part he set apart for God,
> for **HEAVEN** is not accessible to men."
> —*Josephus, Antiquities, Book 3, Chapter 7, Paragraph 7*

So we see that the sanctuary was divided into three parts:

- **HEAVEN was accessible only to the high priest**
- **EARTH was for the priests**
- **SEA was for the "ordinary" people**

Now that we know Israel was referred to as "Heaven and Earth," and that the temple itself was literally considered "Heaven and Earth," we finally understand what Jesus meant. He hadn't just binge-watched the *Left Behind* series and changed His theology overnight, announcing a cosmic demolition of the entire universe. Not at all.

Being a Jew in Israel, speaking to Jews in Israel, who were all thinking as Jews in Israel, Christ simply told them something every Jew in Israel understood perfectly well: Israel and the temple—called "Heaven and Earth"—were going to pass away.

There! Now it makes total sense. Jesus spoke in the normal Jewish idiom of His time—a language that made perfect sense to His audience. It's only to us Westerners, two thousand years later, living thousands of miles away in a culture so radically different it's like comparing ice cream to french fries, that these words sound wildly out of place.

And because of this enormous cultural misunderstanding, billions of believers have spent their entire lives fearing the end of the world, convinced that at any moment "Heaven and Eearth" might literally explode. Help!

Now, let's be diligent about this and do our homework properly. One essential principle for double-checking our interpretation of the Bible is this: *we must compare Scripture with Scripture.* So what do other parts of the Old Testament say about this? Isaiah has some interesting things to say about the new Heaven and Earth.

To begin with, God spoke through Isaiah about the persistent sins of Israel and how He would punish them:

> "I have spread out My hands
> all day long to a rebellious people,
> Who walk in the way which is not good,
> following their own thoughts,
> A people who continually provoke Me to My face...
>
> Behold, it is written before Me:
> I will not keep silent, but I will repay;
> I will even repay into their laps,
> Both your own wrongdoings
> and the wrongdoings of your fathers together," says the Lord.
>
> **...I will destine you for the sword,**
> **And all of you will bow down to the slaughter.**
>
> Because I called, but you did not answer;
> I spoke, but you did not listen.
> **Instead, you did evil in My sight**
> **And chose that in which I did not delight."**
> — *Isaiah 65:2, 6, 12*

God spoke about the coming judgment on Israel. What did He say next, just a few verses later?

> **"For behold, I create new heavens and a new earth;**
> **And the former things will not be remembered**
> **or come to mind."**
> — *Isaiah 65:17*

Just as in Matthew 24, the context of the new Heaven and Earth here is God's judgment on Israel.

1. First, God announced His judgment on Israel.
2. Then He said, "I am creating a new Heaven and Earth."

Was God announcing a brand new physical universe, where there would be no more death, sin, suffering or darkness?

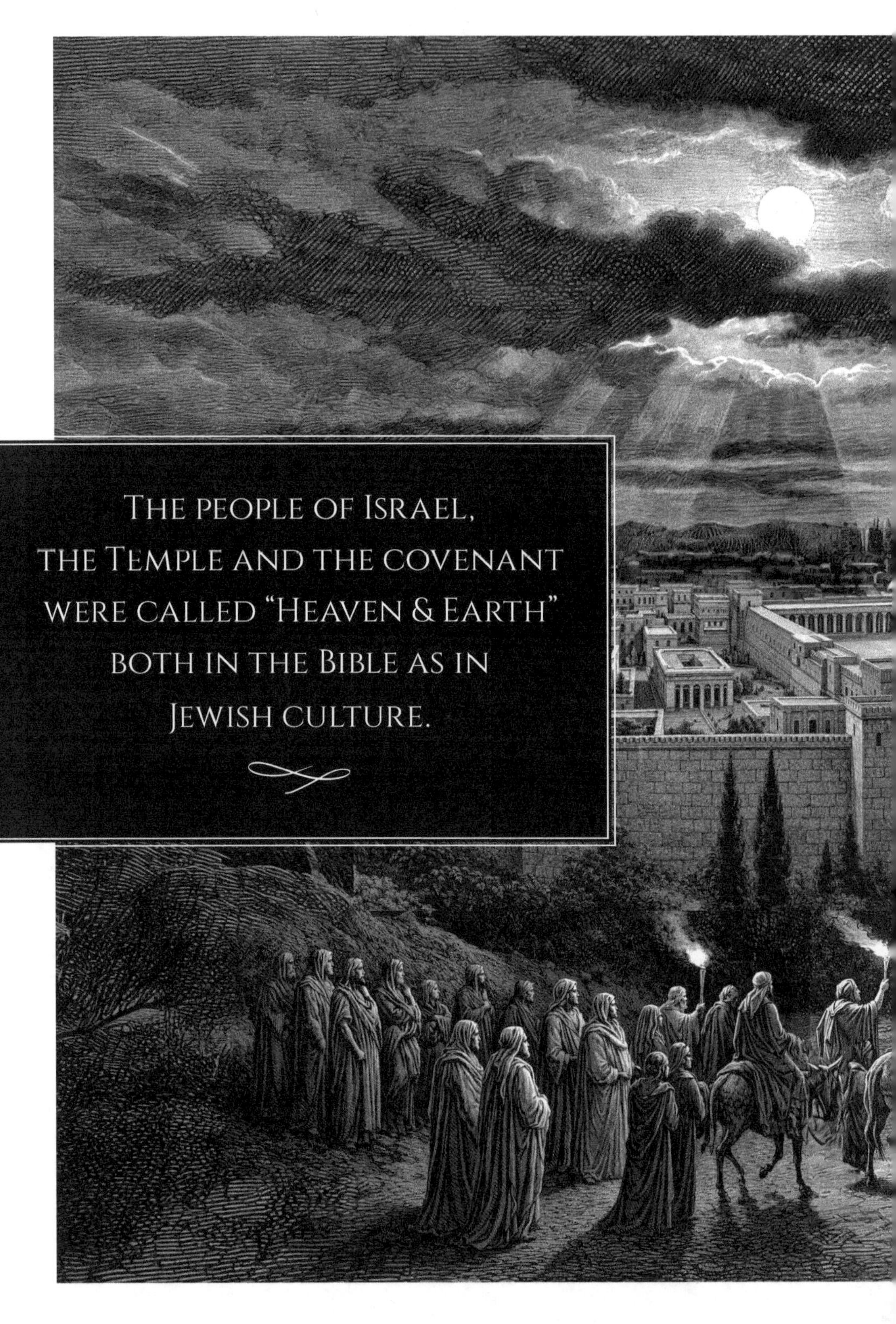
The people of Israel,
the Temple and the covenant
were called "Heaven & Earth"
both in the Bible as in
Jewish culture.

Or did God mean something spiritual, like Jesus explained? Here is what Isaiah said about this "new Heaven and Earth":

- Physical death will still exist — *Isaiah 65:20; 66:24*
- Building houses and farming will continue — *Isaiah 65:21–22*
- People will have children — *Isaiah 65:23; 66:22*
- The Lord will answer prayers — *Isaiah 65:24*
- There will still be sin — *Isaiah 65:20; Matthew 12:32; Rev. 22:15*
- There will be evangelism — *Isaiah 66:19*

That is strange. God creates a new Heaven and Earth, yet there is still death, sin, and life going on as usual. Again, the crystal-clear Word of God radically contradicts the fairytales we've been fed in the Church of our time, where every platform is used to announce that when Jesus returns, the entire creation will instantly transform into a perfect paradise.

Isaiah's description of the new Heaven and Earth confirms that God was speaking about a new *spiritual* dimension, a new *heavenly reality* under which people live—not the "heaven" of the old covenant, but a new heaven, a new spiritual realm in which people live within the new covenant. And not the same "earth," meaning the people of the old covenant, but a brand-new people, reborn by the Spirit of God.

That is indeed the message of the New Testament—the essence of the Christian faith: Jesus Christ has made all things new. In Him, we are a new creation:

> "Therefore, if anyone is in Christ, this person is **a new creation;**
> the old things passed away; behold, new things have come."
> — *2 Corinthians 5:17*

> "For neither is circumcision anything,
> nor uncircumcision, but **a new creation.**"
> — *Galatians 6:15*

The fact that these apostles constantly spoke about the new creation obviously has to do with their awareness that a new Heaven and Earth was coming—*a new creation!* However, they understood that this was not physical, but spiritual. The old covenant would pass away, and a new covenant would come.

"When He said, **'A new covenant,'**
He has made the first obsolete.
But whatever is becoming obsolete and growing old
is about to disappear."
— *Hebrews 8:13*

There is also a *new people of God*, which now consists of all who are in Jesus Christ, as Peter wrote to the Christian Church:

"But **you are a chosen people**, a royal priesthood,
a holy nation, a people for God's own possession,
So that you may proclaim the excellencies of Him
who has called you out of darkness into His marvelous light;
For you once were not a people,
but **now you are the people of God;**
You had not received mercy, but now you have received mercy."
— *1 Peter 2:9–10*

In this new people of God, which has come forth from Christ, there is no longer any racial distinction between Jews and other peoples. Jesus has created a *new man:*

"For He Himself is our peace, who made both groups into one
and broke down the barrier of the dividing wall,
by abolishing in His flesh the enmity,
which is the Law of commandments contained in ordinances,
so that in Himself He might make the two
into **one new man**."
— *Ephesians 2:14–15*

The reconciliation between Jews and other peoples is illustrated by the image of the wolf and the lamb lying down together (Isaiah 11:6). There is no more enmity; together, they form a new people of God—a new man in Jesus Christ. Thus, God fulfilled the promise that the name Israel would remain forever under the new covenant.

"For just as **the new heavens and the new earth,**
which I make, will endure before Me," declares the Lord,
"So will your descendants and your name endure."
— *Isaiah 66:22*

Every time we look up the biblical passages about a new Heaven and Earth, we see that the context is God's judgment on ancient Israel. God would create something completely new in Jesus Christ.

In Christ, the old has passed away, and the new has come.

"My Lord, that is absolutely amazing. It makes so much sense! But why did Peter say, 'the heavens will pass away with a roar, and the elements will be destroyed by fire'? Didn't he predict the total destruction of all of creation through a terrible fire?"

—*Josh*

"But the day of the Lord will come like a thief,
in which the heavens will pass away with a roar
and the elements will be destroyed with intense heat,
and the earth and its works will be discovered.

Since all these things are to be destroyed in this way,
what sort of people ought you to be
in holy conduct and godliness,
looking for and hastening the coming of the day of God,
because of which the heavens
will be destroyed by burning,
and the elements will melt with intense heat!
But according to His promise, we are looking for new heavens and a new earth, in which righteousness dwells."

— *2 Peter 3:10–13*

Yes, I completely agree with you. Again, for us 21st century Westerners, Peter indeed gives the impression here that they were on the verge of experiencing the total destruction of everything that exists.

It is of immeasurable importance that we always remind ourselves of the original audience and the historical and biblical context of this type of Bible passage. After all, we are so accustomed to applying everything the apostles wrote to the first Christians to ourselves, thousands of years later, in a completely different context.

Peter lived in the transition period between the old and the new covenant. In his worldview—and therefore also in his vocabulary—the old covenant was "the old world." *Israel was the only world Peter knew!* And it is of the utmost importance that we understand this. They had no Internet, no travel guides, no televisions showing them the whole Earth, and no paid vacations to explore foreign lands. All they knew was their own tiny little neighborhood called Israel. *That was their world*—literally and figuratively! And on top of that, in their culture, mindset, and vocabulary—just as Jesus, Moses, and Isaiah said—Peter understood that Israel was "Heaven and Earth" in Jewish thought.

So what did Peter mean by "the heavens will pass away with a roar, and the elements will be destroyed by fire"? Let's take a look at this verse in Greek. The Greek word translated as "elements" is stoicheion — στοιχεῖον. Its meaning is: "one of a series, a letter of the alphabet, the elements of knowledge." Does the physical heaven consist of letters and elements of knowledge? Of course not. What does consist of letters and elements of knowledge? The Law—the old covenant.

So Peter was not saying that the physical elements of the universe would be destroyed by fire. He was saying that the elements of the old covenant and the Law would melt away by fire. The temple—or the "heavens"—would be destroyed by fire, and the elements of knowledge, the principles of the old covenant, would perish.

This also refers to the many books and writings that were in the temple, which would melt away in the fire.

"The Earth and the works thereof shall be burned up" refers to the people themselves, who would perish in the fire of judgment. Jerusalem did indeed become a great sea of fire, in which millions of Jews died.

Why did Peter compare this catastrophe to the flood? Because Israel was the "world" for the Jews.

Peter also used the same expression that Peter and Paul used: "But the day of the Lord will come like a thief in the night." (2 Peter 3:10, 1 Thessalonians 5:2). The Jews would think that all was peaceful, and God's judgment would suddenly come upon them, like a thief surprising sleeping people in their beds.

That this day of the Lord would come in their time is also evident from the fact that Malachi prophesied that just before this day of the Lord, someone would appear who would be like Elijah:

> **"Behold, I am going to send you Elijah the prophet before the coming of the great and terrible day of the Lord."**
> — *Malachi* 4:5

Did Elijah indeed come before the destruction of Jerusalem? Absolutely! Jesus Christ said that John the Baptist was this Elijah:

> **"John himself is Elijah who was to come.**
> **The one who has ears to hear, let him hear."**
> — *Matthew 11:15*

John the Baptist was the promised Elijah who was to come before the day of the Lord. Jesus Himself said it plainly. And indeed, right after the coming of Elijah aka John the Baptist, the Lord appeared on the scene, proclaiming the arrival of the "great and terrible day of the Lord."

And Jesus Christ made another important statement regarding the passing of Heaven and Earth:

> **"For truly I say to you, until heaven and earth pass away,**
> **not the smallest letter or stroke of a letter**
> **shall pass from the Law, until all is accomplished!"**
> — *Matthew 5:18*

Do you grasp the enormous weight of what Jesus is saying here? He is declaring nothing less than this: you and I would still be suffocating under the unbearable burden of the law of sin and death *if* "Heaven and Earth" referred to the literal universe. Let that sink in for a moment.

Jesus said that the entire Law would remain in force as long as Heaven and Earth still existed! If He meant the literal Heaven and Earth, then you and I would still have to offer animal sacrifices today for the forgiveness of our sins.

However, we all know that the message of the New Testament is clear: we are saved not by the blood of animals, but by the perfect sacrifice of Jesus Christ.

So why did Jesus say that the entire Law—every jot and tittle—would remain in force as long as Heaven and Earth exist? Because Heaven and Earth indeed represented the old covenant, the old Israel, and the old temple. As long as these existed, the Law was still in force. When God destroyed them, they passed away, and the new era dawned in its full power: we live by the grace of God, guided by the Spirit, who has placed God's love in our hearts. No more old laws carved in stone. No more stone temple where God is separated from people. No more earthly Jerusalem where people must travel to. Everything has become new in Jesus Christ. We are now the temple of God through the Spirit. All believers worldwide are part of the heavenly Jerusalem in the Spirit.

There is even more biblical evidence that there will be no literal destruction of the physical creation. While Jesus Christ said that Heaven and Earth would pass away, He advised believers to flee to the mountains:

> **"Then those who are in Judea must flee to the mountains."**
> — *Luke* 21:21

If Jesus was referring to the physical Heaven and Earth, then His advice would have been nonsense. After all, what good would it do to flee to the mountains if those very mountains were about to come crashing down on top of them—as the entire Earth was being destroyed?

Furthermore, Jesus Christ promised that the meek would inherit the Earth:

> **"Blessed are the meek, for they shall inherit the earth."**
> — *Matthew* 5:5

What bad luck for the meek! First, Jesus promises they will inherit the Earth—and then He announces that it will be destroyed.

Can you see how ridiculous these beliefs really are—ideas we've all mindlessly accepted without ever giving them a second thought?

Let's please trade in that madness for a bit of common sense and finally understand what Moses, Isaiah, Christ, Peter, Paul, and all the other prophets and apostles actually meant: "Heaven and Earth" had a symbolic meaning to them.

God created the Earth for His glory and honor—to fill every heart with wonder and draw all people into worship. The whole Earth is full of His glory. Every bird lifts its song like incense to the greatness of God. The seas shimmer with life, teeming with creatures so graceful, and magnificent that they seem like brushstrokes from a divine imagination. The forests resound with the chorus of living things—mighty elk and gentle deer, whispering leaves and rustling wings—all harmonizing in praise. The meadows sway in the wind, a sea of green and gold crowned with radiant flowers, alive with dancing bees and butterflies like living jewels. Snow-capped mountains pierce the heavens, thunder rolls through deep valleys, and lightning paints the sky with fiery beauty. Rivers sparkle like liquid silver under the sun, carrying life wherever they flow. And above it all, the countless stars stretch across the night like a royal tapestry, each one testifying to the infinite wisdom of their Creator.

God will never destroy His beautiful creation. He promised this to Noah after the flood:

"I establish My covenant with you;
and all flesh shall never again be eliminated
by the waters of a flood, nor shall there again
be a flood to destroy the earth."
— *Genesis 9:11*

Never again, for all of eternity, would God destroy His magnificent masterpiece. He made a sacred vow—not just to humanity, but to every living, breathing thing that would ever be affected: *never again.* From that moment on, God established His covenant to preserve His creation—to guard and sustain the work of His hands forever.

"Then God spoke to Noah and to his sons with him,
saying, 'Now behold, I Myself am establishing
My covenant with you, and with your descendants
after you; and with every living creature that is with you:
the birds, the livestock, and every animal
of the earth with you, of all that comes out of the ark,
every animal of the earth.'"
— *Genesis 9:8–9*

Wouldn't it be terribly false of God if He made that covenant with all of creation—humans and animals—and then ultimately destroyed all of creation in an even worse way, with fire? God is not like that. He made a covenant with all of creation that He would never again bring such great destruction.

He therefore gave Noah and his sons this command:

"Be fruitful and multiply; fill the earth and subdue it."
— *Genesis 9:1*

God blessed Noah and his sons to be fruitful. He still gives us that command. Jesus said to His disciples:

"My Father is glorified by this, that you bear much fruit
and so prove to be My disciples."
— *John 15:8*

God's plan has never been the *destruction* of His creation—but rather it's *restoration*. Jesus did not come to annihilate the Earth but to redeem it. Our calling is not to sit back and expect catastrophe; we are anointed to bring His healing into every part of creation. We are meant to stand in places of authority within society—ending the poisoning of our food, purifying our waters, cleansing the air, and restoring God's order wherever it has been lost. This was God's original mandate to Adam, and it remains His eternal mandate to all who are in Christ, destined to reign with Him as kings and priests.

> **"You have made them into a kingdom and priests to our God; and they will reign upon the earth."**
> — *Revelation 5:10*

> **"But you are a chosen people, a royal priesthood, a holy nation, a people for God's own possession, so that you may proclaim the excellencies of Him who has called you out of darkness into His marvelous light."**
> — *1 Peter 2:9*

> **"...and raised us up with Him, and seated us with Him in the heavenly places in Christ Jesus."**
> — *Ephesians 2:6*

> **"The one who overcomes, I will grant to him to sit with Me on My throne, as I also overcame and sat with My Father on His throne."**
> — *Revelation 3:21*

Again we see that when we stop listening to the wild fantasies of money-greedy preachers who love to spread insane imaginations about the end of the world in order to draw huge crowds of followers on social media, and instead return to Jesus Christ and His true words, the chaotic fog of confusion suddenly lifts. The gospel changes from a message that turns us into escapists and doomsayers, into one that calls us to become people with a clear mission: to bring healing and hope to all of creation.

When we return to Christ, we are transformed from wild-eyed fanatics without vision or hope into courageous overcomers who bring healing to God's creation.

CHAPTER 18

The Terrible Antichrist

"Honestly, I truly love that, Mr. Sörensen. We are the children of God—anointed with His Spirit, guided by His hand, sent to bring His healing to His creation. What an honor! Wow... that's something entirely different from the idea that we're saved by Jesus only to wait until we can escape this world. What a contrast!

But the questions keep raging through my mind. I just can't help it. Like—what's with this terrible antichrist I've been told about all my life? The one who's supposedly coming to lead all of mankind into the abyss of full-blown Satanism and unprecedented darkness? That's what everyone keeps talking about all the time: the antichrist is coming!"

—*Josh*

Oh yes—the antichrist! Hahaha! Everyone in any position of global authority is always the antichrist, right? Every pope is the antichrist. Hitler was the antichrist. Obama. Trump. You name it. That's what fuels this madness—the endless hunt for the "big and nasty" antichrist.

It's what all the spectacular end-time movies are based on, and the centerpiece of so many bestselling novels—like the *Left Behind* series. *Boohooo! Be afraid! Be very afraid! The antichrist is coming!*

But did you know... there is nowhere in the entire Bible a single mention of an antichrist world leader? It's one of those massive myths that has gripped the minds of the masses because it plays to our imagination: a demon-possessed tyrant ruling humanity under a Beast System.

Do you know who in the Bible actually used the word antichrist? Only Apostle John—and only in his letters to the Jewish Christians in Jerusalem. He is the only person in the entire Bible who even mentions the term. Let's see what he actually said:

> **"By this you know the Spirit of God:**
> **every spirit that confesses that Jesus Christ**
> **has come in the flesh is from God;**
> **and every spirit that does not confess Jesus**
> **is not from God; this is the spirit of the antichrist,**
> **which you have heard is coming,**
> **and now it is already in the world."**
> *—1 John 4:2–3*

> **"For many deceivers have gone out into the world,**
> **those who do not acknowledge**
> **Jesus Christ as coming in the flesh.**
> **This is the deceiver and the antichrist."**
> *—2 John 7*

> **"Children, it is the last hour;**
> **and just as you heard that antichrist is coming,**
> **even now many antichrists have appeared;**
> **from this we know that it is the last hour.**
> **They went out from us, but they were not really of us;**
> **for if they had been of us,**
> **they would have remained with us;**
> **but they went out, so that it would be evident**
> **that they all are not of us."**
> *—1 John 2:18–19*

> **"Who is the liar except the one**
> **who denies that Jesus is the Christ?**
> **This is the antichrist—the one who denies**
> **the Father and the Son."**
> *—1 John 2:22*

John was the Apostle specifically appointed to oversee *the Jewish churches in and around Jerusalem.* He was ministering right in the epicenter of Judaism—a region filled with Jewish believers, but also with

Jewish opponents of Jesus. So when John warned that "many antichrists have already come," he was not speaking about future Gentile dictators from Europe or some end-time supervillain. He was referring directly to the Jewish adversaries who had infiltrated the churches in Jerusalem. That's why he said, "They went out from us..." — meaning they had slipped in among the Jewish believers, pretending to be converts, only to later reveal their true intent.

John reminded these believers in Jerusalem that many antichrists had already appeared, exactly as they had been warned.

Jesus Himself had told them to expect false christs to spring up everywhere. John simply confirmed that the prophecy was unfolding right before their eyes. He defined antichrist very clearly: anyone who denies that Jesus is the Messiah come in the flesh. And who denied that? It wasn't Romans. It wasn't Greeks.

It was the Jews who rejected Jesus as the Christ.

These Jews infiltrated the churches with one mission: to pull Jewish believers back into the old system of Judaism and away from the living Christ. They weren't future tyrants—they were present deceivers.

Nowhere does John describe the antichrist as a single future dictator. He never even hints at such a thing. He defines antichrist as a posture of *opposition toward Jesus.* And outside of John's letters, the word doesn't appear anywhere in the entire Bible.

"For real? But what about the Beast, then? Revelation does speak about a Beast that will rule the world, doesn't it? I mean, that's what one of my all-time favorite YouTube prophets keeps talking about—the coming Beast System that will enslave every soul on Earth, from China to Russia, from Europe to Africa, all the way through the Americas.

Nobody will escape the global slave system of the Beast that's supposedly just around the corner."

—Josh

Ah yes—the Beast. That terrifying end-times monster that's supposedly going to devour all Christians. Horrible, right?

Well, let's do what we should always do: go to the actual passage in Scripture, read what it really says, and dig in for some serious investigation of its true meaning. It's a long passage, so brace yourself.

"Then I saw a beast coming up out of the sea,
having ten horns and seven heads,
and on his horns were ten crowns,
and on his heads were blasphemous names.

And the beast that I saw was like a leopard,
and his feet were like those of a bear,
and his mouth like the mouth of a lion.

And the dragon gave him his power and his throne,
and great authority.

I saw one of his heads as if it had been fatally wounded,
and his fatal wound was healed.

And the whole earth was amazed and followed after the beast;
they worshiped the dragon because
he gave his authority to the beast;
and they worshiped the beast, saying,
"Who is like the beast, and who is able to wage war with him?"

A mouth was given to him speaking arrogant words and blasphemies,
and authority to act for forty-two months was given to him.
And he opened his mouth in blasphemies against God,
to blaspheme His name and His tabernacle,
that is, those who dwell in heaven.

It was also given to him to make war with the saints
and to overcome them, and authority was given to him
over every tribe, people, language, and nation.

All who live on the earth will worship him,
everyone whose name has not been written
since the foundation of the world in the book of life
of the Lamb who has been slaughtered.

If anyone has an ear, let him hear.
If anyone is destined for captivity, to captivity he goes;
if anyone kills with the sword,
with the sword he must be killed.

Here is the perseverance and the faith of the saints.

Then I saw another beast coming up out of the earth;
and he had two horns like a lamb, and he spoke as a dragon.
He exercises all the authority of the first beast in his presence.

And he makes the earth and those who live on it
worship the first beast, whose fatal wound was healed.
He performs great signs, so that he even makes fire come down
out of the sky to the earth in the presence of people.
And he deceives those who live on the earth
because of the signs which it was given him
to perform in the presence of the beast,
telling those who live on the earth
to make an image to the beast
who had the wound of the sword and has come to life.
And it was given to him to give breath to the image of the beast,
so that the image of the beast would even speak
and cause all who do not worship the image of the beast
to be killed.

And he causes all, the small and the great,
the rich and the poor, and the free and the slaves,
to be given a mark on their right hands or on their foreheads,
and he decrees that no one will be able to buy or to sell,
except the one who has the mark,
either the name of the beast or the number of his name.

Here is wisdom. Let him who has understanding
calculate the number of the beast,
for the number is that of a man;
and his number is six hundred and sixty-six."
— *Revelation 13*

Is there any passage in Scripture more terrifying than this one? A beast with ten horns, worshiped by the whole Earth, slaughtering the saints? No wonder it's inspired endless books and blockbuster movies. Fear sells—and big fear sells big.

But first, context.

Revelation doesn't describe events thousands of years later.

John wrote to the churches in Asia of the 1st century, not the churches in America of the 21st century.

And he told those believers over and over: "The time is near... these things must soon take place." So none of the events described by John were projected into some vague, distant future. He wrote to the very first churches to encourage them to be strong for what was about to happen.

Now, what was about to occur? It was clearly announced by Jesus Christ and the other apostles: a cataclysmic transition from the old era, where Satan ruled over Israel and the world, to a new era where Christ would be enthroned as King in the Kingdom of God in a new covenant.

The tragedy of the Western Church is its obsession with ripping passages out of their biblical, historical, prophetic, and cultural context—spinning them into wild, futuristic horror stories that have nothing to do with the original text. And because fear sells, these sensationalized "prophecies" have made some evangelical leaders rich beyond measure—building entire empires of deception on the back of this passage.

Mistranslations have been deliberately used to reinforce the fear. In Revelation 13, the Greek word gé—meaning "land" or "region"—has been wrongly rendered as "the whole earth." In context, this refers to *the land of Israel and the Roman Empire*—not the entire world.

But now we must confront the question directly: if the beast John described was not some future world dictator, then who was it?

The answer appears the moment we read Revelation in its historical and biblical context. Suddenly something remarkable becomes clear: John did not describe one beast—but two (Revelation 13:11-12).

So who was the first beast?

In order to answer that question, we must respect the historical context—something that neither famous millionaire preachers nor poor rural pastors seem to do in our time. It appears that much of the Church has been trained to consistently *ignore* the historical and biblical context of Scripture, constantly ripping verses out of their context.

Let's not do that. Instead, let's look at the historical context.

As the beast was fiercely opposing and persecuting Christ and His followers, who could that have been? There is really only one candidate: *the Jews who rejected Christ and His spiritual kingdom*, insisting instead on a military and violent restoration of Israel.

Among them were the Zealots, who were called that because of their intense zeal to establish a powerful military Israel. These Zealots joined forces with the false prophets of first-century Judaism in their opposition to Christ and His Church.

Peter, Jude, and Josephus even referred to those Jewish leaders as "beasts."

> **"But these, like unreasoning animals,**
> **born as creatures of instinct to be captured and killed...**
> **will be destroyed in their destruction."**
> — *2 Peter 2:12*

> **"But these men slander those things**
> **which they do not understand;**
> **and the things which they know by instinct,**
> **like unreasoning animals,**
> **by these things they are destroyed."**
> — *Jude 1:10*

> **"And this place, which is adored by the habitable world...**
> **is trampled upon by these wild beasts**
> **born among ourselves."**
> — *Flavius Josephus Wars 4.4.3*

In Revelation 11–13, this "beast" works alongside false prophets, wages war against the saints, and is given power for forty-two months—the same period that Jerusalem was trampled by the Gentiles during the Jewish-Roman war.

This view finds its roots in both Daniel and Revelation. The prophecies of Daniel 2 and 7 describe a succession of kingdoms—Babylon, Medo-Persia, Greece, and finally a divided fourth kingdom made of iron and clay. Within this final kingdom, Daniel saw a "little horn" rising among ten others, speaking arrogant words and persecuting the saints. When compared with Jesus' words in Matthew 21:43-45, this imagery points toward the religious and political leadership of Israel in the first century, which rebelled against God's Messiah and persecuted the saints.

This also aligns with the forty-six references to the "beast" in Revelation, showing a consistent pattern:

The Jews who rejected Christ became the beast that persecuted those that believed Christ.

The second beast likely was Roman Emperor Nero. The number 666 in Revelation 13:18 points directly to Emperor Nero, whose name in Hebrew letters—קסר ןורנ (Neron Kaisar)—adds up perfectly to 666 through the ancient system of gematria, where each letter carries a numerical value.

Nero demanded divine worship, brutally persecuted Christians, and embodied the spirit of the Beast—power that exalts itself against God and devours the saints.

The theologian N. T. Wright explained in his book "Revelation for Everyone" (Westminster John Knox Press, 2011) that Nero also introduced the "mark of the beast." To buy or sell in the marketplaces, citizens first had to make an offering to a statue of Nero at the entrance. They would then take ash from the altar and mark their hand or forehead. That was the "mark of the beast."

"That's amazing. But if this wasn't about a worldwide calamity—just a local event—then why does Revelation say, 'every people, language, and nation'?"

—Josh

Both Jerusalem and the Roman Empire were teeming with diverse nations and cultures. People came from all over—Egypt, Africa, Europe, the Middle East—to trade, worship, and live under Roman rule. Nero's authority reached them all.

The modern hysteria over the antichrist and the mark of the beast is built on mistranslation, historical ignorance, and shameless exploitation of the Bible. It's time we pulled these fear-driven fables out by the roots and replaced them with the truth: the victory of Jesus Christ and the ever-expanding reign of His kingdom.

Paul was waging war against the same movement. He wrote letters to churches in Galatia that had been infiltrated by Jews who rejected Christ as the fulfillment of God's promises. These men denied that Jesus is the Christ, yet pretended to follow Him in order to infiltrate the churches and lead people away from the gospel—away from the spiritual Kingdom of Christ and back toward the old dream of a political Israel.

John called them antichrists (1 John 2:18).
Paul called them hostile to all people (1 Thessalonians 2:15).
Jesus called them a synagogue of Satan (Revelation 2:9; 3:9).
John described them as the beast (Revelation 13:1–8; 17:7–14).

That is antichrist—those who oppose Jesus Christ.

The same goes for the second beast of Revelation: it's not a twenty-first-century boogeyman but a first-century reality. The mark of the Beast was emperor worship under Nero.

Both the Jews who hated Christ and infiltrated the churches, and Emperor Nero himself, were empowered by the same satanic force to attack the followers of Christ in a desperate attempt to stop His glorious new kingdom from breaking through. They went about devouring all they could. The dragon—Satan—gave power to all whose hearts were hostile to Christ. The Jewish false prophets performed demonic signs to deceive the people, while the religious and political rulers received great power to persecute the Church.

But they were all overcome by the Lamb.

The Kingdom of Christ has conquered the forces of darkness and is advancing throughout the ages. The enemy has been defeated—and we are called to walk in that victory today.

"Oh, come on, sir! You can't be serious. Are you actually telling me that the antichrist already came and went? That's impossible. Paul said the day of the Lord wouldn't happen until there was first a great falling away and the man of lawlessness appeared. Everyone knows that's a future event, right? Don't try to rewrite the Bible!"

—Josh

You're right that Paul wrote about these things. Here's what he actually said:

"...that you not be quickly shaken from your composure
or be disturbed either by a spirit, a message,
or a letter as if from us, to the effect
that the day of the Lord has come.
No one is to deceive you in any way!
For it will not come unless the apostasy comes first,
and the man of lawlessness is revealed,
the son of destruction, who opposes and exalts himself
above every so-called god or object of worship,
so that he takes his seat in the temple of God,
displaying himself as being God."

—2 *Thessalonians* 2:2–4

Now here's where translation matters again. Many preachers have interpreted "apostasy" to mean a great falling away from the faith—basically that most Christians will abandon their belief before Jesus returns. But that is not what Paul said. The Greek word Paul used is apostasia (ἀποστασία), which means *rebellion, uprising, or revolt.* Paul was not predicting that Christians everywhere would lose their faith. He was saying that before the Lord came, a great *rebellion* would break out. And in the midst of that rebellion, a man of lawlessness would rise up—one who would exalt himself like a god.

And that's exactly what happened, just as Paul predicted. In the first century, a widespread Jewish rebellion erupted across the Roman Empire. And within that revolt, certain lawless men rose to prominence.

One of them was Eleazar ben Simon, a ruthless Jewish leader. The historian Flavius Josephus describes him as proud, violent, and utterly unscrupulous. After early victories against the Romans, Eleazar became the leader of the Zealots (Jewish War 2.20.3). He allied with another wicked leader, John Levi of Gischala, equally corrupt and destructive. Together they murdered several high priests, seized control of Jerusalem, and then turned on each other in a bloody power struggle (Jewish War 4.4.1–4.6.3).

Eleazar fits Paul's description strikingly well. He actually moved into the Temple itself and remained there for about three and a half years. He longed for total power—to be revered as though he were a god. His soldiers desecrated the holy things of the Temple, casting lots to install a false high priest named Phannias, who was unwilling but forced into the role (Jewish War 4.3.6–8).

Josephus records that by AD 67, Eleazar had turned the sanctuary into a "place of tyranny and violence." This was the abomination of desolation—prophesied by Daniel, spoken of by Jesus, and confirmed by Paul—set up right in the Temple.

"But Paul said that Jesus would kill the antichrist with the breath of His mouth! How did that happen? Here, read it for yourself:"

—Josh

"Then that lawless one will be revealed,
whom the Lord will eliminate
with the breath of His mouth
and bring to an end by the appearance of His coming..."

—2 Thessalonians 2:8

The question is, what is the "breath of His mouth"? It is the Spirit of God! (Job 33:4). Paul said the Holy Spirit would cause the downfall of the lawless one. History confirms this. Eleazar did not die in glory or triumph—he died under divine judgment. Josephus does not record the precise details of his final moments, but one thing is certain: the man who exalted himself in God's temple, the very embodiment of lawlessness, perished in the very judgment Christ had foretold.

When we look at history, we discover something astonishing—and profoundly liberating: the horrifying beast, the antichrist, and the man of lawlessness are not some 21st-century end-times dictator our modern preachers invented to scare the heck out of us and coax more money from our pockets.

These figures are rooted in the real historical events of the first century, during the great judgment that fell on Jerusalem.

That is wonderful news, because it means we can finally stop fearing that every world leader is "the antichrist" who will lead humanity to its doom.

That paranoid mindset has caused unspeakable suffering. Many people have told me they struggled with crippling depression, nervous breakdowns, and even suicidal thoughts because they lived under a cloud of fear—a future so dark they scarcely dared to breathe.

Once they discovered the plain truth of Scripture, confirmed by history, they were set free and could finally breathe again.

How devastating is the lie that so many preachers spread because it enriches them, while it destroys the hope, vision, dreams, and joy of those they claim to serve.

The message of Christ is the Good News.
But the Church turned it into the Bad News.
Christ proclaimed, "The Kingdom of God is at hand."
But the Church says, "The kingdom of Satan is at hand!"

The gospel of the Kingdom of God was replaced by a gospel of the kingdom of Satan. The message that brings joy to the world became one that steals our joy and casts a shadow of fear.

It's a complete reversal.

Nothing has crippled God's children more than this deception.

It is high time that we return to Christ.

CHAPTER 19

Majestic Millennium

"Incredible! I can't believe nobody ever told me this before. All the puzzle pieces are finally sliding into place! But there's still one huge, towering mystery left. And that mystery, Mr. Sörensen, is... the Millennium! Doesn't the Bible clearly say Christ will come down here with the saints and reign on Earth for a thousand years? You know what I'm talking about—the majestic Millennium! That hasn't happened yet, has it? Care to enlighten me?"

—*Josh*

Indeed, according to the history lessons we all received in school, there has never been such a thing as a thousand-year reign during which Christ and His saints ruled on Earth. On the contrary, we were taught that our past was dark, primitive, and ignorant—and that we are the enlightened ones. But this entire subject stands or falls on one foundational question:

Is the history we've been taught actually true?

I know it sounds outrageous to even ask such a daring question. After all, from a very young age we were trained to unquestioningly accept whatever we were told by the so-called "authorities." But by now it has become painfully clear that these so-called "guardians of knowledge" are anything but trustworthy.

After all, they are the very same authorities who told us that we are nothing more than evolved apes that crawled out of the mud by accident—and that God has no place in our lives.

It is imperative to grasp this fully, because these same people—who insist that you are a meaningless biological accident without purpose or origin—are the ones who have handed us a carefully curated version of what they call "history."

Yes, it may feel unsettling—even frightening—to doubt what we've been taught. But there is no other way to discover the truth. Either we remain locked inside the small prison cell of our minds—a cell constructed by powers that need us confined for our entire lives, so they can easily control us—or we break open the door and step out into the wide, open world of truth that awaits discovery.

The choice is ours.

My life's quest has become to remain as closely connected as possible to the one and only source of real truth—God Himself, who never lies—and to learn how to be led by Him into truths that the forces of deception so desperately try to hide from us.

And one such discovery lies in the area of history.

In this chapter, we will explore a simple but explosive question:

If a system indoctrinates mankind to deny God, why should we blindly trust that same system when it tells us our history?

If the "experts" hide information from humanity to conceal God, could it be that they have also hidden information from us to conceal the thousand-year reign of Christ?

What if crucial parts of our past were altered, twisted, or quietly buried? What if the "official" version is not the full story at all?

We will dig deep into who wrote our history, how trustworthy they truly were, and what agendas they served. Then we will examine the evidence for ourselves—without the veil the so-called "authorities" have placed over our minds.

But before we investigate history, we must start by tossing some of the most ridiculous nonsense about the Millennium overboard. Most Christians today hold to a bizarre sci-fi version of this so-called "thousand-year reign of Christ." In their blockbuster fantasy, Jesus sets up a political world dictatorship, stronger than Hitler and more brutal than Stalin, where every president and king is dragged by the ear to Jerusalem and forced to worship Him—against their will.

Dissenters? Straight to hell! Rebels? Vaporized on the spot. Perfect world peace at gunpoint. Voilà—the Kingdom of God, ladies and gentlemen!

Everyone's got their own private fantasy of the Rapture, the return of Christ, and the Millennium. Ask ten thousand Christians and you'll get ten thousand different scripts. Nobody actually studies the text—they just invent their own spiritual fan fiction and call it doctrine.

This is the problem: *we've let our vain imaginations run the show.* We swallow any fluffy idea that makes us feel good, regardless of whether Scripture actually says it. It's Christian crack cocaine: comforting, addictive, but completely detached from reality. And like addicts, we'll defend our hallucinations with rage if someone dares to take them away.

The sobering reality is that not a single passage of Scripture suggests that Christ will return to Earth to establish a political dictatorship, forcing nations to obey Him against their will, in order to enforce world peace. Jesus Himself made it abundantly clear that His kingdom is not of this world, not tied to geography, not visible to the human eye, and not built through political coercion.

> **"Now He was questioned by the Pharisees**
> **as to when the Kingdom of God was coming,**
> **and He answered them and said,**
> **'The Kingdom of God is not coming**
> **with signs that can be observed;**
> **nor will they say, "Look, here it is!" or, "There it is!"**
> **For behold, the Kingdom of God**
> **is in your midst.'"**
>
> —*Luke 17:21–22*

Jesus dismantled the entire idea of a kingdom you can point to on a map. He insisted His kingdom is invisible to the natural eye—something that can only be seen through the Spirit.

When Pilate interrogated Him, Jesus was crystal clear:

> **"Jesus answered, 'My kingdom is not of this world.**
> **If My kingdom were of this world, My servants would be**
> **fighting so that I would not be handed over to the Jews;**
> **but as it is, My kingdom is not of this realm.'"**
>
> —*John 18:36*

There it is—straight from His own lips. His kingdom is not geopolitical, not military, not territorial—which makes it staggering that millions of Christians still fantasize about Jesus running a world government headquartered in Jerusalem.

The Lord went even further. He explained that the only way to see or enter His kingdom is to be born again by the Spirit:

> **"Jesus responded and said to him,**
> **'Truly, truly, I say to you, unless someone is born again**
> **he cannot see the Kingdom of God.' (...)**
> **'Truly, truly, I say to you, unless someone is born of water**
> **and the Spirit, he cannot enter the Kingdom of God.'"**
> —*John 3:3, 5*

So let's state it plainly: flesh and blood will never inherit the Kingdom of God. You can't storm Jerusalem with an army and you can't vote it in at the United Nations. It is spiritual—discerned by the Spirit of God.

The idea that we'll need to book flights to Jerusalem to worship Jesus is about as biblical as Hansel and Gretel. Don't you know that you are now the temple of God, where He dwells?

> **"Do you not know that you are a temple of God**
> **and that the Spirit of God dwells in you?"**
> —*1 Corinthians 3:16*

> **"Or do you not know that your body**
> **is a temple of the Holy Spirit within you,**
> **whom you have from God?"**
> —*1 Corinthians 6:19*

No need to pack your bags for Jerusalem, folks. You don't need to buy a first-class ticket to the Holy Land to worship Jesus. He said plainly:

> **"...a time is coming when you will worship the Father**
> **neither on this mountain <u>nor in Jerusalem.</u> (...)**
> **The true worshipers will worship the Father**
> **in spirit and truth; for such people the Father seeks**
> **to be His worshipers."**
> —*John 4:21, 23*

Paul put the final nail in the coffin of all these childish fantasies:

"Now I say this, brothers and sisters, that
flesh and blood cannot inherit the Kingdom of God."
— 1 Corinthians 15:50

The natural man can't even grasp it, because it's spiritually discerned:

"A natural person does not accept the things
of the Spirit of God, for they are foolishness to him;
and he cannot understand them,
because they are spiritually discerned. (...)
But we have the mind of Christ."
— 1 Corinthians 2:14–16

What does this mean? That the popular picture of a visible kingdom on Earth with Jesus ruling like Caesar from a throne in Jerusalem is not just a slight misinterpretation—*it's a total reversal of everything He said.*

So after clearing away all the fairy tales and Sunday-school cartoons, the question still stands: *what, then, is the real Millennium?*

To understand the true meaning of the thousand-year reign, we must first remember what the world actually looked like before Christ sent His apostles into it. This requires a deep dive into the darkest depths of our history—into realities so disturbing that most of us have never even heard of them.

What stands out above all about the world before Christ is this: humanity was not living in some noble age of wisdom, enlightenment, or moral progress. *It was a blood-soaked nightmare.* Every culture. Every continent, without exception. Human sacrifice was the norm, not the exception. Demonic worship was mainstream religion. Violence, slavery, and sexual perversion were stitched into the very fabric of society. To be human in that world meant to live in fear, darkness, and constant vulnerability to cruelty.

In Europe, the Druids constructed massive wooden figures—"wicker men"—stuffed them full of living people, and burned them alive as offerings to their gods. Entire communities watched while their neighbors screamed and roasted in the flames.

In South America, the Chimu cut open the chests of children and ripped out their still-beating hearts. Archaeologists have unearthed mass graves of over 140 children, sacrificed all at once in a single ritual.

The Incas strangled, buried alive, or exposed their most beautiful children to the freezing mountains as offerings to demons. The Moche tied naked victims, slit their throats, and collected their blood in ceremonial vessels.

In Africa, people were buried alive, strangled, mutilated, and drowned in rituals to appease spirits and empower kings. Archaeologists confirm that ritual killing, ancestor sacrifice, and blood offerings were deeply entrenched across the continent.

And then—Rome. The "pinnacle" of ancient civilization. Citizens gathered for entertainment as gladiators hacked each other to pieces, prisoners were burned alive, and Christians were thrown to wild beasts. After the Spartacus revolt, Rome crucified six thousand men and lined their bodies along the Appian Way for miles. Emperor Nero had the charming habit of dipping Christians in oil, hanging them on stakes, and setting them ablaze to light his gardens at night.

Public executions doubled as theater. Criminals—or anyone labeled inconvenient—were humiliated, stripped, raped, or dismembered on stage. Some "mythological reenactments" even forced naked women into grotesque spectacles of ritualized rape before slaughter. This was "entertainment" for the most advanced empire the world had ever seen.

Sexual depravity was not hidden—it was institutionalized. In Corinth, thousands of women and young girls served as "sacred prostitutes" for Aphrodite. Families dedicated their virgin daughters to be defiled by strangers in temple rites. Roman emperors like Tiberius, Caligula, and Nero reveled in incest, child abuse, and sadistic orgies. In both Greece and Rome, the sexual exploitation of young boys was celebrated as a cultural norm.

There were also the wild, secretive festivals dedicated to Dionysus, god of wine and ecstasy. Participants consumed large amounts of wine and entered states of frenzy (mania). Orgies included group sex, cross-dressing, and ritual role reversal. Some reports describe animal sacrifice, public nudity, and sexual trance-dancing.

Roman Emperor Tiberius kept young boys ("little fishes") on Capri to swim between his legs and perform sexual acts. Caligula reportedly had incestuous relations with his sisters and turned his palace into a brothel. Nero married two men (one as groom, another as bride) and staged orgies in his Golden House. Roman elites hosted lavish feasts that ended in group sex, often with slaves, prostitutes, or captives. Orgies sometimes depicted mythological reenactments of sexual acts. Sex was used for power assertion, humiliation, or political manipulation.

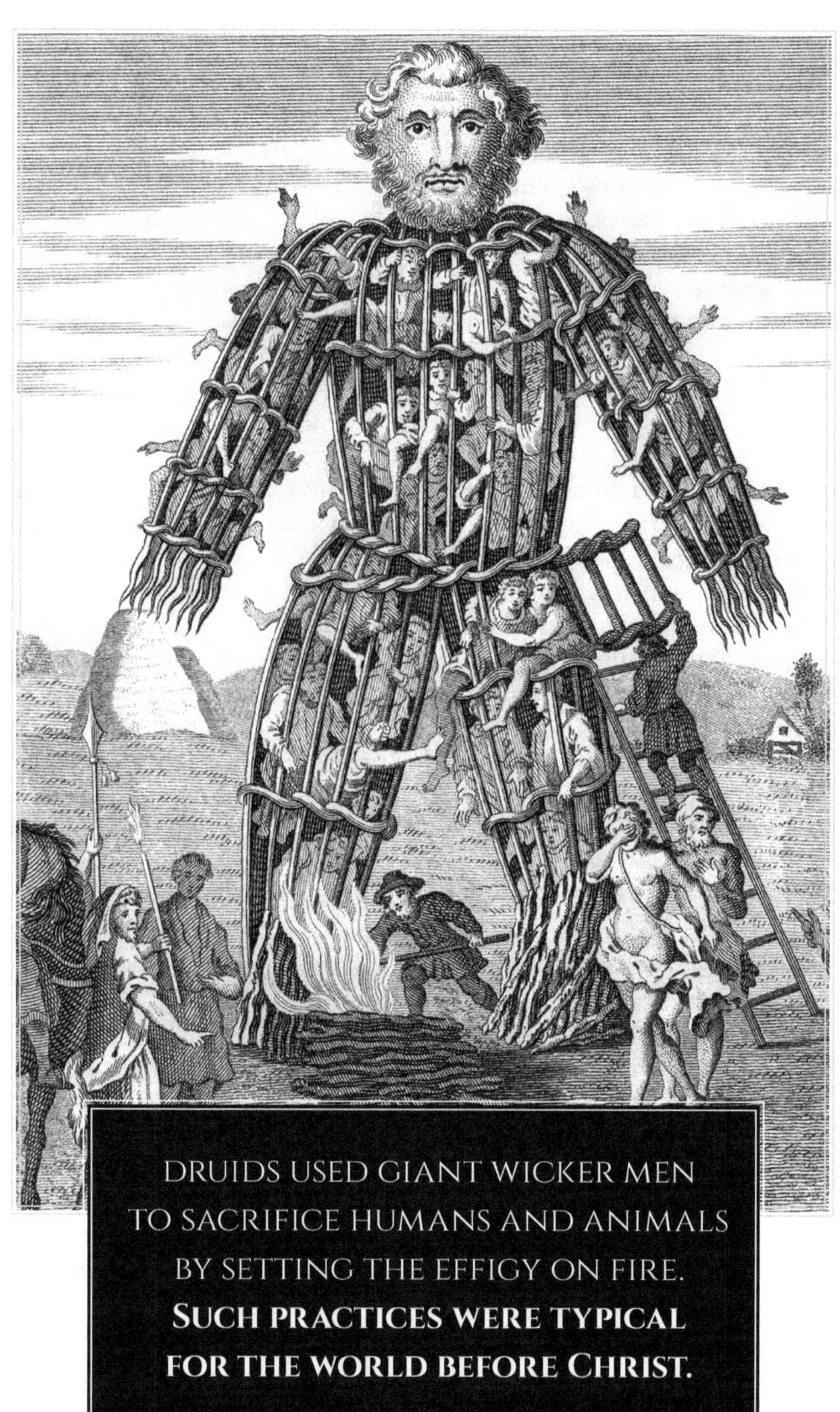

DRUIDS USED GIANT WICKER MEN
TO SACRIFICE HUMANS AND ANIMALS
BY SETTING THE EFFIGY ON FIRE.
**SUCH PRACTICES WERE TYPICAL
FOR THE WORLD BEFORE CHRIST.**

In Greece, there was a common, institutionalized practice where adult men ("erastes") courted adolescent boys ("eromenos"). Seen as a rite of passage and a form of educational bonding, but usually involved sexual relationships. The practice was idealized in Athenian culture and even referenced by Plato and Socrates.

In Rome, sex with underage slaves (boys and girls) was also common. Male citizens could legally use slaves for sex at any age. Catamites (young boys kept for sex) were part of elite Roman households.

Both in the Roman and Greek empires there was a multitude of brothels and sexual markets. The brothels (Lupanaria) were legal and widespread throughout Rome. Slaves were branded and rented by the hour, often kept in horrific conditions. Some brothels were decorated with explicit murals showing available sex acts and prices. Slaves had no rights over their bodies and were used for any sexual whim. Female and male slaves were often publicly raped as punishment or entertainment. Households kept specialized sex slaves for family use or to lend to guests.

Public punishment of supposed criminals (anyone could be convicted as a criminal) included public stripping, rape, or being paraded naked. Roman law permitted sexual torture of slaves during investigations. Public performances sometimes included mock rapes or real sexual acts, especially in lower-class venues.

This overview is only about the Roman and Greek empires, which were considered the most civilized. In other parts of the world, it was even worse.

Take, for example, Scandinavia. In Sweden, humans were sacrificed on a regular basis at the Temple of Uppsala, and their bodies were left to rot in the trees as offerings. In Denmark, people were ritually murdered by slitting their throats, breaking their bones, and by drowning. The Norse believed sacrifices could appease gods, ensure fertility, victory, or good harvests.

All throughout the world, human sacrifice, extreme torture, indescribable sexual perversion, and bloodthirsty violence were absolutely normal. People didn't even consider it evil but thought of it as a normal part of life.

Humanity was in unspeakable darkness: every culture, every nation, North, South, East, and West. All of mankind was submersed in an intensity of satanic horror that we truly don't have the slightest idea about. Kings were usually accompanied by sorcerers, priests, witches, and diviners, who advised the kings with their dark witchcraft.

In South America the Aztecs cut open the chest of living victims, and ripped out their beating heart.

In every culture of the world, human sacrifice, demon worship, extreme sexual perversion, bestiality, bloodthirstiness, and unspeakable cruelty were considered normal.

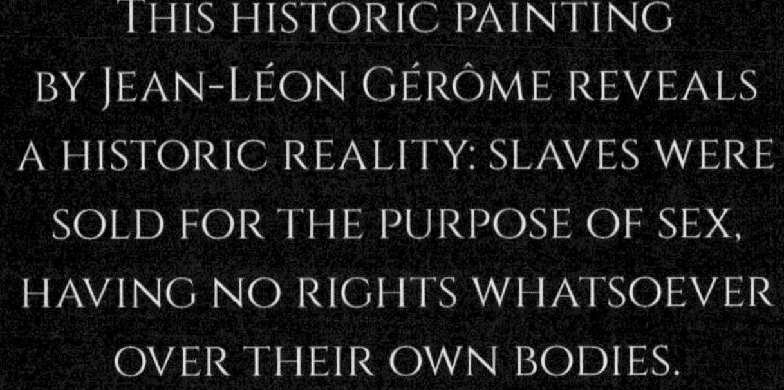

This historic painting by Jean-Léon Gérôme reveals a historic reality: slaves were sold for the purpose of sex, having no rights whatsoever over their own bodies.

History documents that some of these occult practitioners had so much demonic power they could transform themselves into any shape they desired, be it an owl, bat, or wolf. That is not legend or folklore but shocking reality. Even the Bible describes how the magicians of Egypt were able to turn a stick into a living snake (Exodus 7:8–12). Do we even grasp a tiny fragment of the incredible severity of the evil that had been ruling on Earth since Satan deceived mankind and the fallen angels perverted all life? Just imagine how dark the human soul is to sacrifice their own babies to be burned alive to their cruel demons.

I will give you one example from history that illustrates, perhaps better than anything else, just how grave the horror was that once ruled the entire Earth. Have you ever heard about the so-called "terafim"? These were household idols that appear repeatedly in Scripture (Genesis 31:19; 1 Samuel 19:13; Ezekiel 21:21). To the modern reader, they sound like little figurines, but the reality was far more gruesome.

Ancient Jewish writings, early Christian commentators, and Near Eastern traditions reveal that terafim were often fashioned from the preserved heads or bodies of sacrificed children, used as demonic oracles inside the home.

The Jewish Encyclopedia (Vol. 12, p. 108–109) describes terafim:

> **"The teraphim were made of the head of a first-born, which, after being slain, was shaved and then salted and spiced. After a golden plate on which magic words were engraved had been placed under the tongue, the mummified head was mounted on the wall, and it spoke to the people."**

Early Christian writers like Theodoret and Epiphanius repeated similar descriptions. Archaeological evidence from surrounding Near Eastern cultures supports rituals where preserved remains were used for spirit consultation. Families placed these terafim in their houses as guardians and guides, believing the spirits inhabiting the idol would give direction, bring good fortune, or curse their enemies. The terafim were treated as sacred household prophets — voices from the other side.

But the "voice" was nothing more than a demonic spirit speaking through the corpse of a murdered child.

Can you imagine if this practice were considered normal today?

Can you fathom slaughtering your younger brother, cutting off his head, and hanging it on the fireplace mantle so demons could speak through it? That is how severe evil was.

Can you imagine the heartbreak, emotional trauma, and mental terror mankind suffered from the moment they were born into this hell?

Let's look at another historic example.

Did you know that in ancient Rome people willingly took part in certain rites where they invited demons to enter them, so they would turn into raging, ravenous wild beasts—devouring one another and committing the most unimaginable acts of sexual violence? In Rome these "parties" were called the Bacchanalia; in Greece they were the Dionysian mysteries; and similar cultic festivals spread across Asia Minor. Participants drank themselves into a stupor, consumed hallucinogenic mixtures, and chanted invocations specifically designed to open the door of their souls to demons.

Once the frenzies took hold, the crowds were swept into uncontrollable fits of aggression, cruelty, and derangement. They lost all sense of self, all moral restraint, all humanity. What followed was an eruption of the worst impulses hell could ignite in the human soul.

> **"Once plunged into the madness of the rite,**
> **they became as though possessed... committing deeds**
> **more foul than the human tongue can relate."**
> *—Livy, Ab Urbe Condita, Book 39.8–18*

Early Christian theologians like Tertullian, Clement of Alexandria, and Augustine wrote that these rituals were demonic invasions, designed to strip away the last traces of conscience and plunge entire cities into moral ruin. Some acts ended in death. Others ended in lifelong trauma. And the priests called it "holy worship."

Even the Bible records atrocities so cruel, that it's almost impossible for us to imagine they truly happened. One of the most chilling windows into that ancient depravity is found in the Bible, Judges 19. In Gibeah, a weary Levite and his concubine sought shelter for the night. Hardly had darkness fallen when a mob of men surrounded the house — shouting, pounding, demanding the man be dragged out so they could abuse her. When the Levite's concubine was handed over, Scripture says:

> **"They raped her and abused her all night until morning..."**
> *—Judges 19:25*

By dawn, she collapsed at the doorway—reaching for safety she would never attain. She died there — alone, broken, discarded.

We all know the story of Sodom and Gomorrah, where the same happened: angels in human form visited Lot, and the entire population came out demanding they be handed over for rape.

> **"Before they had gone to bed, all the men from every part of the city of Sodom—both young and old—surrounded the house. They called to Lot, "Where are the men who came to you tonight? Bring them out to us so that we can have sex with them."**
>
> — *Genesis 19:4-5 (NIV)*

And remember what we discussed earlier in this book: the Roman and Greek world—the greatest civilizations of their time—featured rape by animals as public entertainment, women publicly violated on platforms carried through the city, and leaders keeping multiple sex slaves as a normal part of life.

Do you see it?

Can you feel the suffocating horror of it?

This was *Hell on Earth.*

And into this pitch-black nightmare, Christ came. He began His ministry by driving out demonic spirits from thousands upon thousands of people and by healing multitudes who were sick. In doing so, He effectively broke the rule of Satan over their lives.

> "Now when evening came, they brought to Him many who were demon-possessed; **and He cast out the spirits** with a word, and healed all who were ill."
>
> —*Matthew 8:16*

> "And He healed many who were ill with various diseases, a**nd cast out many demons;** and He was not permitting the demons to speak, because they knew who He was."
>
> —*Mark 1:34*

> "And He went into their synagogues preaching and **casting out the demons** throughout all Galilee."
>
> —*Mark 1:39*

Christ openly declared that by driving out the satanic spirits from the people, He was establishing the Kingdom of God.

"But if I cast out the demons by the finger of God,
then the Kingdom of God has come upon you."
—*Luke 11:20*

He then sent out His followers to do the same:

"Now after this the Lord appointed seventy-two others,
and sent them in pairs ahead of Him to every city
and place where He Himself was going to come. (...)
Whatever city you enter and they receive you,
eat what is served to you; and heal those in it
who are sick, and say to them
'The Kingdom of God has come near to you.' (...)
Now the seventy-two returned with joy, saying,
"Lord, even the demons are subject to us in Your name!"
And He said to them, **"I watched Satan fall**
from heaven like lightning."
—*Luke 10:1-18*

Can you see what is happening here? Jesus Christ did not come to install some dull religious system filled with lifeless rituals that make people look ridiculous in the eyes of their community. He didn't come to tell us to hide in our churches and wait for an escape hatch.

No! No! No!

Christ invaded our hellish world—ruled by Satan and his demons, where humanity was being terrorized in unimaginable ways—and like a true warrior, He went from place to place shattering Satan's rule. He drove out demons. He broke their diabolical grip on people. He liberated the prisoners and announced that a new era had begun: the Kingdom of God.

And He sent His followers to go and do the same. The result was astonishing: Satan himself fell from his place of authority over mankind.

Christ came to end the reign of Satan and proclaim a new era of deliverance and healing for humanity. That is why he was called "the light of the world", "the new day", and "the savior".

After Christ took His rightful place as King of kings and Lord of lords in the Kingdom of God, Revelation 20 declares something utterly staggering: the very mastermind of all human misery—the fountainhead of every cruelty, every depravity, every demonic nightmare—Satan himself was seized and bound for a thousand years:

"Then I saw an angel coming down from heaven,
holding the key of the abyss and a great chain in his hand.
And he took hold of the dragon, the serpent of old,
who is the devil and Satan,
and bound him for a thousand years;
and he threw him into the abyss
and shut it and sealed it over him,
so that he would not deceive the nations any longer,
until the thousand years were completed;
after these things he must be released for a short time."
—Revelation 20:1–3

During this thousand-year period, Satan could no longer deceive the nations as he once had. *That's the turning point of history.* Before Christ, the devil dominated the world through human sacrifice, demonic religion, perversion, and terror. After Christ, his grip was broken

During that time the souls of the saints, who had been beheaded because they refused to worship Emperor Nero as god, reigned with Christ for a thousand years.

"Then I saw thrones, and they sat on them,
and judgment was given to them.
And I saw the souls of those who had been beheaded
because of their testimony of Jesus and because of the word of God,
and those who had not worshiped the beast or his image,
and had not received the mark on their foreheads
and on their hands;
and they came to life and reigned with Christ
for a thousand years.
The rest of the dead did not come to life
until the thousand years were completed.
This is the first resurrection.
Blessed and holy is the one who has a part
in the first resurrection;

> over these the second death has no power,
> but they will be priests of God and of Christ,
> and will reign with Him for a thousand years."
> —*Revelation 20:4–6*

Notice this carefully: John does not say that Jesus is sitting on a throne in Jerusalem. He sees the *souls* of the martyrs reigning with Christ. This is a *heavenly* reign, not an *earthly* dictatorship. From His throne in heaven, Christ rules. From their thrones in Heaven, His saints rule with Him, alongside the believers on Earth. As the followers of Christ went out into the entire world, carrying light, love, hope, healing, restoration, and deliverance, the world began to undergo a slow—but unstoppable—metamorphosis. For the first time in recorded memory, humanity began to climb out of darkness. Temples of blood sacrifice fell silent. The gladiator games were abolished. The exposure of infants was outlawed. Bestiality and sexual perversion were condemned rather than celebrated. Slavery was confronted and, over time, dismantled. The sick were cared for. Hospitals were founded. The poor were given dignity. Orphans and widows were protected. Mercy replaced terror as a governing virtue, and love—once unthinkable as a foundation for society—began to reshape the world.

Christ's reign did not produce a "perfect paradise"—because if everything were perfect, there would be no need to reign at all. Reigning presupposes resistance. It assumes disorder, darkness, and evil that must be restrained. Yet make no mistake: *the world transformed.* Not just a little. It was a passage from night to day—from indescribable terror into the first true dawn of hope the world had ever known. Entire cultures shifted from celebrating cruelty to building schools, hospitals, and orphanages. For the first time in history, people began to speak openly of the dignity of human life, the equality of souls before God, and the moral obligation to love one another.

This was the reign of Christ breaking into history.

It was not a political empire marked by borders, flags, or armies. It was something far more powerful—and far more threatening to the powers of darkness: the slow, relentless expansion of a spiritual kingdom that transformed nations from the inside out.

And Jesus had said it would be so:

> **"The Kingdom of God is like a mustard seed,**
> **which a man took and sowed in his own garden;**

and it grew and became a tree,
and the birds of the sky nested in its branches."
—Luke 13:19

A mustard seed, insignificant at first, then unstoppable. That is the kingdom Christ described, and that is exactly what unfolded in history.

Before Christ, the world was a nightmare of blood and terror. But after He bound Satan and released His apostles into the nations, history took a turn the world had never seen before. For the first time, societies began to breathe air that was not poisoned by demonic cruelty.

The thousand-year reign of Christ was not a perfect utopia—it was the steady, undeniable transformation of the world by the Kingdom of God.

Schools began to appear where none had existed before. Monks and nuns painstakingly copied manuscripts by hand, preserving the knowledge of the ancient world that would otherwise have vanished forever. They taught children who would have been left to rot in ignorance—peasants, orphans, the poor—because they believed every soul mattered. Literacy was no longer reserved for elites. The conviction took hold that every person should learn to read and write, because every soul should be able to read the Word of God for themselves.

From this vision emerged the very first universities in Europe. Oxford, Paris, Bologna, Salamanca—these were not secular inventions, but Christian foundations. Theology stood at their center, and all other disciplines—law, medicine, philosophy, science—were ordered around the pursuit of truth under God. The modern university itself was born from a Christian worldview.

Hospitals sprang up where there had previously been only indifference to suffering. Before Christ, the sick were abandoned, hidden away, or left to die. Now they were seen as neighbors. The first hospitals in Europe were established by Christians who believed that caring for the suffering was a sacred duty, an act of worship. Orders like the Benedictines, Augustinians, and later the Knights Hospitaller devoted their lives to tending the sick, the wounded, and the dying.

Lepers—once feared, shunned, and cast out as untouchables—were now approached with compassion. Christians built leper houses, not to isolate them in cruelty, but to care for them with dignity. This was unheard of in the ancient world.

Orphanages appeared, offering refuge to abandoned children who would otherwise have died on roadsides, in fields, or on trash heaps. Christians took in the unwanted, the discarded, the invisible—because Christ had done the same for them.

And slowly, the value of human life itself began to change.

Infanticide and child sacrifice—once common, accepted, and even celebrated—were outlawed. The casual disposal of inconvenient lives was confronted and condemned. Slavery, so deeply woven into the fabric of every ancient civilization, was no longer viewed as "natural" or unquestionable. It was challenged at its moral roots. This struggle took centuries, but it was ultimately Christians—men and women driven by the gospel—who dismantled it. Figures like William Wilberforce, fueled by faith, finally brought the transatlantic slave trade to its knees.

In Rome, the gladiator games—where human beings were slaughtered for entertainment—were brought to an end when Christians stood against the bloodlust of the empire. Tradition records that a monk named Telemachus stepped into the arena to stop the killing and was murdered by the crowd. His death ignited outrage, and soon after, the games were abolished.

It was the fruit of Christ's reign advancing through history—relentlessly, and irresistibly—through ordinary people who believed that Jesus was King, and that His kingdom had come.

Wherever the kingdom spread, public torture, demon worship, and ritual sacrifice were driven underground.

Even the treatment of women was transformed. In the Greco-Roman world, women were little more than property. But the teaching of Christ—that men and women are equal in value before God—laid the groundwork for a revolution. Marriage was redefined as a covenant of love and fidelity. Sexual immorality, once paraded as normal, was rebuked. For the first time, there was a moral framework that honored purity, dignity, and family.

The belief that all are equal before God eventually formed the basis of legal codes across Europe. The Magna Carta itself rests on principles rooted in Christian teaching. Compassion for the poor, the weak, and the oppressed became virtues instead of burdens. Charity became a calling for the community.

But here is the great irony. Later generations—especially in modern times—began to label this period "the Dark Ages."

EARLY CHRISTIANS POURED
THE LOVE OF CHRIST
INTO HUMANITY FOR
THE FIRST TIME IN HISTORY.

THE SERVANTS OF CHRIST BROUGHT HEALING TO EVERY NATION, TRANSFORMING HUMAN SOCIETY FROM PURE HELL INTO COMMUNITIES WHERE THE LOVE OF CHRIST WAS INTRODUCED.

Dark? Really? Compared to what? Rome's orgies and mass crucifixions? Greece's child prostitution and ritual sacrifice? *The world before Christ was the real dark age.* What Christianity brought was light: schools, hospitals, law, mercy, human dignity. But history has been rewritten to hide this reality. The very era when Christ reigned through His saints has been smeared as "backward" and "barbaric," when in fact it was the beginning of human civilization as we know it today.

This is the reign of Christ. Not a political dictatorship from a throne in Jerusalem, but a spiritual kingdom that spread like a seed, transformed nations, and reshaped the world.

While no movement is perfect—and some used Christianity as a mask for empire or greed—the authentic message of Jesus Christ brought undeniable transformation:

- **It lifted nations out of unspeakable darkness.**
- **It established moral order and dignity.**
- **It brought healing, education, and hope.**
- **And most importantly, it revealed a personal God who loves each human being and calls us to love one another.**

"But Mr. Sörensen, the Bible clearly speaks of exactly a thousand years! The period you are referring to wasn't exactly a millennium, so it can't have been the thousand-year reign!"

—*Josh*

That objection only holds if Revelation 20 is read like a mathematics textbook rather than as the prophetic vision it clearly is. Scripture itself provides the necessary interpretive framework. Throughout the Bible, the phrase "a thousand" is not used as a literal stopwatch measurement of exactly 365,000 days, but as a symbolic expression—denoting a long, complete period of time, or an immense and effectively uncountable multitude. Let's look at the evidence:

- God keeps covenant to "a thousand generations." Not 30,000+ years, but unending faithfulness. — *Deuteronomy 7:9*

- God owns the cattle on "a thousand hills." Not 1,000 and no more—but all the hills. It's poetic fullness. — *Psalm 50:10*

- "A day in Your courts is better than a thousand elsewhere."

Not mathematically 1,000 days, but immeasurably better. — *Psalm 84:10*

• "A thousand years in Your sight are like yesterday." What feels long to us is nothing to God. — *Psalm 90:4*

• "Thousands upon thousands" stand before the throne. Clearly countless multitudes, not literal headcounts. — *Daniel 7:10*

• "With the Lord one day is like a thousand years, and a thousand years like one day." God is outside time itself. — *2 Peter 3:8*

The point is this: for a long period of time Christ reigned, Satan was restrained, and the world was transformed. An era when the power of Christ reshaped human history, bringing light into a world that had been suffocating under millennia of extreme darkness.

Again, nothing was perfect. There was corruption in the Church, evil in the hearts of people, and attempts to overthrow Christ's kingdom. In fact, the very statement that Christ and the saints *reigned* tells us there was evil that needed to be reigned in. If everything were already perfect, there would be no need for reign—no need for rule, judgment, or correction. Perfection requires no government; it runs on autopilot.

The concept of reigning means that divine authority entered a dark, broken world, confronted entrenched evil, rebuked destructive powers, and began a process of transformation.

The magnificent glory of Christ's reign is revealed by a remarkable fact: not even the Nicene Council could stop it from transforming the world. Though the Roman Empire attempted to steal the presence of Christ from His Church, this dark scheme could only partially restrain it. Throughout the world, sincere followers of Christ continued to manifest the reality of His presence in extraordinary ways, radically transforming entire nations.

That is precisely the kind of Millennium history records—not a mythical utopia, but a world profoundly and visibly changed through the reign of Christ and His saints, unfolding in glorious abundance across nations and centuries.

Christ is King, in the face of his diabolical adversaries.

CHAPTER 20

Satan's Little Season

"Mr. Sörensen, open your eyes! How can you possibly say the world is getting better? Have you lost your mind? Please—look around. The world has never been darker. Pornography is destroying the heart and mind of billions who are no longer even capable of forming healthy relationships. Godly families have become rarer than gold. Healthy marriages are almost mythical, as it seems nearly everyone has been divorced at least once. Children are being taught in school that they can be a boy or a girl—even a dog or a cat! Corruption plagues every public office and has practically become a job requirement. Our food is laced with chemicals that quietly destroy our bodies, and nobody seems to care. Hollywood floods the minds of young and old alike with perversion, violence and despair. Depression is crushing children who should be laughing. Mental illness is ravaging society, yet most people can't even see it happening. Nearly one million precious people commit suicide every single year, and millions more attempt it. Healthcare has mutated into a cold, predatory business that bankrupts the sick while enriching criminals in white suits. The news has devolved into a dark propaganda machine, manipulating uninformed masses into blind obedience to nefarious puppet masters behind the scenes. Faith in Christ has almost completely evaporated as society is bombarded day and night with anti-Christ, anti-God indoctrination. Sin is everywhere you look; satanism is now openly celebrated on stage; and humanity feels more lost, more broken, more desperate than ever before.

How can anyone look at this world—this hurting, bleeding, collapsing world—and still believe things have improved?"

—*Josh*

I feel your pain, Josh. And I can't tell you how glad I am that you see what is happening in our world today. So many people are living in a darkness so deep that they don't even recognize the indescribable madness swarming all around them. They swim in oceans of poison and call it "delicious." They welcome demons into their lives and think it's "magical." They pervert every form of purity and celebrate it as "liberation." The blindness is so thick, most people can't even distinguish the worst expressions of evil from the wonderful reality of goodness. They call darkness "light" and expel truth as if it were deception. Never before has such devastating, all-encompassing confusion darkened the mind of the human race.

So thank you, Josh. Thank you for seeing what others refuse to see, for noticing what most have been conditioned to ignore, and for calling out what so many have been taught to accept.

It indeed raises the burning question: *what on Earth is happening?* How is it possible that the wonderful transformation of humanity is suddenly reversing back into the same ancient satanic forces that were once cast out by the Church? What is going on here?

We get the incredible answer when we keep reading the Scriptures. As we saw in the previous chapter, Christ and the saints were the highest spiritual authority in the world for a long period of time, powerfully transforming all of human society everywhere on Earth. Where humans once ate one another as a common practice, slaughtered their own children as sacrifices to demons, worshipped evil spirits and practiced sorcery, indulged in unimaginable sexual perversion—where people were even raped publicly as entertainment—and where anyone with some level of wealth owned sex slaves even for their guests, while the most brutal forms of violence and bestiality dominated every culture... all these horrors came to a screeching halt the moment the children of God arrived with the kingdom of Christ on their banner. They built the first schools, hospitals, and orphanages, and established a level of well-being, peace, and goodness previously unknown in history. Thanks to the massive force of heaven invading hell on earth, the world was radically transformed. This, beyond a doubt, is what Revelation 20 spoke about—the Millennial reign of Christ. Nothing was perfect of course, but light was breaking forth with unprecedented force.

It is imperative that we get this solidly fixed in our minds, because it forms the foundation for understanding what happened next—and why we are suddenly witnessing a roaring renaissance of evil across the world.

Revelation 20 exclaims that after the thousand-year reign something terrible would happen:

after being bound and locked up for a "thousand years" Satan would be released all over again!

> "Then I saw an angel coming down from heaven,
> holding the key of the abyss and a great chain in his hand.
> And he took hold of the dragon, the serpent of old,
> who is the devil and Satan,
> and bound him for a thousand years;
> and he threw him into the abyss
> and shut it and sealed it over him,
> so that he would not deceive the nations any longer,
> until the thousand years were completed;
> after these things **he must be released for a short time...**
>
> **When the thousand years are completed,**
> **Satan will be released from his prison,**
> **and will come out to deceive the nations**
>
> which are at the four corners of the earth, Gog and Magog,
> to gather them together for the war;
> the number of them is like the sand of the seashore."
> — *Revelation 20:1–8*

Satan had to be released one last time, to once again deceive all the nations of the world and gather them together for a final war against Christ and His kingdom.

"...to gather them together for the war; the number of

them is like the sand of the seashore. And they came up on the broad plain of the earth and surrounded the camp of the saints and the beloved city..."

— *Revelation 20:7-9*

That is exactly what we are seeing today. After a long period during which the kingdom of Christ expanded in incredible ways around the world, all of a sudden we are witnessing an unprecedented, all-out attack on Christ and His people, all around the world. Satan has been released again to wage war against the saints and the "beloved city," which is the heavenly Jerusalem that we mentioned earlier.

"Oh no! Please tell me this isn't true! This is so horrible. Why would God decide to release the demon of demons, the greatest dragon of them all... the deceiver of all nations, the devourer of mankind, the source of all evil, the Father of Lies, the murderer from the beginning... the worst of all evils—*all over again?* Isn't that immensely cruel of God?"

—*Josh*

Yes, it's an excruciating question — one I struggled with as well, Josh — and I can't tell you how grateful I am that God eventually gave me a satisfying, though by no means easy, answer. Are you ready for this? I need to warn you, because it doesn't fit our Disney-World, feel-good, cotton-candy theologies that pretend faith is painless and life is a fairy tale. So brace yourself... this is hard-core reality. This is why God released Satan all over again, one last time:

God is fully determined to permanently uproot all evil — once and for all.

He desires a creation cleansed completely of wickedness, purified for all eternity. But in order for that to happen, He must allow humanity to pass through several cycles of choosing Him or choosing Satan. It's like a cosmic cycle of rinse and repeat.

Clearly, God can't just put an end to evil as easily as sweeping a floor with a broom and kicking all the dirt under the carpet. As we have seen, the forces of evil are far too strong, and the number of people willingly choosing it is far too great.

Just look at the fact that the entire world — every single nation, every culture from east to west and north to south — once lived in a state of evil so total it is almost beyond comprehension... a world where people raped anyone who came near them, slaughtered their own children as offerings to the demons they worshipped, tortured their enemies in ways too gruesome to describe, drank the blood of their sons and daughters, and enslaved whoever they could capture to be used for the most bestial forms of sexual abuse... if you grasp that this was normal life for most of humanity, while crowds cheered as men were dismembered in gladiator arenas, and lined up to watch crucifixions, burnings, and hangings of victims — often completely innocent... And if you remember that witches, warlocks, diviners, and sorcerers served as advisers to the rulers of nearly every civilization — the Africans with their witch doctors, the South Americans with their blood-soaked priesthoods, the Celts and Vikings with their ruthless druids, the Indians with their shady shamans, and countless others...

Only then do you begin to see the true depth of the darkness that ruled the Earth before Christ — a darkness so severe that modern man can scarcely imagine it.

And even today—after humanity passed through a long era in which the Church transformed this world from the darkest depths of demonic depravity into a place where life is protected, marriage is honored, children are safeguarded, food is abundant, the poor are cared for, education is available to all, and a thousand other blessings poured into the world through Christ—after all that goodness had taken root in human society—we now witness something shocking.

The moment Satan is released again, we immediately see a total reversal: society sinks straight back into the same darkness that Christ had ended—not even that long ago.

All around the world there is an explosion of "pride parades," where millions of people publicly celebrate perverse sexuality. And increasingly, these public displays of sexual depravity are beginning to resemble the dark rituals of the ancient world. In Israel, Tel Aviv pride parades showcase public acts of extreme sexual obscenity on stage. Deranged men contort their naked bodies in ways that mimic violent, aggressive sexual acts. If this trajectory continues, it won't be long before—under the banners of "acceptance," "equality," and "inclusion"—they begin allowing actual sexual acts, even rape, to be performed publicly on stage, just like what was "normal" before Christ ever came into this world. Truly, Satan's old demons are trying to resurrect the horrors of the past.

That is what drives the LGBTQA+ movement which tells toddlers they are not a boy or a girl, but can be a cat or dog — and can have sex with anything and anyone they desire. It's behind drag shows where child predators dressed like demonic witches enter classrooms to teach defenseless children about sex. It's behind school programs teaching six-year-olds how to masturbate, perform sex acts, and watch pornography. (The following evidence report documents what is going on in schools around the world: StopWorldControl.com/children.)

Ending the cancer of evil is not as simple as we might think—not even for God, the Almighty, eternal Creator of all life. As difficult as this may be to hear, delivering this world is not merely a matter of removing a few demons or eliminating a handful of wicked people. Evil must be uprooted *from the very heart of creation itself;* otherwise, it will inevitably return—only in different forms. That is why God must allow humanity to make a choice. After the light of Christ has illuminated the entire world, Satan is permitted to bring back the ancient darkness—so that it may become unmistakably clear, once and for all, who gladly returns to the old horrors and who remains steadfast in Christ.

Humanity is being given a choice—final and irrevocable.
And God is watching.

The good news is that this final release of Satan is short-lived. Scripture describes it as "a short time," which the King James Version translates as "a little season."

"...till the thousand years should be fulfilled:
and after that he must be loosed **a little season."**
— *Revelation 20:3, KJV*

"Mr. Sörensen, do you actually have solid proof that we are living right now in what Scripture calls 'Satan's Little Season'? Can this claim be demonstrated from real, documented history?"
—*Josh*

Absolutely. It would be ridiculous to make claims of this magnitude without presenting profound and compelling evidence. That is exactly what I will present in the following pages. But first I must ask one important question:

Why did none of us ever hear that the coming of Christ had already taken place—and that it was followed by a Millennium so powerful, so civilizing, so liberating, that whole civilizations were raised out of brutality and darkness into blessing and light?

Instead, every one of us was taught the exact opposite. From childhood onward, we were informed that the centuries after Christ were the darkest in human history. Our schoolbooks called them "the Dark Ages." We were told they were bleak, ignorant, backward, violent, and hopeless—an era to be pitied, mocked, and forgotten.

But why?

Why did no teacher ever whisper even a hint that those centuries were, in reality, the fruit of the Millennial reign of Christ—the very era Scripture promised, when His kingdom would flood the Earth with light, justice, learning, and compassion?

Why were we given a version of history that inverted the truth so violently?

Why did no one ever tell us that what the world calls "dark" was, in fact, the brightest season humanity had ever known?

Why were we never allowed to learn about the Millennium... and instead taught its opposite?

These questions are the beginning of an earthquake that should shake every one of us to the core:

Could it be that—just as we were lied to about the origin of creation, forced to bow before the doctrine that life emerged from absurd chance without a Creator—we were also lied to about our history?

Could it be that the same powers who erased the hand of God from the beginning of the world have also erased the hand of Christ from the shaping of the Christian world?

Could it be that what was truly an age of light was deliberately renamed 'darkness'—and that the era transformed by Christ was intentionally rewritten as a time of ignorance and misery?

And could it be that this deception was designed to sever us from our true heritage, blind us to what Christ accomplished on Earth, and prepare the world for Satan's final assault?

As I've shown again and again in this book, virtually everything we're told in our world today is a lie—*a full blown lie.* Deception has even infiltrated the most sacred realm of human life: the Body of Christ. Not even the Bible has been safe from the twisting and mutilating hands of the great deceiver. *So, why would history be spared?* If I were Satan, fresh out of a thousand-year abyss, and I knew I only had one last chance to deceive humanity, my first move would be to scrub the record clean of that glorious era when Christ reigned and my kingdom was shattered.

And—surprise, surprise—that's exactly what happened.

Every trace of that golden era has been carefully removed from our history books. Instead, a full-blown lie has been imprinted on our minds.

While the facts reveal how Christians transformed the world from indescribable horror, perversion, satanic bloodlust, and rampant witchcraft into Christian nations where the poor, weak, and broken were cared for, and where education, food, science, and justice flourished, the history books falsely call that era the "Dark Ages."

But let's test that claim.

What does history truly reveal when we honestly examine the available evidence?

One of the most compelling examples of how the era of Christ's reign stands in stark contrast to Satan's Little Season is the *architecture.* On the following pages you will see glimpses of the splendid works of grandeur that were built during the time when Christians held primary authority on the Earth.

Look closely at those expressions of majesty.

Were those indeed the "Dark Ages"?

Never before, since the dawn of time, were such magistral masterpieces of heavenly beauty built on Earth as during the "thousand-year reign." And once Satan was released again, we observe an immediate end to that opulence—and a rapid reversal back into darkness.

During the Millennium beauty was normal. Architecture was breathtaking. Majestic buildings, intricate detail, and artistry that lifted the soul toward God. Cities were exhibitions of splendor and grandeur, and the central theme everywhere was Christ—His apostles, His kingdom, even Heaven itself. Humanity lived immersed in the knowledge of the Saviour.

Compare that to our "advanced" civilization. Ugliness reigns.

Cities are concrete wastelands. Lifeless boxes, soulless glass towers, depressing concrete jungles designed by people allergic to beauty.

Christ inspired humanity to build splendor.
Satan inspires humanity to build prisons.

The same collapse is obvious in the arts. Once, artists trained for decades to master their craft. Their souls burned with a passion to express the inexpressible majesty of the Almighty through their sublime works of art. They longed to touch the hearts of the beholders and inspire a deep sense of awe. Art was a gateway for heaven to transform mankind.

But once Satan was released again, a terrifying transformation took place. All of a sudden vulgarity and insanity were paraded as "brilliance," with morons cashing in millions for utter garbage.

A spiritual blindness descended on mankind—so thick that people began applauding this demonic absurdity as the height of their "advanced" culture.

Take a good look at the following examples...

The Cathedral in Sienna, Italy

Never before, since the dawn of time, were such magistral masterpieces of **heavenly beauty** built on earth as during the "thousand-year reign".

During the Millennium, architecture around the world was marked by majesty and magnificence, reflecting the **glory and beauty of Christ.**

The Church of the Savior on Spilled Blood, Russia

Artists and architects strove for the highest level of resplendence, driven by awe for the greatness of the Almighty and a deep desire to **glorify Him through their work.**

The Berliner Dome, Germany

The Cathedral Church of Milan, Italy

No amount of effort was too much for these masters of beauty as they filled the world with awe-inspiring masterpieces, for they were **captivated by Christ.**

Humanity witnessed a whole new level of previously unimaginable artwork, all created with the sole intent of giving glory to Jesus Christ and drawing people **to worship His Majesty.**

The Cathedral of Our Lady of Strasbourg, France

ONCE SATAN WAS RELEASED AGAIN, ARCHITECTURE WORLDWIDE **LOST IT'S GLORY** AND TURNED INTO DEAD AND DEPRESSING DISPLAYS OF UGLINESS AND CHAOS.
LIKE THIS CHURCH IN FRANCE.

The Church of Sainte-Bernadette du Banlay, France

Instead of revealing the splendor of the Most High, the Church worldwide lost its beauty and became an expression of **DARKNESS AND BONDAGE.**

St. Francis De Sales, USA

St. Klementz, Switzerland

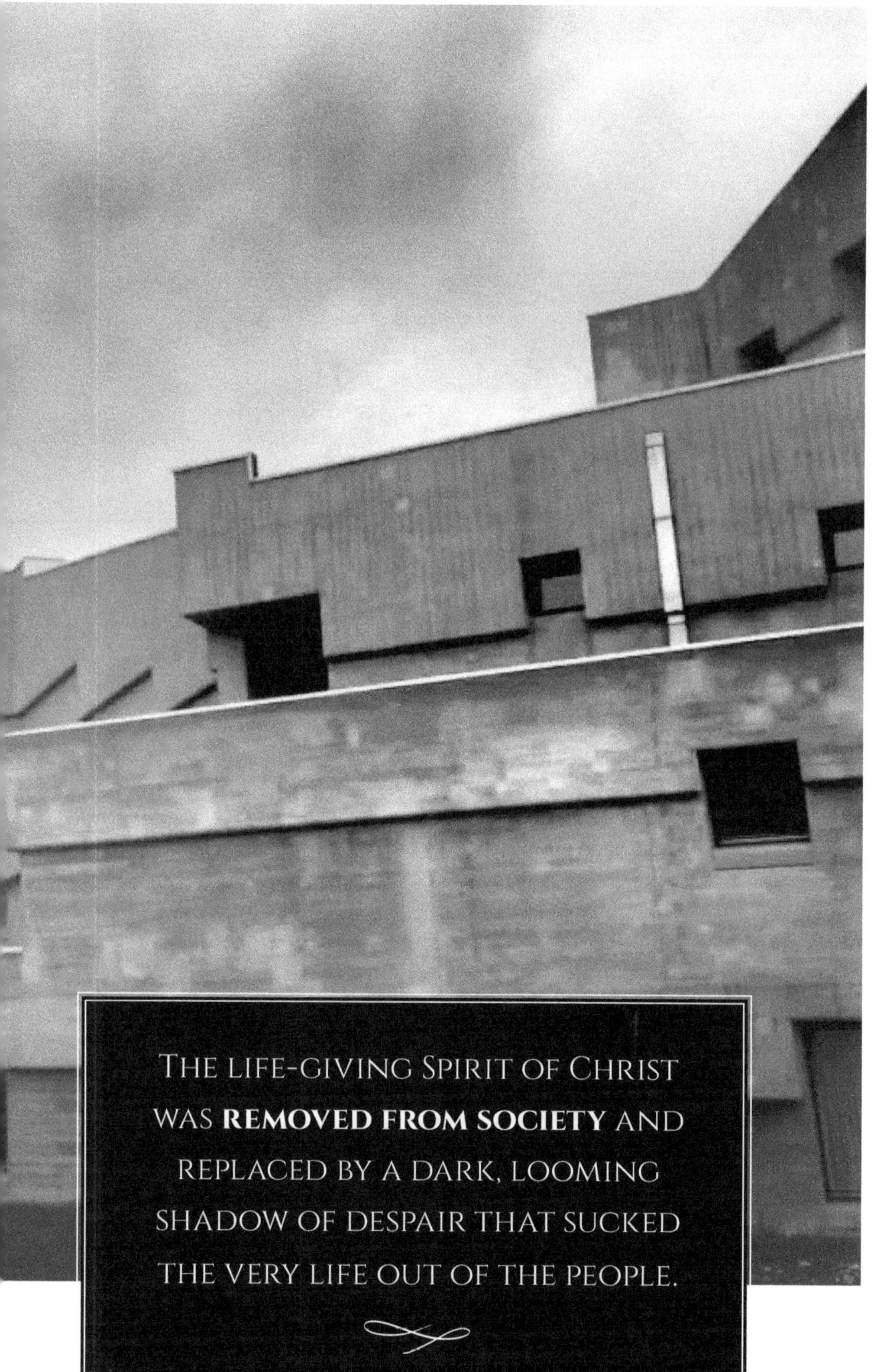

THE LIFE-GIVING SPIRIT OF CHRIST WAS **REMOVED FROM SOCIETY** AND REPLACED BY A DARK, LOOMING SHADOW OF DESPAIR THAT SUCKED THE VERY LIFE OUT OF THE PEOPLE.

"My Inner Beast" by Jens Galschiøt

"Marthe" by Berlinde De Bruyckere

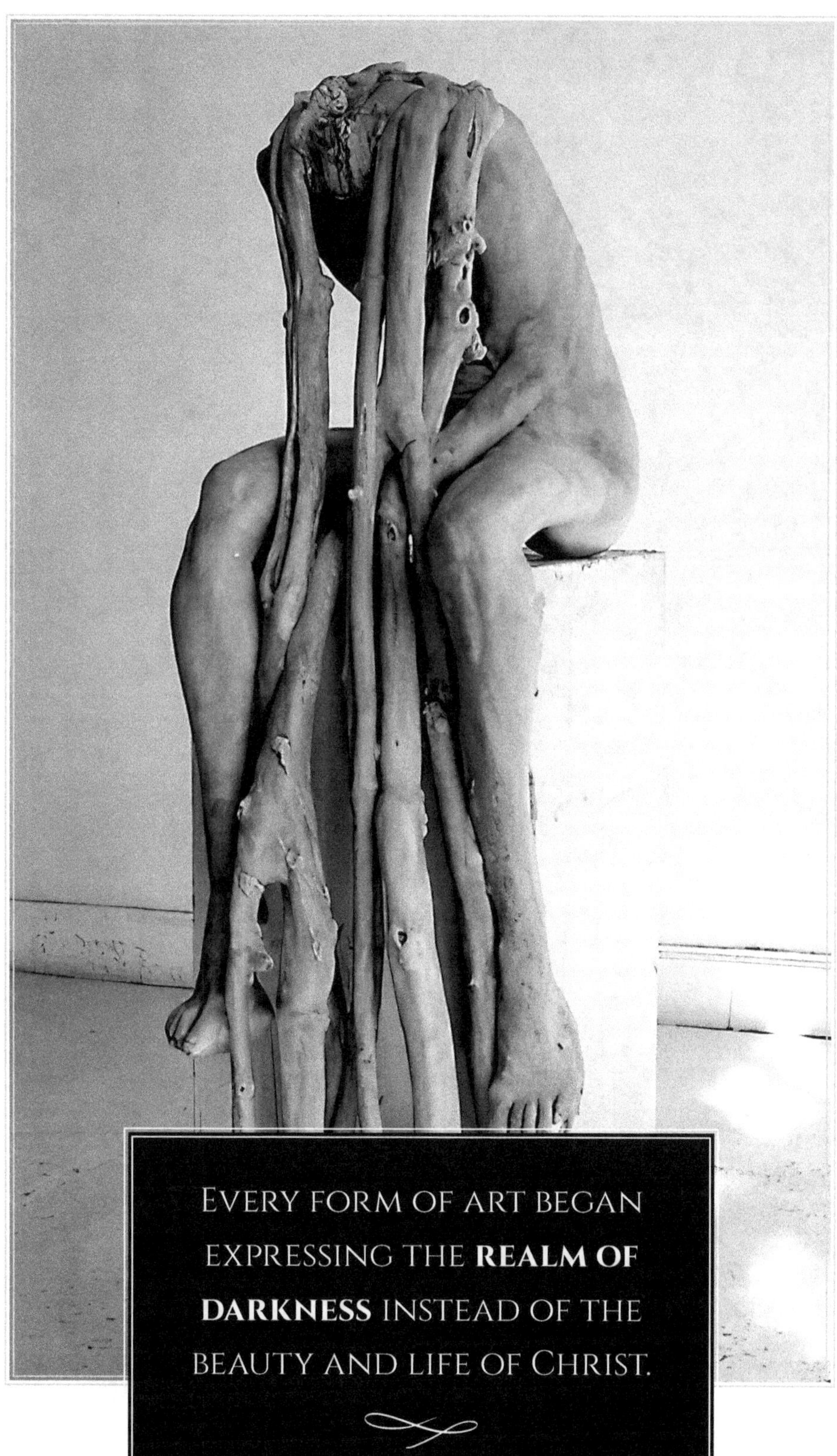

EVERY FORM OF ART BEGAN EXPRESSING THE **REALM OF DARKNESS** INSTEAD OF THE BEAUTY AND LIFE OF CHRIST.

Untitled (1970) by Cy Twombly. Cost of Painting: $69.6 million

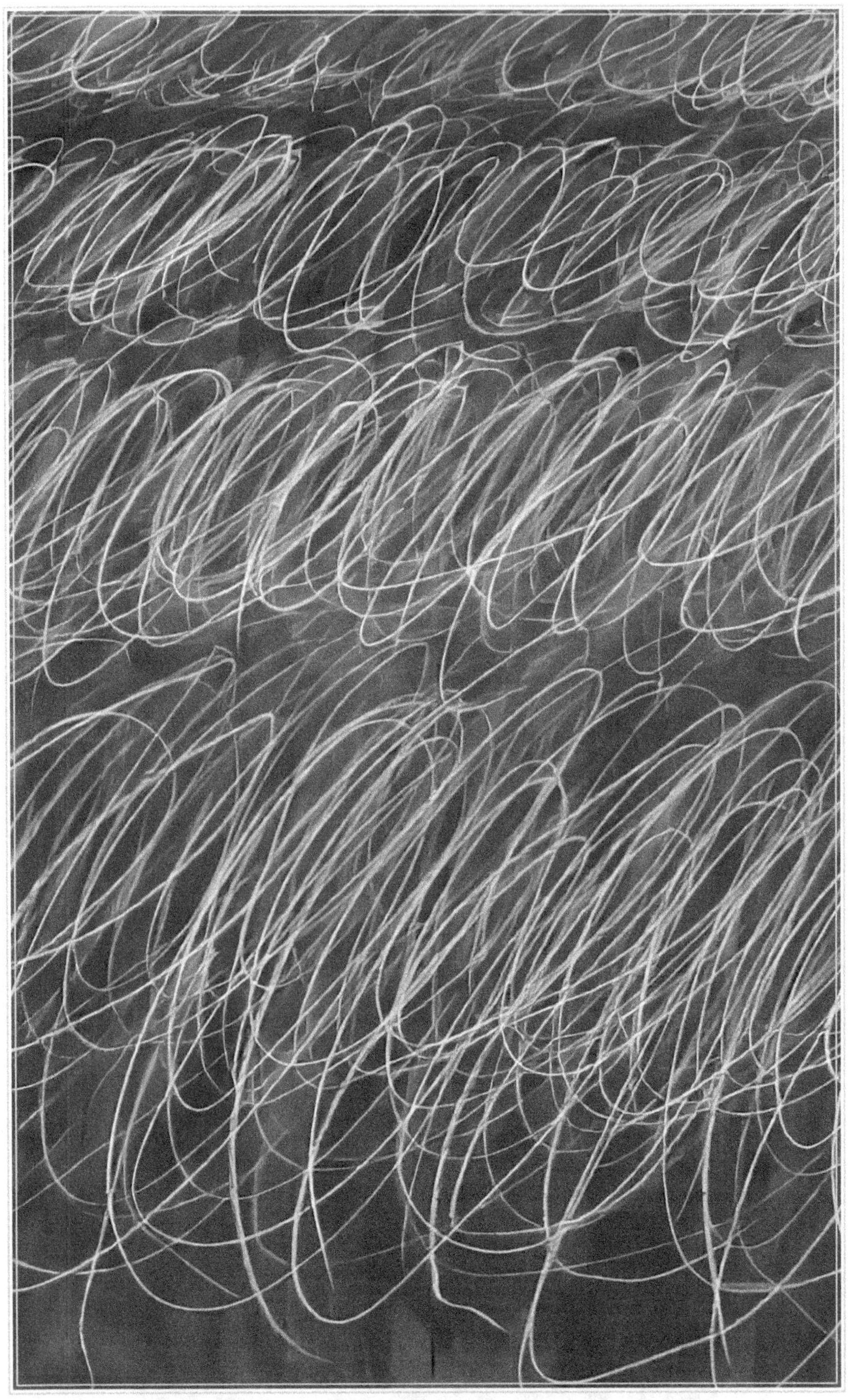

"Comedian" by Maurizio Cattelan

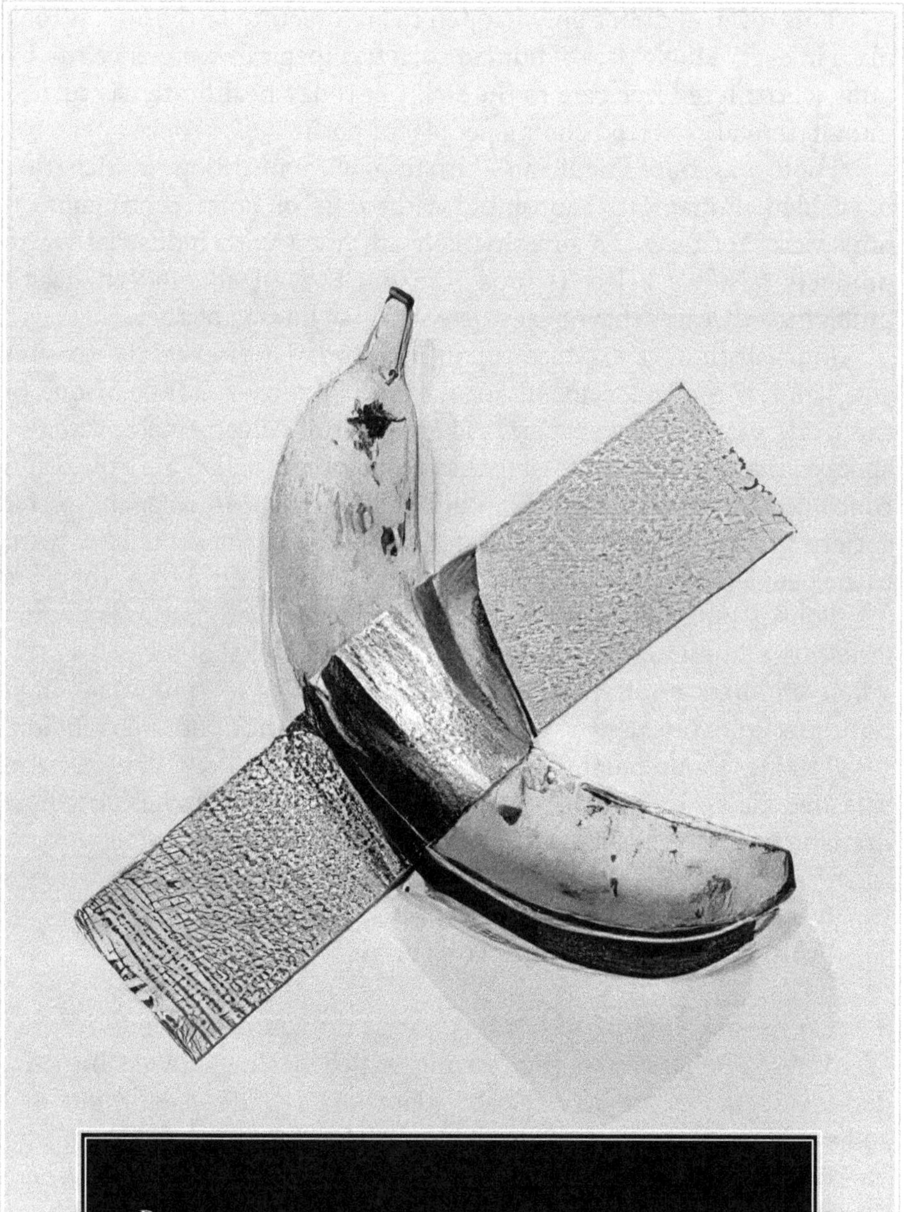

BREATHTAKING WONDER GAVE WAY TO **RIDICULOUS INSANITY**—LIKE A DUCT-TAPED BANANA SELLING FOR $120,000 OR UGLY SCRIBBLING SOLD FOR $69.6 MILLION.

This reversal didn't only happen in architecture or the arts; it took place in every single part of human society. Hospitals were once run by nuns who offered free care to the sick, yet today healthcare has turned into a criminal cartel, poisoning people for profit.

Food was once medicine—bursting with nutrition so rich that it enabled humans to hand-build cathedrals or cross continents on horseback. Yet now the supermarkets are filled with industrial waste products falsely labeled as food, causing 85% of all modern health problems—diseases that never existed in all of human history.

Journalism once exposed corruption; today it protects the corrupt and slanders the innocent. In 2014, Udo Ulfkotte — editor of one of the world's largest newspapers, the Frankfurter Allgemeine Zeitung — shocked the world by confessing that all major journalists are bribed and controlled by the CIA, American billionaires, governments, and secret societies. Their job, he revealed, is to "always lie and never tell the truth to the people." See this documentary: StopWorldControl.com/thenews

Politics once honored prayer and the fear of God, but today many leaders are implicated in child trafficking and global abuse networks, where children are literally used as a commodity to "purchase" high positions in government, the judiciary, police, finance, and even religion.

Talking about religion—once a force that cast out demons and smashed idols—today it has fallen so far that many churches now host drag shows and bless sin in God's own name.

**It is a complete inversion—a civilizational reversal.
From an invasion of light to a renaissance of darkness.**

Let me ask you, in all honesty: what do you think were the true "Dark Ages"? Was it the era during which healing flowed into the darkest depths of an indescribably depraved world—casting out evil and establishing goodness, love, and peace for the first time since Satan overwhelmed all of creation? Or the time we are living in today, where we see a massive reversal back to the ancient perversion, with millions of people worldwide presenting themselves in pride parades as total madmen, walking around naked, displaying perverse sexual acts for all to see, dragging little children in their wake, as a full blown promotion for pedophilia and child abuse?

What are the true Dark Ages? The era when Christians went about casting out evil, tearing down demonic strongholds of child sacrifice and cannibalism, turning entire nations to Christ? Or today, when the

Church hides from the world, terrified of what is happening around them, crying out to escape through a rapture?

What is the real Dark Age? Is it the time when barbaric cultures were taught to read for the first time, learning to respect one another and lifting themselves to new heights of unimaginable wonder as the truth of heaven enlightened their darkened minds? Or is it our time, when children in school are taught that boys are girls, that children can choose to be a cat or a dog—utterly destroying their minds, their souls, their identities, and their future family life forever?

During the so-called "Dark Ages" of the Millennium, music lifted the soul. Gifted musicians developed their divine abilities to create musical masterpieces that stirred the heart so deeply that their classical works have been treasured for centuries as heavenly gifts. Compare that to the music of today—sounds of horror that torture the soul into societal rot, inflicting pain and suffering on the hearts of those who listen. Insane figures scream hideous nonsense on dark stages, while millions of children lose their minds on drugs that kill their brain cells, shattering their nervous systems and poisoning their hearts for life.

Tell me then—what were the real Dark Ages?

The contrast between those ages—when Christians ended human slavery, abolished the blood-thirsty gladiator games, established well-being for all, and founded the first schools and hospitals—and today, when everything good is being torn down and all truth violently concealed from humanity—is indescribable. It is truly the difference between day and night. A beautiful dream turned into a horrifying nightmare.

I believe it is evident that we are in Satan's Little Season.

"What you are saying is very interesting, Mr. Sörensen. I had never thought about it this way. But how is it possible that I have never heard this perspective before? I have always loved history, and I even spent entire afternoons in the public library reading books filled with dramatic tales of the eras that lay behind us. But all that taught me is how horrible the past centuries supposedly were, and how wonderful our era is."

—*Josh*

Yeah, it's weird, isn't it? For me it was also a long journey of waking up to how badly I had been misled about our past. Just like you, Josh, I loved reading about the adventures of knights, and the suffering of poor peasants whose lives—so we were told—were nothing but hell from their first breath to their last.

So when I finally studied real history, I too struggled to wrap my head around it. Mind you, I was raised in one of the most historic cities in the world—"Bruges the Beautiful" also called the "Venice of the North" due to its many wondrous canals. A breathtaking medieval city so stunning it feels like an open-air museum. Marvelous buildings, glorious fortresses, impressive city gates and fortified walls. And the museums! As a kid I spent entire days running around them, taking all the wonders into my young soul, hungry for knowledge and understanding.

I stood in awe before the magnificent tapestries depicting fantastical scenes of richly dressed hunters alongside gorgeous chatelaines. Everything around me radiated splendor and majesty.

Yet my mind was filled with the conflicting beliefs I was taught at school—this overwhelming beauty and brilliance was somehow from the so-called Dark Ages. A time where people were stupid and underdeveloped. They knew nothing and we, the enlightend ones, know everything.

But one day, my crooked worldview suddenly took a terrifying blow when I read the following statement from an online researcher:

"All of our history has been written by a small group of Freemasons connected to a handful of Freemason-controlled universities."

This observation rattled me to my core, and I immediately set out to investigate it. What I found is shocking, to say the least. Let me tell you what I discovered...

We were taught that "history" is a neutral record of facts, written by noble scholars who simply wanted to preserve truth. But did you know that nothing could be further from reality? Just as everything in our world is infested with lies, manipulation, and deception, so it is with history itself.

As the saying goes, history is "His Story."
Whose story? The story told by the man with the power.

Who is that man? In reality, it is not a single individual at all, but a small network of men—elite families, political dynasties, and ideologically aligned academic circles. Together, they decide which version of history will be told to the world, shaping our understanding of the past in order to manipulate us into accepting their future.

It is no different from the theory of evolution. We were told that God does not exist so that humanity would become spiritually disconnected and powerless—making people vulnerable to the forces of evil that can then drive us straight off a cliff.

When it comes to history, they made sure that almost nobody knows that our world was dramatically transformed by Jesus Christ. Why? Because that truth would completely wreck their plan for the future—a future in which there is no place for Jesus Christ. And so, they erased Him from "his story."

So who are "they"? I will give you a few names.

Throughout the 19th and 20th centuries, much of Western academia, publishing, and education was heavily funded or influenced by dynastic powers such as the Rothschilds, Rockefellers, Morgans, Mellons, and Carnegies — families whose global empires required humanity to adopt a very specific worldview.

This selective presentation of history is exemplified by the Rothschild family, which has funded and influenced historical research and education through institutions like the University of Oxford and the British Museum. For instance, the Rothschild family has been accused of manipulating the narrative of World War I, downplaying their role in financing the war effort.[1]

Similarly, the Rockefeller family has exerted profound influence over American history through its control of powerful institutions such as the Rockefeller Foundation and the Council on Foreign Relations, using these platforms to shape educational priorities and promote specific narratives across schools, academia, and the media.[2]

Even the most seemingly objective sources, like the Encyclopedia Britannica, have been influenced by these elites; for example, the encyclopedia's entry on the Rothschild family was written by a Rothschild himself.[3]

The elites exert tremendous influence over history, determining what is remembered and what is forgotten.

They drenched the American university system with billions of dollars, strategically flooded medical schools with funding, endowed entire faculties, dictated textbook production, and underwrote the writing of history itself. They built an academic empire designed to ensure that whole disciplines would bow to an ideology engineered to serve elite interests.

This was confirmed by Theodore R. Sizer (1932–2009) one of America's most respected education scholars and reformers—a professor at Harvard University, former dean of the Harvard Graduate School of Education, and founder of the influential Coalition of Essential Schools. Far from being a fringe critic, Sizer worked at the very heart of elite academia, giving his observations particular weight. In *Horace's Compromise* (1984), a landmark study of American secondary and higher education, he candidly acknowledged how large philanthropic foundations reshaped the intellectual landscape of universities.

Sizer stated plainly:[4]

> **"With their financial largesse, these foundations have helped set the research agenda, determine what counts as significant knowledge, and shape the institutional structure of higher education itself."**

Simply said: elites determine what the public knows.

Another authority exclaimed the same idea: Andrew Carnegie (1835–1919) was one of the most powerful industrialists in American history. He believed that education should be deliberately shaped to serve the needs of their new and preferred modern society. Through the Carnegie Foundation for the Advancement of Teaching, his wealth was used not merely to support schools, but to restructure the entire educational system by defining standards, accrediting institutions, and aligning curricula with industrial and administrative priorities. The Foundation made its objective unmistakably clear:[5]

> **"One of the chief functions of the Foundation is to bring about a greater degree of uniformity and standardization in American education."**

This statement reveals that the transformation of education was not accidental, but intentional—designed to replace diverse, independent forms of learning with a centralized and standardized system aligned with the needs of an emerging industrial order.

In plain English:

Andrew Carnegie made sure that all children were taught the same information in school—information selected by himself.

Simultaneously, across the Atlantic, the Rothschild dynasty carried out its own long-term cultural engineering project. Through sprawling philanthropic networks, they quietly molded the intellectual memory of Europe. For more than a century, their foundations have funded archives, endowed academic chairs, influenced research priorities, and preserved the texts they deemed indispensable for shaping the next generation of European thinkers.

Even in recent years, the Rothschild Foundation Hanadiv Europe funded Oxford University's Bodleian Libraries to preserve, catalogue, and prioritize *selected* textual collections. The public was told this was "charitable preservation," but in reality it continued a tradition of steering the academic focus of the Western world, determining what is studied, what is remembered, and what quietly disappears into oblivion.

The same thing happened within Christianity. Why have you never heard about the historical record from the first century that documents in detail how all the prophecies of Jesus Christ and the apostles came to pass—exactly as foretold, in the precise manner, location, and timing predicted? Because powerful people with vast money and influence deliberately kept these records out of the Christian seminaries, Bible schools, theological faculties, and academic institutions.

For the same reason, you will never find a truly powerful book that proves the existence of God—or that teaches you how to actually experience God—in a public library. Such works are quietly excluded and systematically weeded out, while you will find shelves filled with thousands of writings designed to steer you away from the Creator and straight into the abyss of atheism.

We see the exact same method of subversion at work in the realm of science, where the entire global scientific establishment has been coerced into denying the existence of an intelligent Creator, Instead, they are forced to embrace a new "state religion": the doctrine that all life emerged from blind chance, a cosmic accident championed by their carefully manufactured prophet, Charles Darwin. Any scientist who dares to question this dogma—who suggests that the staggering complexity of nature or the breathtaking design of the human body points to a Designer—is immediately branded a heretic. Careers are destroyed, tenure is revoked, research funding evaporates, and they are expelled from the academic community with ruthless efficiency. This was exposed in the documentary *Expelled: No Intelligence Allowed* (2008) by Ben Stein, which revealed how countless scientists and professors were blacklisted simply for acknowledging the possibility that nature might have been created. The message is clear: bow to Darwin, or dissapear.

In other words, the intellectual landscape of the modern West did not arise by accident. It was cultivated, curated, and controlled by some of the wealthiest families in human history, whose influence continues unabated to this very day.

Many people say, "Humanity is drifting away from God." But that is not accurate. A far more precise description is this: *humanity is being driven away from God.* Television programs are carefully produced with this purpose in mind. Books in libraries are selectively removed or added. School and university curricula are meticulously written. Museums are filled with carefully selected artifacts, each accompanied by curated explanations. Cultural activities are strategically organized—and so on.

All with one and the same objective:

to steer mankind away from Jesus Christ and His Kingdom.

When we examine history more closely, we find that much of this anti-Christian manipulation has flowed through specific institutions. Among them are Oxford, Cambridge, Harvard, Yale, Columbia, Princeton, and the London School of Economics. These universities produced—and continue to produce—the majority of textbook authors, historians, diplomats, policymakers, and cultural gatekeepers who shape how the world thinks, teaches, and remembers.

One of the most explicit and influential architects of this elite mind-shaping system was Cecil Rhodes (1853–1902). Rhodes was a renowned British imperialist, meaning he was an avid promoter of the British Empire's agenda of world domination. Beyond his imperial ambitions, he was also a diamond magnate, the founder of De Beers, Prime Minister of the Cape Colony, and one of the most powerful men of his age. Educated at Oriel College, Oxford, he believed unashamedly in rule by a chosen elite—and he understood something most conquerors never grasp: lasting power is not secured by land, armies, or wealth alone, but by education, ideology, and institutions.

Rhodes openly envisioned a world governed by a tightly connected ruling class, unified by a shared worldview and strategically positioned to direct nations from within. His solution was not brute force, but something far more effective:

the colonization of the human mind.

While empires rose and fell on battlefields, Rhodes designed a system that would outlive armies by shaping what future leaders would be permitted to know—and what must be erased from their awareness.

That vision lives on most visibly through the Rhodes Scholarships, deliberately created to identify, groom, and network future global leaders at Oxford—men and women who would go on to shape governments, academia, media, and culture across the world. Rhodes understood a chilling truth of empire: armies may conquer territories, but institutions conquer minds. He stated his ambition in his 1877 Confession of Faith:[6]

> **"I contend that we are the finest race in the world**
> **and that the more of the world we inhabit**
> **the better it is for the human race."**

His understanding of "inhabiting the world" also included "inhabiting the mind of the world." For unless you control what people believe, you have not truly conquered them.

In order to accomplish the conquest of the human mind, Rhodes founded the Round Table Group—an elite network operating largely in secrecy, dedicated to steering global affairs through *influence* rather than visibility. This hidden structure was later exposed by historian Carroll Quigley, a Georgetown professor and mentor to President Bill Clinton, and one of the very few scholars ever granted access to the group's private archives. Quigley revealed that behind governments, behind nations, behind presidents and parliaments, there existed *a quiet empire*, a hidden order of men who believed they had the right to rule the world.

Then he put their agenda into words:[7]

> **"The powers of financial capitalism had another**
> **far-reaching aim, nothing less than to create**
> **a world system of financial control in private hands**
> **able to dominate the political system of each country**
> **and the economy of the world as a whole."**

Quigley described how this world system would operate:[8]

> **"This system was to be controlled in a feudalistic fashion**
> **by the central banks of the world acting in concert,**
> **by secret agreements... with the Bank for International**
> **Settlements at the apex of the system."**

And then the revelation becomes even more stunning. Quigley had seen the documents, the correspondence, the hidden plans:[9]

> **"I know of the operations of this network**
> **because I have studied it for twenty years**
> **and was permitted for two years, in the early 1960s,**
> **to examine its papers and secret records."**

He was not whistleblowing. He was informing—almost justifying—what he believed was the natural evolution of global power:[10]

> **"I have no aversion to it or to most of its aims...**
> **my chief difference of opinion is that**
> **it wishes to remain unknown."**

Think about that for a moment...

A historian with direct access to the world's most secretive financial archives tells us plainly that a global elite does exist, that it moves in coordinated unity across nations, that it operates through central banks and hidden agreements, that its ambition is nothing less than world domination through financial control—and that it prefers to remain unseen behind the curtain. Here we have the definition of what is commonly referred to as the "Deep State" or "Shadow Governments." And it is not presented as a conspiracy theory. This is the sworn testimony of a man operating at the highest levels of the elite—someone who was granted access to their most secret papers and handled them with his own hands.

What Quigley uncovered was a coordinated structure of global power rising like a counterfeit kingdom, preparing the world for the greatest deception ever to come.

His revelations were powerfully confirmed by men who stood at the highest summits of politics and banking. James A. Garfield, the 20th President of the United States—a man who dared to confront the hidden rulers of finance—issued a warning that now echoes like thunder from the grave. Speaking in Congress before his assassination in 1881, President Garfield declared:[11]

> **"Whoever controls the volume of money in any country**
> **is absolute master of all industry and commerce."**

Another U.S. President, Thomas Jefferson, warned with prophetic clarity about the rise of private banking power:[12]

> **"I believe that banking institutions are more dangerous to our liberties than standing armies."**

And decades later, after the creation of the Federal Reserve, President Woodrow Wilson cried out in sorrow at what had been unleashed:[13]

> **"A great industrial nation is controlled by its system of credit. Our system of credit is privately concentrated. The growth of the nation, therefore, and all our activities are in the hands of a few men."**

They are the confessions of presidents—men who saw the monster rising. Some of them were killed in cold blood because they dared to oppose these dark forces—forces that sought to manipulate governments in pursuit of global domination.

And the gravity of their warnings becomes undeniable when we recognize that the same financial force they feared in America had already reached its full, terrifying maturity in Europe.

During the 19th century, the Rothschild banking dynasty rose to a level of dominance the world had never before witnessed. They did not merely lend money—they financed kingdoms. They arranged the debts of nations, underwrote the cost of wars, rescued collapsing treasuries, stabilized currencies, and supplied lifelines in moments when entire governments trembled on the edge of ruin. When kings needed armies, when parliaments needed budgets, when empires gasped for survival, they all came knocking on the same door.

The Rothschilds amassed their unprecedented wealth through ruthless strategies that exploited mass panic. They became masters at provoking sudden market collapses—and profiting from the chaos that followed. As prices spiraled downward in a terrifying freefall, other investors—terrified of losing everything—sold their holdings in blind panic. Then, at the darkest moment, when the market had been reduced to ashes and stocks were worth next to nothing, the Rothschilds swept in and purchased everything. When the markets inevitably recovered—as they knew they would—they rose like a rocket, becoming unimaginably wealthy, while everyone else was left impoverished, broken, and ruined.

Through these immense financial levers, the Rothschilds became the invisible power behind the visible thrones of Europe.

Monarchs changed, cabinets rose and fell, but the banking houses of Frankfurt, London, Paris, Vienna, and Naples remained the constant, unshakable presence—quietly steering the fate of nations through the simple, devastating logic of credit and debt.

What makes all of this even more remarkable is that the elites who rose to such unprecedented financial power were not spiritually neutral—at least not in the way they presented themselves to the world. Throughout modern history, the Rothschilds and other elite figures have repeatedly surrounded themselves with imagery, symbolism, and performances that many observers interpret as openly Satanic.

One of the most striking examples is the now-infamous Surrealist Ball hosted by Marie-Hélène de Rothschild on December 12th, 1972, at Château de Ferrières—one of the family's colossal mansions. These events were usually shrouded in secrecy, yet photographs of this particular evening somehow surfaced. They reveal a spectacle that left millions around the world stunned: Rothschild greeting guests while wearing the head of a horned animal—a symbol long associated in Western tradition with occultism and satanic ritual.

Inside, the table décor displayed dismembered baby dolls, cracked infant-like skulls, and nude mannequin bodies arranged in ways that many viewers could not interpret as anything other than symbolic nods to human sacrifice (see photos on the following pages).

On another occasion, Jacob Rothschild was photographed standing beside avant-garde performance artist Marina Abramovic, in front of a painting titled "Satan Summoning His Legions from Hell." Abramovic is known for work featuring imagery of children covered in blood, simulated cannibalism, and satanic themes.

Her shocking "Spirit Cooking" ceremonies showcased full-sized cakes formed as naked human bodies, consumed by elite attendees—a spectacle of cannibalistic symbolism presented to the world as "art."

Meanwhile, various members of the Rothschild family have repeatedly been photographed wearing jewelry with occult symbols—including large golden depictions of horned figures and inverted motifs long associated with satanic imagery.

Although these things do not constitute legal proof of satanism, they do reveal a disturbing pattern—one that any honest observer recognizes instantly. When individuals who sit atop global financial systems repeatedly surround themselves with symbols of darkness, death, cannibalism, human sacrifice, and violent abuse, it raises legitimate questions about the beliefs and practices of these people. If they're already bold enough to parade this before the entire world, then what, in heaven's name, are they doing behind closed doors, hidden from every witness, every camera, every shred of public accountability?

And the timing is impossible to ignore.

During the very era in which it appears Satan was "released for a little season," with a raging fury to destroy the kingdom of Jesus Christ, the people who rose to global power—controlling nations, economies, and cultural institutions—were the same people openly surrounding themselves with symbols traditionally associated with Satan.

"That is all so shocking, Mr. Sörensen. But do you know what strikes me? My entire life I was programmed to dismiss the idea of a hidden rule by evil people as nothing more than a 'conspiracy theory'—wild fairy tale nonsense invented by mentally unstable people who see ghosts under every rock, and spin wild fantasies out of an overheated imagination.

And now here you are—quoting it straight from multiple Presidents of the United States, and from the very founders and architects of the world's central banking system. And then on top of that, showing how these same elites openly flaunt their allegiance to Satan.

I can't believe I've been so gullible my whole life—never once looking deeper into anything, always just swallowing whatever the TV fed me. What an awakening this is!"

—*Josh*

I know. It *is* wild. And once you finally gather the honesty and courage to stop burying your head in the sand and actually look at the real world — not the fantasy world you see on TV — it can be terrifying to see what's out there. That shock alone is what causes most people to slam their eyes shut. They would rather live inside a comfortable illusion — even if it is a prison tightening around them on every side — than bravely lift their head and face the guardians of this world who keep humanity locked into their system of control.

Jacob Rothschild posed with Marina Abramović in front of a painting titled **"Satan Summoning His Legions from Hell."**

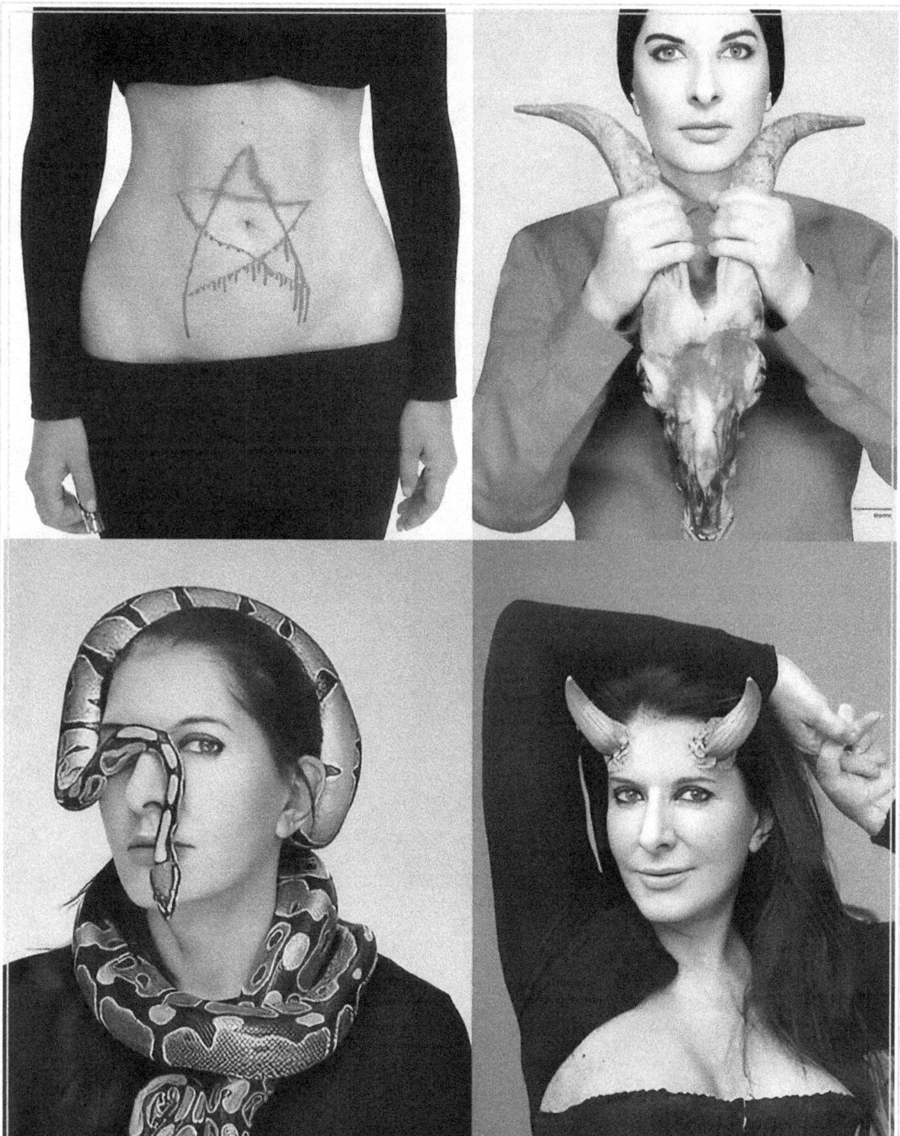

Marina Abramović is notorious for art steeped in symbols long linked to **satanism and dark occult ritual imagery.**

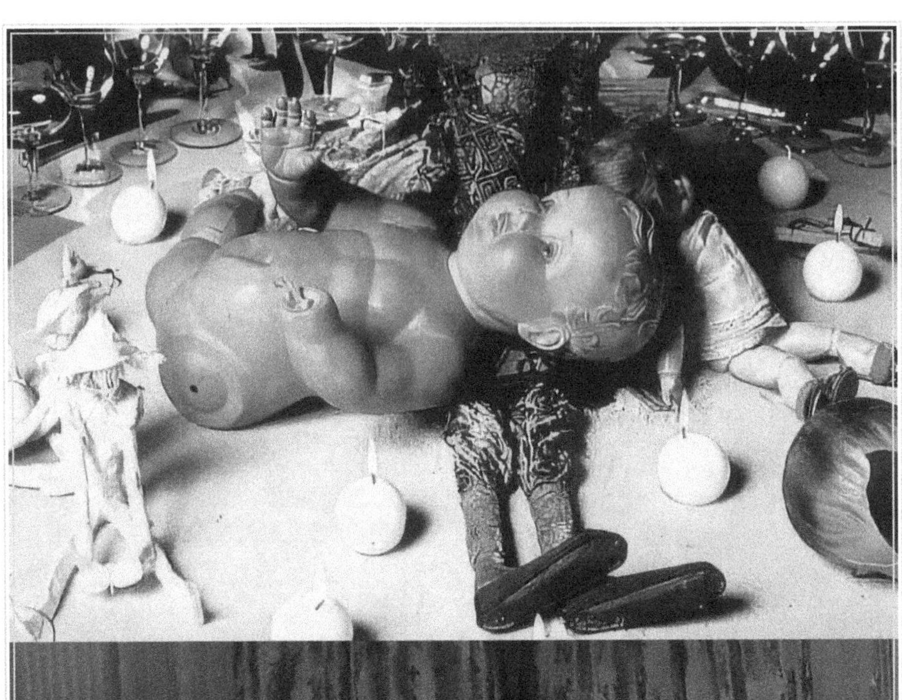

A ROTHSCHILD "SURREALIST BALL" DISPLAYED DISMEMBERED BABY DOLLS AND NAKED MANNEQUINS—**CLEAR SYMBOLS OF SATANIC RITUALS AND CANNIBALISM.**

Baroness Philippine W. P. de Rothschild often wore a necklace depicting a devil, goat, or ram's head—**classic symbols of Satan.**

Baroness Mathilde de Rothschild collected more **skulls and sculptures of the devil** than any other person in all of history.

SHE OWNED **A SCULPTURE OF A DEVIL** LIFTING THE TORCH OF LOVE AS IF TO BLESS HUMANITY, WHILE SECRETLY CONCEALING A SKULL OF DEATH BEHIND HIS BACK.

Let us continue uncovering the undeniable proof—straight from history and the words of world leaders—that Satan has indeed been unleashed once again with a plan to subjugate mankind.

One of the most revealing—and least understood—figures in this dark architecture is Walter Lippmann, the man who quite literally designed the blueprint for modern media propaganda. Lippmann wasn't just a journalist; he was a political philosopher, a presidential advisor, a founder of The New Republic, and one of the most influential voices of the twentieth century. His ideas became the operating system of Western media, politics, and psychological manipulation.

In 1922, Walter Lippmann published a book that quietly rewired the modern world: Public Opinion. In its pages, Lippmann argued that ordinary people were essentially incapable of understanding reality. The masses, he claimed, wandered through life inside a mental fog of "pictures in their heads"—pre-fabricated illusions constructed for them by those who supposedly understood how the world truly worked. Everyday citizens, he insisted, were too busy, too emotional, too easily distracted to make informed decisions about their own lives or their own nations. Therefore—and here Lippmann is shockingly blunt—society must be guided by a small ruling elite, a "specialized class," who would decide on behalf of everyone else.

And how should this elite maintain its power?
By shaping the public mind.

Lippmann argued that modern democracy could not function without intermediaries who mold the public's perception of reality. Ordinary people, he said, inhabit a "pseudo-environment" constructed through media, stereotypes, and tightly controlled information—making them dependent on those who interpret events for them. It is in this context that he delivered his most chilling admission:[14]

> **"That the manufacture of consent is capable of great refinements no one, I think, denies. The process by which public opinions arise is certainly no less intricate than it has appeared in these pages, and the opportunities for manipulation open to anyone who understands the process are plain enough..."**

"Sir, I find this language a bit too complex for my humble brain. What do these guys even mean by the term 'the manufacture of consent'? Care to help this simple soul understand the lofty language of these elites?"

—*Josh*

I had the same reaction the first time I read this. These elites love dressing their schemes in fancy academic words so nobody understands what they're actually saying. So let me put this in simple terms. When they talk about 'the manufacture of consent,' they mean something very straightforward:

teaching people what to think — without letting them know they're being taught what to think.

It means shaping public opinion so subtly, so constantly, so professionally, that people honestly believe their thoughts are their own... even though those thoughts were planted in them by the rulers of the information world. It's the polite, academic way of saying:

"We will manipulate the minds of the people until they agree with us."

It is nothing less than the creation of a mandated narrative that everyone silently agrees upon. Whatever the rulers declare — through television, school textbooks, science, religious indoctrination, political speeches, and media propaganda — is blindly and unquestioningly accepted. You bow your mind before whatever they demand you believe. And those who dare to raise a finger, ask a question, think for themselves, or wonder why we are all required to accept a predetermined set of beliefs... are instantly branded as "weird," "unstable," "untrustworthy," or even "dangerous." They become outcasts. Today we mock them with a weaponized label: "conspiracy theorist."

People who see the corruption of the system and try to warn others are silenced with this ridiculous word — a verbal muzzle designed to shame truth-seekers into compliance.

That is precisely what it means to manufacture consent:

an entire population quietly agrees to remain inside a mental prison. And anyone who tries to escape that prison is punished — not by the rulers, but by the mob they have been taught to imitate.

You are not immediately attacked by the criminal politicians or the financial overlords. No — the first blow comes from the people closest to you. They have consented to believe only what they are told, and anyone who dares to deviate from the imposed narrative becomes a threat to their fragile sense of safety. So they lash out. They mock. They accuse. They distance themselves. They try to silence you — not because you are dangerous, but because your awakening threatens their illusion.

This is perhaps the most painful persecution of all: being attacked not by enemies, but by those we love.

And it reveals just how successful these men have been in their strategy of "manufacturing consent" to keep the public in its place. Generations have been conditioned to defend their own captors, to safeguard the very system that enslaves them, and to tear down anyone who dares to question it.

And again, we see the exact same spirit dominating the Church: either you believe what you are told—for example about the return of Christ and Israel—or you will be slapped with every ugly label they can throw at you: "false teacher," "false prophet," "deceiver," "antisemite", and more. Not because they have honestly weighed the evidence, but because those accusations are a weapon designed to intimidate you, silence you, and make sure you shut up, sit down, and fall back into line.

Lippmann did not describe this as a conspiracy—he presented it as the unavoidable machinery of mass society, where those who control information also control the boundaries of what the public sees, understands, and ultimately consents to.

He stated this plainly:[15]

> **"The common interests very largely elude public opinion entirely, and can be managed only by a specialized class whose personal interests reach beyond the locality."**

Simply translated: "People are dumb, so they must be ruled by an elite class". He literally called the public a "wild herd":[16]

> **"The public must be put in its place...**
> **so that each of us may live free of the trampling**
> **and the roar of a bewildered herd."**

His ideas became the backbone of modern public relations, political messaging, corporate advertising, and government propaganda. And the man who carried Lippmann's worldview out of the ivory tower and into the bloodstream of society was even more influential — Edward Bernays, the undisputed father of modern public relations. A nephew of Sigmund Freud, steeped in the psychological machinery of human desire and subconscious manipulation, Bernays became the perfect fusion of propaganda and psychoanalysis. Corporations hired him. Governments paid him. Intelligence agencies studied him. Media conglomerates followed his blueprint. He understood something terrifying:

if you know how the human mind works, you can shape entire populations without them ever realizing it.

In *Propaganda* (1928), Edward Bernays openly admitted that modern democracy does not rest on the conscious judgment of the people, but on *the covert power of a hidden elite.* He declared that "the conscious and intelligent manipulation of the organized habits and opinions of the masses is an important element in democratic society," and he described the small ruling class behind this machinery as an "invisible government" — the men who quietly steer nations by shaping what the public sees, thinks, and believes. Bernays publicly declared:[17]

> **"We are governed, our minds are molded, our tastes formed, our ideas suggested, largely by men we have never heard of."**

But the architects of global influence didn't stop with controlling news, shaping opinion, and manufacturing consent. If Bernays taught the elite how to mold the mind of the masses, another towering figure rose to explain how to mold the entire human being—body, will, emotion, and character. That man was Bertrand Russell.

Russell, one of the most celebrated philosophers of the 20th century, took the next logical step: if propaganda could steer the thoughts of adults, then education, medicine, and even diet could be engineered to sculpt the minds of children and future generations at the deepest possible level. In 1952, he calmly described a future in which scientific power would be used not to liberate mankind, but *to program it.* In *The Impact of Science on Society*, in the chapter "Scientific Technique in an Oligarchy," he imagined a dictatorship that would achieve what earlier tyrants only dreamed of—shaping human beings *from the inside out:*[18]

"Diet, injections, and injunctions will combine, from a very early age, to produce the sort of character and the sort of beliefs that the authorities consider desirable, and any serious criticism of the powers that be, will become psychologically impossible. Even if all are miserable, all will believe themselves happy, because the government will tell them that they are so."

Does this not shake your soul? One of the most influential thinkers of the twentieth century openly declared that control over what people eat, control over what is injected into their bodies, and control over what authorities command them to obey would be deliberately fused into a single system—engineered to produce a humanity perfectly conditioned for submission. A world where resistance is no longer crushed by force, but quietly engineered out of existence from the inside. The people have been mentally engineered to love and defend their prison.

And these were not the mutterings of some wide-eyed conspiracy hermit hiding in a basement with a tinfoil hat. Russell was a Nobel Prize–winning philosopher, a respected statesman, a titan of the academic world. Yet here he stood, describing with surgical calm a future in which governments would craft the human soul through pharmaceuticals, schooling, and the manipulation of information itself.

He outlined the very system we are watching unfold today: the poisoning of the Western food supply with industrial toxins labeled as "food," the forced injections that deliver undisclosed substances into the bodies of billions, the corruption of courts and judges to protect the powerful and persecute dissenters. Russell did not warn about a distant dystopia. He predicted the world we now inhabit—a world where the authorities shape thought, desire, and even happiness itself, all while insisting it is for our own good.

For Russell, none of this was accidental. It was the design—with a single, chilling purpose:

weaken humanity physically, mentally, and morally until people become defenseless, dependent, and easily controlled servants of the ruling class.

At the very same time, another world-leading figure stepped onto the stage: Dr. John Rawlings Rees, the founder of the Tavistock Institute and one of the most influential psychiatrists of the twentieth century.

While Russell outlined the philosophical blueprint, Rees provided the psychological and institutional strategy for carrying it out.

In *Strategic Planning for Mental Health* (1940), Rees made his objective unmistakably clear:[18]

> **"We must aim to make our particular point of view permeate every educational activity in our national life: primary, secondary, university, and technical education...**
> **Those who provide the education, the principles upon which they work, and the people upon whom they work must all be objects of our interest...**
> **Public life, politics, and industry should all of them be within our sphere of influence...**
>
> **We have done much to infiltrate the various social organizations throughout the country...**
>
> **Similarly, we have made a useful attack upon a number of professions. The two easiest of them naturally are the teaching profession and the Church; the two most difficult are law and medicine....**
>
> **If we are to infiltrate the professional and social activities of other people, I think we must imitate the Totalitarians and organize some kind of fifth column activity....**
>
> **Let us all, therefore, very secretly be 'fifth columnists.'"**

It is interesting that Rees considered the Church easy to infiltrate. Hear, hear, all you pastors and priests!

Now, what is the "fifth column" he refers to? In military terms, a fifth column refers to a hidden force operating from within—a covert network embedded inside a nation, working quietly to weaken it from the inside out.

Rees was calling for nothing less than a stealth infiltration of every sector of society. Teachers, clergy, journalists, civil servants, and professionals in every field were to be subtly influenced—or replaced—by operatives shaped by psychiatric doctrine, spreading new values under the guise of "mental health."

It brings to mind the sculpture once owned by Baroness Mathilde de Rothschild: a devil proudly holding a torch of light, while concealing a skull behind his back. The symbolism is obvious. It perfectly reflects what Apostle Paul warned about in Scripture:

> **"No wonder, for even Satan disguises himself as an angel of light."**
> — *2 Corinthians 11:14*

This is how Satan has always worked. He presents himself as a benefactor—one who promises progress, enlightenment, and a better world—while hiding intentions that are as dark and deadly as hell itself.

Another example of this is the Fabian Society—a socialist elite devoted to remaking civilization not through revolution, but through slow, calculated, technocratic control. While Rees focused on infiltrating institutions, the Fabians focused on redefining the ideas that would guide those institutions.

History, media, education, and academia were their first targets—the gateways to the human mind, and therefore the foundations of mass control.

One of their most prominent members, H. G. Wells, was far more than a novelist. He was a strategic thinker operating at the highest levels of British political and academic power—an architect of the worldview that shaped elite institutions like the London School of Economics. Wells advised statesmen, helped craft public policy, and influenced the educational philosophies that trained future leaders.

In his 1928 manifesto *The Open Conspiracy,* Wells laid out a blueprint for a future world. Through systematic propaganda and a "conspiracy" operating in full view, he proposed the creation of a world that is politically, socially, and economically unified, culminating in a global revolution aimed at "peace," "welfare," and universal "happiness"—what he called a "world commonwealth." But beneath the utopian veneer, his program required something far darker: total mind control of the entire human population.

The world had to think only what the architects of the new order allowed—and nothing else.

Wells' own words expose his intention in the 1928 manifesto *The Open Conspiracy:*[19]

> **"From its outset the Open Conspiracy will be setting itself to influence the existing educational machinery, but for a long time it will find itself confronted in school and college by powerful religious and political authorities..."**

The new world, Wells argued, must "guard its children from the infection of earlier beliefs and national identities", raising them instead within a "unified progressive world community," indoctrinated from birth. In other words, everything Christ and His kingdom had accomplished worldwide had to be erased to make way for a new global kingdom—ruled by elites who openly show their allegiance to Satan.[21]

> **"The character of the Open Conspiracy will now be plainly displayed...**
>
> **It will be frankly a world religion.**
>
> **This... will be definitely and obviously attempting to swallow up the entire population of the world and become the new human community."**

H. G. Wells — a man who stood at the very heart of British intellectual and political power, advising statesmen, shaping institutions like the London School of Economics, and operating as a strategic voice within elite policy-making circles — openly called for nothing less than a new global faith to replace Christianity:

> **"a world religion... attempting to swallow up the entire population of the world."**

"Aha, now I see it. The full picture comes into focus. These men hid the Millennium of Christ from all of us because they wanted the world prepared for a different reign — one in which they become the kings over mankind, without anybody ever realizing it. Is that right?"
—*Josh*

You hit the nail on the head, Josh. That is exactly what happened in our world. And what that future reign looks like is revealed with piercing clarity in Revelation chapter 20. Once Satan was released, his desire erupted into a single, all-consuming obsession: to once again force the entire world under his rule, leaving not one place of escape. His ambition was nothing less than the destruction of the Kingdom of Christ on Earth — a ruthless assault on the children of the Heavenly Father — and the total deception of humanity all over again, luring mankind back into his web of darkness, corruption, and spiritual enslavement.

That the driving force behind all of this is spiritual, becomes even clearer when we examine one key organization—one that openly gives voice to the culmination of these efforts. That organization is the Lucis Trust, founded in 1922 by Alice and Foster Bailey.

On the surface, the Lucis Trust presented itself as a publishing foundation promoting "world goodwill." They presented themselves as holy angels dreaming of a better world. In reality, it advanced a universalist spirituality that rejected Christ and prepared humanity for the arrival of a coming global leader they called the World Teacher.

To that end, Lucis Trust issued a spiritual summons called The Great Invocation, a prayer intended to condition the nations for this figure:[22]

> **"From the point of Light within the Mind of God**
> **Let light stream forth into the minds of men.**
> **Let Light descend on Earth.**
>
> **From the point of Love within the Heart of God**
> **Let love stream forth into the hearts of men.**
> **May the Coming One return to Earth.**
>
> **From the centre where the Will of God is known**
> **Let purpose guide the little wills of men—**
> **The purpose which the Masters know and serve.**
>
> **From the centre which we call the race of men**
> **Let the Plan of Love and Light work out**
> **And may it seal the door where evil dwells.**
> **Let Light and Love and Power restore the Plan on Earth."**

At first glance, the Great Invocation sounds like a beautiful prayer. It could have been whispered by any of our beloved pastors or priests. But that is only because we have no idea where it came from. Behind these words stands one of the most influential occult figures of the modern world: Alice Bailey, a woman who spent decades writing under the direct "dictation" of an entity she called Djwhal Khul — one of the so-called Ascended Masters. She did not hide this; she boasted of it. In her own books, she describes these beings as powerful disembodied intelligences guiding humanity toward a "new era."

Another ancient name for Satan is Lucifer — "light-bearer" — the deceiver who comes disguised as illumination. It is no accident, then, that Alice Bailey's organization originally bore the unmistakable title Lucifer Publishing Company. Only after public concern grew too large to contain did they quietly rename it "Lucis Trust," preserving the same root meaning while masking its true allegiance.

And this same organization — born from the occult, guided by demonic "Masters," explicitly invoking Lucifer as a bringer of light — crafted the Great Invocation as a magical formula to prepare the world for their coming global messiah: the "World Teacher."

Bailey taught that Christianity must be reshaped, blended into a universal religion, and ultimately submit to this new spiritual ruler who would emerge in Israel to unite all nations and all faiths.

A counterfeit Christ.

Most Christians have no idea that this Invocation — created by an occultist, dictated by demonic entities, and calling upon the "Masters" who rebel against the true God — is now recited daily in over eighty languages, promoted and distributed by the United Nations, and used inside government buildings, diplomatic programs, schools, and spiritual initiatives across the world.

Do you understand what is really happening here?

Is it dawning on your heart why God's voice thundered over me with a shaking, audible command to write this book and expose the strategy of Satan himself? This is why the Lord declared to me:

"This is the heart of the enemy!"

The most terrifying part of it all is that hundreds of millions of Christians — including tens of thousands of pastors, evangelists, teachers, prophets, worship leaders — are shouting "Hallelujah!" right in the middle of this Satanic plot. They preach the very essence of the enemy's plan: a coming "return of Christ" to rule the world from Israel. They proclaim it non-stop at their conferences, they teach it in their Bible studies, they publish it in their Christian bestsellers, and they produce multi-million-dollar films that steer the Church straight into the jaws of deception. A plan conceived in the very mind of the highest-ranking demons, who dare to call themselves "Masters."

The Satanic strategy is simple: make sure everyone — all Christians, all Jews, all Muslims, all Buddhists, all Hindus, all New Agers, all atheists, all spiritual seekers, all skeptics — will eagerly welcome this coming World Teacher, each under the banner of their own belief system.

- New Agers will embrace him as the bringer of "light and love."
- Jews will enthrone him as their long-awaited Messiah.
- Muslims will receive him as the fulfillment of their prophecies.
- Christians will worship him as their "Jesus" finally returning.

And yet... it is pure Satanism.

The way this staggering deception has seized the mind of the Church is—as I have demonstrated in the first chapters of this book—through grotesque distortions of Scripture, violent abuse of isolated verses, shameless theological fraud, mistranslations of the Bible, and a never-ending tsunami of false prophecies about the Rapture and the return of Christ, designed to keep billions of believers living in constant expectation every single day of their lives.

And when the truth is proclaimed by real servants of God — the ones who still fear the Lord, who still dare to challenge the darkness — they are met with hissing hatred, furious persecution, and violent opposition... not from atheists... *but from pastors, prophets, and preachers.* The very people who occupy the platforms of a Church so deeply compromised that she is no longer worthy of the name "Body of Christ." She has betrayed her Bridegroom a thousand times, and now lies in the arms of His greatest enemy.

Is this the Antichrist of Scripture? No—not in the way modern dispensationalism portrays him. As we have documented from both Scripture and history, the "antichrists" mentioned by John were Jews who rejected Christ and denied that He had come in the flesh. Likewise, the Beast of Revelation referred to the combined rebellion of apostate Judaism and Emperor Nero, who together sought to destroy the early Church. So this modern global agenda is not the Antichrist predicted in prophecy, because those prophecies were fulfilled long ago.

However—and this is critical—it is absolutely animated by the same spirit. The same hatred of Christ. The same desire to overthrow His Kingdom. The same impulse to establish an alternative order ruled by the enemy of God.

This is why the patterns repeat: widespread deception, centralized power, counterfeit spirituality, and the attempt to re-engineer humanity in the image of darkness rather than light. It is not "the" Antichrist, but it is unmistakably antichrist in character, driven by the same adversary.

"I don't understand you, Mr. Sörensen. First you accuse the Church of stealing our hope for the future by producing Hollywood-style blockbuster narratives that depict a totalitarian world under the reign of Satan — and now you're doing the exact same! This is not the glorious future of hope you spoke about earlier!"
—*Josh*

I agree, Josh. At first glance it does look eerily similar — but the difference is as stark as the contrast between night and day. The popular end-time stories that flood the Church today paint a future of pure nightmare — with no hope, no redemption, no victory. In their version, the only salvation is the Church's *escape* to heaven, abandoning — and effectively betraying — the rest of humanity to darkness.

According to this doctrine, Satan is far too powerful for the Church, so the Church must flee from him in a rapture. Therefore believers are told it is utterly useless to try and stop the influx of evil or build a better world, because everything is doomed for destruction anyway.

This doctrine was devised by the very same dark forces we have been exposing — designed specifically to eliminate the resistance of the Church and pave the way for a smooth establishment of Satan's totalitarian rule on Earth.

As you will see throughout the rest of this book, our mission is not to step aside and let it all happen while we wait for Jesus to return and solve this catastrophic mess. The answer lies in doing the exact opposite: *we are called to rise up with Jesus Christ once again and reign with Him.*

Our mandate is to reclaim our positions of authority, power, and influence, and to restore the Kingdom of God on the Earth — even more glorious than during the Millennium.

That is the final phase described in the book of Revelation. After Satan is released for a short time, he gathers the nations of the world for an all-out war against Christ and His Kingdom. But then, suddenly, fire comes down from Heaven—signifying the judgment of God falling upon Satan and all who serve him. He is removed once and for all, and a new day breaks forth: *a whole new era of restoration.*

> **"And they came up on the broad plain of the earth**
> **and surrounded the camp of the saints and the beloved city,**
> **and fire came down from heaven and devoured them.**
> **And the devil who deceived them**
> **was thrown into the lake of fire and brimstone,**
> **where the beast and the false prophet are also;**
> **and they will be tormented day and night**
> **forever and ever."**
> — *Revelation 20:9-10*

This time, Satan is not removed for a period of time, only to be released again. No. What we are about to witness is the *permanent deliverance of all creation.* That is the great and glorious hope we will explore in the chapters ahead.

But first, we must conclude our exposé of the evidence for the Little Season. For only if we know—without a shadow of doubt—that we are indeed living in the final phase of Satan's Little Season can we stand on the solid foundation of the radiant hope that Satan will soon be removed forever, and that a beautiful new world will emerge.

So let us finish our exposé.

Satan's Headquarters

How can we know for sure that the international network of control is indeed ruled by Satan himself? There is one remarkable indicator. Many of the forces pursuing global governance, centralized finance, world-reshaping ideology, and planetary management are connected—structurally and historically—to a very small geographical area: **the City of London.** This is not London, the capital of the UK. The City of London is a tiny sovereign enclave of roughly one square mile with its own government, its own laws, its own police force, and a unique constitutional status separate from the British Crown. It is not subject to ordinary British jurisdiction. It is the *financial heart of the world.*

Located here are ancient and powerful institutions:

- The Bank of England
- Lloyd's of London
- Rothschild & Co.
- Standard Chartered
- The London Stock Exchange
- Major Masonic Grand Lodges and historical Masonic centers

The City of London operates with a level of sovereignty unmatched anywhere else on Earth. This tiny square mile is a world unto itself — a jurisdiction above jurisdictions, a kingdom above kingdoms. Its vast networks of power — financial, legal, political, ideological, and fraternal — function entirely outside the constraints that bind every other nation.

Simply put: they are untouchable. No court can prosecute them, no government can restrain them, no law can lay a finger on them.

They submit to no external authority. Their institutions and officials enjoy a legal elevation so far above ordinary accountability that it effectively grants them free rein to commit any crime they choose, without consequence. It is a fortress of immunity — a citadel where earthly power shields itself from earthly justice.

But what makes this even more astonishing is its symbolism.

The City of London is marked by fourteen boundary statues of a *dragon*, each guarding the entries to the sovereign territory. These dragons, standing on pedestals and holding the City's red-cross shield, are the heraldic guardians of the City. The City's motto reads:

"Domine dirige nos"
"Lord, guide us."

Yet the symbol representing the City is not a cross, not a lamb, not a lion, not an angel, not a saint or knight—but a *dragon*. And Scripture leaves no ambiguity about the identity behind that symbol:

"The great dragon… that ancient serpent, called the Devil and Satan, who deceives the whole world."
—*Revelation 12:9*

THE CITY OF LONDON IS A SOVEREIGN CITY-STATE UNTOUCHABLE BY ANY EARTHLY AUTHORITY. ITS BORDERS ARE MARKED BY FOURTEEN STATUES OF A DRAGON, THE **"DECEIVER OF THE NATIONS."**

It is profoundly revealing that one of the primary command centers of global finance, global influence, and global restructuring openly identifies itself with the very creature Scripture names as the deceiver of the nations: the great dragon, the ancient serpent, the Devil and Satan.

As I stated before, the Lord called me to expose this international network of Satanism to help lay the foundation for a worldwide movement of resistance and deliverance. That is why I launched my platform StopWorldControl.com. On this website, you can read revealing reports and watch powerful documentaries—all 100% evidence-based—exposing this agenda for world domination. This information is not meant to instill fear, but to awaken hope. For once the plans of the wicked are brought into the light, they can be dismantled.

It is time for the Church to step out of its ignorance and begin to look at the world with open eyes. Only then can we become the heroes of humanity that God has called us to be: warriors who defeat the armies of hell, dragon-slayers who strike down the serpent of old through the power of Jesus Christ and the Spirit of the Most High God.

Some ignorant pastors proudly proclaim, "We should only look at what God does and never pay attention to Satan." Well, congratulations, dear brother. It is exactly this mentality that has left the Church so profoundly deceived. Because we refused to understand the schemes of our greatest enemy, we lost all discernment. Our deadly ignorance gave him free and unchallenged access right into our midst.

This outrageously foolish idea that the Church should remain totally unaware of what Satan is doing in our world is nothing less than this declaration: "Ignore everything God's watchmen on the wall are seeing. Ignore what all truth-speakers are revealing. Be deaf and blind to it all, and pay attention only to what is nice and pleasant." That mentality is directly responsible for the mass invasion and near-total destruction of the Church in our time.

It is time we stop behaving like toddlers and become mature men and women of God, unafraid to look Satan in the eye and pierce his demonic heart with the blazing sword of the Lord: *the undefiled truth.*

"Mr. Sörensen, you have convinced me that indeed we must be living in that final 'little season' of Satan. But do you also know when exactly Satan was released, after the thousand-year reign of Christ?"

—*Josh*

I wish I could pinpoint the exact day and hour, Josh. Wouldn't that be something? And perhaps in the future some God-led researcher will uncover a clearer answer. But while I cannot identify the precise moment, I do know this: it appears to have happened somewhere near the end of the 18th century or during the early 19th century. That is the period when all the deceptions we have discussed suddenly began erupting out of the abyss of darkness—exploding almost simultaneously and flooding humanity without restraint.

This is important to understand: every single lie born in the twisted mind of the great dragon did not spread slowly or with limited reach. What characterizes the deceptions of this era is their *immediate worldwide impact*. They appeared out of nowhere, were promoted with unprecedented funding, enforced by overwhelming political and cultural power, and defended by the most ruthless silencing of all opposing voices. *They became mainstream almost overnight.*

In recent years, a growing number of documentaries and books have appeared, some even suggesting that enormous, potentially worldwide natural catastrophes were part of this avalanche of darkness. There is indeed evidence pointing to large-scale mud floods that covered entire cities and quite literally buried Christian civilizations beneath layers of earth and rubble.

Personally, I have not yet been able to investigate these claims thoroughly enough to present them with the rigor they deserve. I therefore leave this aspect open to those who dare to explore the forbidden realm of hidden history. In the future I hope to write a follow up book, titled "The End Of Evil" in which I will explore this in far greater depth.

Because it is undeniable: extraordinary events occurred around the turn of the nineteenth century. Profound upheavals unfolded simultaneously across many realms—spiritual, philosophical, political, geological, social, financial, and beyond. An indescribable eruption of darkness suddenly engulfed the entire Earth with unstoppable force.

Satan did not infiltrate "part of the nations." He deceived *all* the nations of the world. The word used in Revelation 20 for "nations" is τὰ ἔθνη — ta ethne. It doesn't mean one nation, or a region, or a tribe. It means *all peoples... all ethnic groups... the entire world population.* When Scripture says Satan is released "to deceive the nations," it reveals that his final assault is worldwide—no continent untouched, no culture exempt, no people group beyond his reach. This is not a local skirmish. It is a worldwide deception targeting every ethnos under heaven, fulfilling with terrifying precision what John saw in the Spirit.

Revelation describes the vastness of the army of darkness: "their number is as the sand of the sea." And is that not exactly what we see? Not thousands, not millions, but billions of people — swept into this tidal wave of deception, corruption, and darkness — rising up in unison against the Kingdom of Christ.

Schoolteachers imposing indoctrination... police officers enforcing tyranny... scientists denying their Creator... doctors participating in mass poisoning... politicians selling their nations... farmers spreading toxins across the land... bankers tightening the chains of debt... pastors preaching lies from their pulpits. Every field of human society has been overwhelmed by a tsunami of corruption, perversion, and moral collapse. Nothing has been left untouched. The majority of mankind has joined this rebellion wholeheartedly — not reluctantly, not unconsciously, but with passion, conviction, and pride. "Their number is as the sand of the sea." It is the living fulfillment of the prophecy — a total uprising against God, waged by a world that no longer knows Him, no longer wants Him, and no longer fears Him.

Satan will not rest until every last trace of life is wiped away — until all of God's creation is turned into a wasteland of ash and ruin; a world where no blade of grass can grow, no child can laugh, no creature can breathe freely again.

But God will not allow it.
This is not the end of the story.
This is the end of Satan's story.

He was not released to *fulfill* his ambitions. He was released only to *expose* them, and to reveal, one final time, who on Earth would join him in this rebellion. The Almighty allowed this brief season, not as a triumph for darkness, but as a final unveiling. Every heart has been tested. Every allegiance revealed. The masks have fallen.

And Scripture promises that at the very height of this global heist, at the pinnacle of perversion, at the crescendo of corruption, God Himself will intervene. Not temporarily, as when Christ appeared in the clouds to inaugurate the first phase of His Kingdom, but with a final, eternal judgment that removes Satan forever.

All of creation has now witnessed what Satan is capable of. Every heart has shown its true loyalty. And now it is time.

"And they came up on the broad plain of the earth
and surrounded the camp of the saints
and the beloved city, and fire came down from heaven
and devoured them.
And the devil who deceived them was thrown
into the lake of fire and brimstone...
and they will be tormented day and night
forever and ever."
— *Revelation 20:9–10*

The fire coming down from Heaven is not a literal fire, but—like the fire at Pentecost—it is a fire that burns in the hearts of those who have remained faithful. Through them, a blazing wave of deliverance sweeps across the Earth, rising in the souls of millions just as it once rose in the apostles. It is a fire that judges evil, exposes lies, breaks chains, and brings down strongholds. It is the same fire that ends Satan's Little Season and begins a new dawn. And this worldwide outpouring of holy fire is what we will explore at the end of this book.

But before we can reach that glory, we must confront one final aspect of Satan's Little Season:

How did Satan subvert the worldwide Christian Church?

What you are about to read now will be devastating to many. Because the moment you turn this page, you cross a threshold into the realm where shadows breathe and ancient powers whisper. You are about to enter the dragon's den, the chamber where the oldest deceiver has brewed his darkest poisons, where the kettles of Hell simmer with doctrines forged in fire.

This is the womb of deception, the furnace where Satan has crafted the lies that have swallowed whole generations of believers.

Satan was released
only to reveal,
one final time,
who would join him
in this rebellion.
The Almighty allowed
this brief season,
not as a triumph
for darkness, but as
a final unveiling.
Every heart has
been tested. Every
allegiance revealed.
The masks have fallen.

CHAPTER 21

How The Church Was Hijacked

"You know, sir... all this deception that swept over the entire world makes me wonder. Was the massive invasion of the Church — the one you described in the first chapters — also part of Satan's strategy during the Little Season? Do these waves of infiltration have anything in common? Could they all be pieces of the same strategy of world domination?"

—*Josh*

Absolutely! It was indeed part of the massive worldwide invasion. The Church was hijacked in the exact same period that Darwin rose to prominence to invade science and proclaim to the world that there is no Creator. It happened within a single historical moment—the explosive century between 1830 and 1930—when every pillar of human society was hit by an unstoppable tsunami of deception that suddenly and swiftly rewired the entire world.

And of course it makes perfect sense. If Satan wanted to become the new ruler over all of mankind, he first had to eliminate his greatest and most dangerous opponent: the Church of Jesus Christ. They were the ones who had brought deliverance, healing, and transformation to the world during the time Satan was bound. And so, the moment he was released, he hurled himself at them with such staggering force that the very foundation of God's Word splintered across almost every church on Earth, tearing open a yawning abyss of deception beneath billions of unprepared believers. And he hand-picked specific people who would become his surgical instruments—used to insert his deadly deceptions directly into the body of Christ.

One man chosen to be Satan's vessel for this assault on the Kingdom of Christ was *John Nelson Darby,* born from the elites in 1800 to an Anglo-Irish aristocratic family of wealth, privilege, and worldly power. Darby first trained to become a lawyer—a profession built on the art of twisting information, shaping narratives, and manipulating facts to win battles in court. After mastering this craft of cunning he made his abrupt and curious pivot into the priesthood of the Church of Ireland. Once Darby had secured his place within the Church, he swiftly discarded the historic faith and fashioned his own breakaway sect, the Plymouth Brethren—a theological laboratory where ideas unheard of in two thousand years of Christianity were suddenly manufactured and released.

Darby's movement soon mutated into what became known as the Exclusive Brethren, a name that perfectly captures its spirit: isolationist, secretive, authoritarian, and cult-like to the core. It became a sealed world where the warmth of Christian fellowship was replaced with fear, control, and silence. The gifts of the Holy Spirit were forbidden, musical instruments were banished, and women were forced into complete silence—barred from speaking, praying aloud, or lifting their voices in praise—seated apart like shadows along the perimeter, as if Christ had never welcomed them into His kingdom. The result was a community that resembled not the early Church, but a carefully engineered cage.

It was in this totalitarian cult that Darby unleashed the teaching that would cripple billions of believers for generations: the Rapture—a doctrine designed to strip the Church of her calling to expand the Kingdom of Christ, and turn Christ's victorious army into fearful spectators waiting to be evacuated.

But Darby didn't stop there. He went on to deliver a second, even more lethal blow to the Kingdom of Christ.

He began proclaiming that God's promises are not fulfilled in Jesus Christ, but would instead find their fulfillment in a political Israel that Darby declared would soon rise again.

Darby literally took the Christian Church and turned her 180° around—from focusing on Jesus Christ to directing her attention toward an entirely different entity: a new state of Israel.

To justify this shift, Darby engineered an entirely new interpretive system he called "dispensationalism." This framework divides history into isolated "dispensations". According to this system we are currently living in a dispensation called "the Church Age." Only after this Church Age ends, will the Kingdom of God finally arrive—not through Christ reigning through His people, but through a restored military nation-state of Israel.

Darby taught that the Kingdom of God is not spiritual, but geo-political, with Jerusalem as the centre of world power.[1]

"The Most High... makes Israel the centre
for the government of the earth...
Jerusalem is the centre on earth."[2]

"When the kingdom shall be established...
Canaan and Jerusalem are its earthly centre."[3]

And he sealed it with his most extreme statement:[4]

"That government will extend over the whole earth,
but the royal nation and the seat and centre of government
will be the Jewish people.
To Jerusalem, as the centre alike of worship
and government, all nations will flow."

John Nelson Darby predicted a Jewish political world-rule, headquartered in earthly Jerusalem—a vision that stands in direct contradiction to the words of Jesus Christ, the teachings of Paul, and the witness of Scripture from beginning to end.

Christ said the exact opposite:

"The hour is coming when neither on this mountain
nor in Jerusalem will you worship the Father...
But an hour is coming, and now is,
when the true worshipers will
worship the Father in spirit and truth."
—*John 4:21, 23*

Jesus dismantled the notion of a geopolitical kingdom:

"The Kingdom of God is not coming
with signs to be observed; nor will they say,
'Look, here it is!' or, 'There it is!'
For behold, the Kingdom of God is in your midst."
—*Luke 17:20–21*

He made clear that the kingdom is a spiritual dimension, that can only be seen after being born from the Spirit:

"Unless one is born again he cannot see
the Kingdom of God."
—*John 3:3*

Apostle Paul confirmed that God's kingdom is spiritual:

"For the Kingdom of God is... righteousness and peace and joy in the Holy Spirit."
—*Romans 14:17*

The apostles affirmed the same spiritual reality that the new Jerusalem comes from above and is spiritual:

"The Jerusalem above is free; she is our mother."
—*Galatians 4:26*

"For our citizenship is in heaven."
—*Philippians 3:20*

The writer of Hebrews reveals Abraham was not seeking an earthly political homeland at all:

"For he was looking for the city...
whose architect and builder is God."
—*Hebrews 11:10*

"But now they desire a better country,
that is, a heavenly one."
—*Hebrews 11:16*

Despite standing in stark contradiction to the core truths proclaimed by Jesus Christ and His apostles, Darby's teachings infiltrated the Church with astonishing success, until they were embraced not as error, but as Christianity itself. His doctrines—of a sudden rapture and a mandated allegiance to a political state of Israel—were elevated to untouchable dogma, reshaping the foundation of modern Christianity and redirecting the faith of hundreds of millions of believers.

"Can you tell me more about the background of John Nelson Darby? What kind of spiritual influence did he have in his life, for example?"
—*Josh*

Well, hold on to your seat because this is where things get dark and and mysterious.

Darby's father owned a world-famous estate called Leap Castle and was therefor known as "John Darby of Leap Castle". The Darby family first acquired the estate in the mid-17th century (approx. 1649–1659) and owned and resided in the castle for roughly 250 to 270 years, until it was burned during the Irish Civil War in 1922.

Now, this wasn't a regular historic fortress. It was permeated by *horror* and the *occult*.

Leap Castle has been described as the most haunted castle in Europe, due to numerous accounts of disturbing supernatural manifestations reported on the property over the centuries.

The estate bore the weight of generations of bloodshed and terror—a legacy so dark that even seasoned investigators have spoken of it in hushed tones. Murderous feuds soaked its stones. Torture chambers echoed with screams. It was a place where violence and treachery did not simply pass—but left behind something that lingered.

IrishCentral.com, surveying more than a century of eyewitness accounts, wrote:[5]

> **"Leap Castle is one of the most haunted places in Ireland... The spirits, of which there were at least nineteen, were quite real... The most terrifying of all the castle's supernatural entities was what she called 'It' and 'The Thing,' and which others have termed 'The Elemental.'"**

The Little House of Horrors summarizes it even more bluntly:

> **"No other place in Ireland can beat the number of ghosts that reside in this place."**

No one can grasp the spiritual atmosphere surrounding John Nelson Darby without confronting the reality of his ancestral home. This was not a place whispered about by superstitious villagers—it was a bastion that investigators from around the world have documented as one of the most demonically charged locations in Western history. Witnesses describe encounters not with "ghosts" but with entities that look and behave nothing like human spirits. These manifestations were so shocking that those who saw them struggled to find words.

One encounter stands above the rest: Mildred Darby, a member of the Darby family itself, met the infamous Elemental face-to-face. In her own published account she wrote:[6]

> **"I felt somebody put a hand on my shoulder... The thing was about the size of a sheep... its face was human—to be more accurate, inhuman... its lust—in its eyes, which seemed half decomposed in black cavities—stared into mine. The horrible smell... came up into my face, giving me a deadly nausea."**

This was not a shadow. It was a *being*. And it did not merely appear; it brought with it a stench of decay so strong that witnesses gagged.

And the deeper researchers dug, the worse the picture became. Modern investigations confirm what older accounts claimed: Leap Castle housed at least nineteen identifiable spirits, each associated with violence, tragedy, or atrocity. Paranormal teams documented shadow figures materializing in corridors, violent poltergeist activity shaking stone walls, and an acidic, rotting odor that signaled the presence of the Elemental.

The castle's most infamous murder—the killing of a priest by his own brother while saying Mass—left a stain so deep that the chapel where it happened became known as the Bloody Chapel. One source states, "Leap Castle has a very violent and bloody history... said to be the most haunted castle in Ireland, possibly even Europe."[7]

The restorations of the early 1900s revealed horrors greater than any legend. Workers clearing the Bloody Chapel uncovered the unimaginable:

JOHN NELSON DARBY CAME FROM A FAMILY THAT RESIDED IN A CASTLE WORLD-FAMOUS FOR ITS EXTREME, AND TERRIFYING DEMONIC MANIFESTATIONS.

more than 150 human skeletons stacked in the oubliette beneath the floor. For centuries victims had been impaled on wooden spikes and left to die.

As one investigator said, "It's got all the ingredients for a lot of activity—not just one thing... It's on intersecting ley lines. It's got the history: 150 remains were pulled out of the castle by the current owners."[8] It was a burial pit, a torture chamber, and a spiritual lightning rod combined.

The accounts continued into the modern era. Visitors described apparitions "with a face like a rotting corpse," disembodied voices calling them by name, and a suffocating pressure so intense it felt like an invisible weight crushing the chest. Doors slammed by themselves. Stones were thrown across empty rooms. Investigators from *Ghost Hunters International* and *Most Haunted* recorded full episodes documenting violent activity that defied explanation. Elliot O'Donnell devoted entire chapters to its horrors in *Haunted Houses of Britain and Ireland* (1926). Folklorist V. M. Cooper chronicled its manifestations in *Famous Haunted Houses of Ireland* (1935). Mildred Darby's chilling reports were published in *The Occult Review* (1909). The record is vast—far too extensive to dismiss as myth.

Some historians and researchers have speculated that parts of Leap Castle were used for occult rituals or even satanic ceremonies. No official documentation has surfaced, but the patterns of activity—ritual violence, non-human entities, ley-line intersections, mass death, and consistent manifestations of a creature like the Elemental—speak loudly enough.

"Are you serious, Mr. Sörensen? Do you actually believe these stories of superstition and ghosts? You've got to be kidding me, right?"
—*Josh*

No, Josh. I am not kidding. I am dead serious. These events are abundantly, repeatedly, historically documented—recorded over centuries by witnesses, investigators, journalists, folklorists, and even members of Darby's own family. And frankly, none of this should surprise us. Anyone familiar with the Scriptures knows this: the existence of evil spirits is woven into the very fabric of the biblical narrative. Christ and the apostles confronted demonic forces constantly.

"Jesus rebuked him, saying, 'Be quiet, and come out of him!' And when the demon had thrown him down... it came out of him without doing him any harm."
—*Luke 4:35*

"And He was casting out many demons and was forbidding the demons to speak."
—*Mark 1:34*

And the apostles continued His work:

"Paul... said to the spirit, 'I command you in the name of Jesus Christ to come out of her!' And it came out at that very moment."
—*Acts 16:18*

Paul even said that the supernatural ability to discern different kinds of spirits is a specific gift of the Holy Spirit—an essential weapon for the Church in a world where demonic forces are real and active (1 Cor. 12:10).

The demonic influence in the life of John Nelson Darby becomes even more undeniable when we turn from his biography to his writings. There we discover a vocabulary that did not come from Jesus, or Paul, or the prophets, but from the shadowed corridors of Luciferian mysticism, Masonic ritual, Theosophical philosophy, and Kabbalistic esotericism.

Take, for example, his repeated use of **"the Architect."**

This is not a biblical title. It is the central name of the Masonic deity—"The Great Architect of the Universe." In Freemasonry and Theosophy, God is not the God of Abraham, Isaac, and Jacob. He is an impersonal cosmic builder, a metaphysical engineer—the Architect.

This is Masonic vocabulary. It belongs to secret oaths, veiled symbols, and hidden rites—not the Kingdom of God. And yet Darby used that very term—exactly as the lodge uses it—throughout his writings.[9]

"The traces of God, of **the Architect,** are there; but it is a ruin."

Then there is his use of **"the Absolute."** In Theosophy, the Absolute is an impersonal divine essence—an abstract, distant, unknowable cosmic principle at the core of all existence. Nothing could be further from the God revealed in Scripture. Yet Darby casually writes:[10]

"The essential being of Godhead cannot change...
the Absolute, as men speak..."

Darby also used the expression **"the vital force."** In occult healing systems, Kabbalistic magic, Eastern mysticism, and esoteric spirituality, "vital force" refers to a hidden life-energy that can be manipulated by rituals, crystals, spells, or occult techniques. It is the cornerstone of pagan healing arts. And Darby applies this language to the death of Jesus:[11]

"But though He died it was not because His **vital force** was exhausted..."

Darby sprinkled his writings with terms like "divine mind," "divine essence," and "divine energy." These are all pillars of Theosophical and Kabbalistic doctrine. Theosophy defines occult practice as "the study of the Divine Mind in nature"—a cosmic intelligence permeating all things. Kabbalah speaks of divine essence flowing through the universe like mystical energy. New Age mysticism calls it "universal vibration."

And Darby echoes them:

"...to lead the way to fuller investigation of **the divine mind."**

"He was Himself in the unity of **the divine essence."**

"...where God is in **divine energy..."**

He goes further, using phrases like "secret wisdom," "divine principle," "active energy," and more. Kabbalah calls itself the secret wisdom of God. Theosophy speaks endlessly of divine principles—impersonal spiritual laws, not the personal God of the Bible.

Yet Darby writes:

"the **secret wisdom** of God..."

And again:

"...he obeys by an inward **divine principle..."**

The list of occult terms used by Darby and his fellow Brethren leaders stretches into the dozens—divine architect, divine light, divine law, divine plan, divine union, universal principle, the One, God-consciousness, mystical body, radiance of light, all-seeing eye, active energy, and on and on.[12]

Darby also constructed a framework of "ages" and "dispensations" that mirrored the esoteric cycles of occult and mystical traditions long before he ever put pen to paper. He spoke of "the Church parenthesis," a concept that resembles occult views of hidden cosmic intervals, and of "the heavenly calling versus the earthly calling," language rooted far more in mystical dualism than in biblical covenant theology. These terms were unheard of in the early Church, the Reformers, or the Puritans. They appeared suddenly with Darby—and they bear unmistakable fingerprints of esoteric thought, vocabulary far more at home in secret societies than in the writings of the apostles.

The man who moved the Church away from Jesus Christ and His kingdom, to a political Israel... is the very same man whose writings drip with occult vocabulary—phrases borrowed from lodges, temples, and esoteric brotherhoods.

The famous 19th-century preacher and critic Samuel Prideaux Tregelles, who personally knew Darby, wrote:[13]

"Darby's system does not arise from Scripture, but from a secret philosophy imposed upon Scripture."

Even Charles Spurgeon warned publicly:[14]

"Brethren, I regard much of the new prophetic teaching as a delusion... I am sick of it."

The great Welsh revivalist John Jones famously wrote:[15]

"Darbyism teaches men to flee the battlefield and call it faith."

Darby never aimed his ideas at ordinary believers, but went straight for the shepherds. Capture the pastors, and you capture the Church. And so he traveled relentlessly to select groups of influential leaders in private, tightly controlled settings where he could slowly, methodically reshape their worldview.

Conquering America

After the Church in Europe was invaded, it was America's turn. And the man who carried the torch from Darby's hands and transported the entire system of deception from East to West, embedding it into the heart of the United States, was *Cyrus Ingerson Scofield.*

Evangelical history often introduces Scofield as a gifted pastor and Bible teacher who merely helped ordinary believers "understand the Word." But the real Scofield story begins in a place almost no prophecy teacher dares to enter: the dark terrain of his documented early life, marked by scandal, fraud, desertion, and ambition so ruthless that even friendly biographers were forced to admit he was "secretive about his past and not above distorting the facts of his shadowy years."[16]

Before Scofield ever opened a pulpit Bible, he was a lawyer and rising politician in Kansas. In 1873, at only twenty-nine, he was appointed U.S. District Attorney for Kansas—the youngest federal attorney in the nation. Yet his meteoric ascent imploded almost instantly. Contemporary records are blunt. Wikipedia documents:[17]

"Nevertheless, that same year Scofield was forced to resign 'under a cloud of scandal' because of questionable financial transactions, which may have included accepting bribes from railroads, stealing political contributions ... and securing bank promissory notes by forging signatures."

The Topeka Daily Capital, in an exposé dated August 27, 1881, described him as a man infamous for "forgeries and confidence games," reporting that after abandoning his destitute family he resurfaced in St. Louis, where "a series of St. Louis forgeries" landed him in jail for roughly six months. This was not whispered rumor—it was printed news, public record, and local memory for decades.

And yet, astonishingly, this man—marked by crime, corruption, fraud, and forgery—rose from the shadows to become America's Darby, the herald of a new theology that would reshape the entire landscape of American Christianity and carry a foreign interpretive system into the heart of the Church as if it were holy writ.

Even mainstream evangelical historians admit that Scofield's notes were simply Darby's system rephrased and popularized.

But his masterstroke was not the sermons he preached nor the books

C. I. SCOFIELD—WHO HIJACKED THE AMERICAN CHURCH—WAS A MAN MARKED BY CRIME, CORRUPTION, FRAUD, AND FORGERY.

he wrote—it was the creation of the Scofield Reference Bible (1909; revised 1917), the first massively successful modern study Bible to weave commentary directly into the biblical text itself. Scofield's notes were not tucked away in a separate commentary volume where they could be weighed and tested. They appeared *on the same page as Scripture*—sometimes so extensive that the footnotes visually dominated the inspired text. And into those footnotes Scofield quietly inserted Darby's entire framework: dividing history into rigid dispensations, separating Israel from the Church, postponing the kingdom, splitting redemption into two programs, and projecting Christ's triumph into a future political state of Israel:[18,19]

"The prophets foretell the future restoration and glory of [Israel] under King Messiah."

"Land promises that God gives to Israel... are to be interpreted geographically and eternally."

Scofield's commentary on Isaiah 2 claims that:

- **The Messiah will rule the world from Israel**
- **For this purpose Israel will be rebuilt as a powerful nation that will lead the entire world**
- **This is predicted by the prophets in the Bible**

Scofield literally taught the Church of America:[20,21]

"Jerusalem becomes the earthly center of the divine kingdom; Christ reigns there in visible glory."

"The nations are ruled through restored Israel."

The absolute foundation of Cyrus Scofield's theology is the claim of an *eternal and indivisible separatio*n between the Jews and the Church of Christ. Based on this premise, he builds the argument that all of God's promises regarding the restoration of Israel are not fulfilled in Jesus Christ, but instead apply entirely to a future political state of Israel.

That doctrine stands in direct opposition to the very words of Jesus Christ and the apostles, who declared that Christ came to *abolish* the dividing wall:

> **"For He Himself is our peace,**
> **who made both groups into one**
> **and broke down the barrier of the dividing wall...**
> **so that in Himself He might make the two**
> **into one new man."**
> —*Ephesians 2:14–15*

> **"There is neither Jew nor Greek...**
> **for you are all one in Christ Jesus."**
> —*Galatians 3:28*

> **"There is no distinction between Jew and Greek;**
> **for the same Lord is Lord of all."**
> —*Romans 10:12*

Cyrus Scofield and John Nelson Darby shamelessly rejected this fundamental Biblical truth. They boldly proclaimed that the Church must look to a newly established state of Israel as the place where Christ would return to rule the world. Again, an idea that stands in sharp contrast to the words of Jesus Christ, who opposed the notion of a political kingdom centered in ethnic Israel. He said:

> **"My kingdom is not of this world."**
> —*John 18:36*

> **"The Kingdom of God is not coming**
> **with signs to be observed...**
> **for behold, the Kingdom of God is in your midst."**
> —*Luke 17:20–21*

One of the most foundational truths revealed in the New Testament is that God's attention is no longer on earthly Jerusalem, and that His children now belong to a new, heavenly Jerusalem—which is our mother:

> **"The Jerusalem above is free; she is our mother."**
> —*Galatians 4:26*

The letter to the Hebrews reveals that Abraham and the other Old Testament patriarchs were not looking for a geopolitical restoration at all, but were waiting for a heavenly city built by God Himself:

> **"He was looking for the city which has foundations, whose architect and builder is God."**
> —*Hebrews 11:10*

> **"But you have come to Mount Zion**
> **and to the city of the living God,**
> **the heavenly Jerusalem, and to myriads of angels,"**
> —*Hebrews 12:22*

Cyrus Scofield taught the opposite: that Jerusalem is not primarily spiritual, but that everything revolves around the old, earthly city—from which a future Messiah would rule the entire world.

In essence, Darby and Scofield launched a worldwide assault on the very heart of Jesus Christ and His kingdom.

They proclaimed to the whole Church that from now on everyone had to deny Jesus Christ as the fulfillment of God's promises and instead look forward to a new political state called Israel.

"But how were they able to gain such incredible influence? I mean, these ideas became the bedrock of modern Christianity! What force accompanied these men that they overthrew the entire Church—not just in their own town, or even their own nation, but all around the world?"
—*Josh*

The answer is short and simple: *Oxford*. The moment Oxford University Press published the Scofield Reference Bible, it conferred an instant, untouchable academic legitimacy that no pastor, seminary, or Christian institution dared to question.

And Oxford was no neutral ground. Throughout the 19th and early 20th centuries, Oxford University was a nexus of elite influence, shaping the theological, political, and ideological direction of the English-speaking world. It was also the very institution where the Rothschild family—one of the most powerful financial dynasties on Earth—held deep historical ties, long-standing endowments, and cultural influence through philanthropy, political patronage, and academic appointment networks.

While no formal document has surfaced proving that the Rothschilds directly financed Scofield's project, the convergence of influence is impossible to ignore. During the very years when the Rothschilds were strategizing to establish a new political Israel, the Scofield Bible was published from the very university where their influence reigned supreme.

Within decades, the Scofield Reference Bible sold in the millions and became the default Bible of American evangelicalism. Scofield's theology bled into boardrooms, pulpits, capitols, and national policy.

His single footnote under Genesis 12:3—"And I will bless those who bless you, and the one who curses you I will curse"—became one of the most devastating insertions in modern Church history. By redefining God's promise to Abraham's seed as a divine shield around a future political state, Scofield rewired the conscience of entire generations. Blessing modern Israel was equated with blessing God Himself, and questioning Zionism became synonymous with resisting the Almighty.

As with Darby, Scofield and his system encountered sharp and public critique. In a 1945 article in *Ministry Magazine* the dispensational scheme of the Scofield Bible was called

> **"heresy of a very terrible kind....**
> **the organising principle of dispensationalism**
> **of the Scofield Bible is essentially heretical."**

Another voice: Professor Albertus Pieters (in *A Candid Examination of the Scofield Bible*) pointed out:

> **"The entire 'dispensational scheme'... when subjected**
> **to examination in the light of Holy Scripture,**
> **breaks down completely—yet it is accepted by multitudes**
> **today as the undoubted teaching of the Bible."**

Those early critics never had a real chance. They were drowned out almost immediately by a tsunami of promotion—because this takeover of the Church was backed by the richest people on Earth.

That is how Satan seized total control over the Christian Church around the world. But today, I hear the voice of the Spirit of God speaking loud and clear: it's time to end this invasion and turn the Church back to the truth.

It's time to return to Jesus Christ.

JOHN NELSON DARBY AND CYRUS SCOFIELD SHIFTED THE CHURCH AWAY FROM CHRIST AS THE FULFILLMENT OF GOD'S PROMISES AND MADE EARTHLY JERUSALEM THE CENTERPIECE OF PROPHECY, CLAIMING THAT A MESSIAH WOULD COME TO RULE THE WORLD FROM WITHIN ISRAEL.

CHAPTER 22

THE END OF THE END TIMES

"So that's what happened... the Church has literally been invaded by someone who was deeply involved in the occult, and who was raised in the most demonized castle in Europe, where people were ritually murdered en masse! And he was powerfully supported by elites who proudly display their allegiance to Satan. Goodness gracious... No wonder the Church is in ruins! My, oh my...

I will need time to process all of this. I understand that not all my questions can be answered in one book. It is already so much, all at once!

But can I ask one more question, sir? From the moment I entered the church, I was hammered with the idea that the end of the world is at hand. 'We are in the last days!' my fellow believers said. 'These are the end times!'But if Christ already came, and all those events happened in the past, then we can hardly still be in the last days, can we? Can you explain to me what the Bible truly means with the term 'end times?'"

—Josh

It is true, Josh, that we cannot answer all questions in a single book. But I have come to realize that we don't *need* to answer every little detail.

When you step into a car, you don't know everything about how the engine works either, do you? Or when you board an airplane, do you understand how to make it fly? Or when you go to a bank and entrust your savings to them, do you have any insight into how their computers process your money and what happens to it? No—we never need to know all the facts before we can trust something. So it is with the truth as well. Once I had a good grasp on the fundamentals of the actual message of the Bible, I knew I could believe it. And then I trusted the Lord that He would continue to reveal deeper insights when needed, as I walk my journey with Him. And it wouldn't surprise me too much, if other dramatic disclosures will surface in the future.

Did you know that the Vatican has hidden thousands of ancient spiritual manuscripts that the world is not allowed to read? What are they hiding from humanity?

If Apostle John said the entire world could be filled with books describing everything Jesus Christ said and did (John 21:25), why then are we left with only four short gospels?

"Oh no! Please don't say things like that, sir! You are going to get yourself lynched for sure. You cannot doubt the canon of the Bible. It's 66 books and not one more or less."

—*Josh*

Really? Says who? The same people who told us to wait our entire lives for the return of Christ? They are the ones who compiled the 66 books and decided to leave out dozens of other books.

Have you ever wondered what is concealed by the Roman Vatican?

Why are they obscuring shelves filled with thousands of ancient manuscripts—many of which relate to Christ, His message, and His kingdom? Why are scholars not allowed to study these holy books? Could it be that questions raised by the Bible might be answered in those hidden books? Because when we truly study the Word of God with great sincerity and a deep hunger for understanding, we inevitably encounter frustrating limitations. Often, the Bible doesn't give us answers, but rather raises a great number of questions.

For example, why did Paul say:

"Or do you not know that the saints will judge the world? Do you not know that we will judge angels?"

— *1 Corinthians 6:2-3*

Come again, Paul?

You don't mean... no, this can't be. Surely you *don't* mean...

Yes. That is *exactly* what he said.

We, the followers of Christ, are supposed to judge the angels. Where did Paul get that outrageous idea from? What did he know that the Church has been completely ignorant about for centuries?

Another example is the Apostle Peter who wrote about angels being bound in Tartarus:

> **"For if God did not spare angels when they sinned, but cast them into hell and committed them to pits of darkness, reserved for judgment."**
>
> —*2 Peter 2:4*

The Greek word that was translated as "cast them into hell" is tartarosas— ταρταρώσας, which means "to cast into Tartarus". But what on Earth—or better, what underneath the Earth—is Tartarus? What is Peter referring to? Nowhere else in the Bible is there any reference to Tartarus.

Do you see what I mean? Clearly, Paul and Peter were reading ancient manuscripts that most of the Church doesn't even know about. Documents that, for example, gave deeper insight into the spiritual realms and the different layers of the underworld.

This becomes more clear than ever when we find out how crooked our Bible translations really are. All modern Bible versions use one single word "hell" to translate several different Greek words that all refer to entirely different realms. The original text speaks about Hades (ᾅδης), Gehenna (γέεννα), Tartarus (ταρταρόω), the Abyss (ἄβυσσος) and the lake of fire (λίμνη τοῦ πυρός). But all these words are ridiculously translated as "hell," while they refer to totally distinct places.

Gehenna refers to the Valley of Hinnom outside Jerusalem and isn't even a spiritual realm. It's where corpses of the dead were burned.

Hades is the realm of the dead, equivalent to the Hebrew Sheol.

The lake of fire is the final place of eternal damnation for Satan, the false prophet, and all who followed them.

The Abyss is a bottomless pit, a place of confinement for spirits.

Tartarus is a deep prison for fallen angels.

These are five clearly separate dimensions. Yet, for some reason, they are all translated as "hell" in our Bibles.

Doesn't that disturb you?

Why have Bible translators obscured these distinctions?

It is clear that there is a strategy to hide important insights from the Church, in order to keep her powerless and ignorant.

Now, does this mean we should go searching for *occult* knowledge, like the Gnostics? Of course not. This is not secret knowledge, it is revealed truth that was *mistranslated.*

I am thankful for the great work that Bible societies are doing to bring the Word of God to the world. But I am shocked how they allow certain translators to obscure deeper meanings from us.

This also brings us to the question: what does the Bible truly mean by the term "the end times" or "the last days"? The grave confusion that terrorizes hundreds of millions of believers in our day, is also the direct result of incredibly wrong mistranslations.

Take, for example, Matthew 13:40 and Matthew 24:3, where Jesus and the apostles discussed the "end of the world":

> **"As therefore the tares are gathered and burned in the fire; so shall it be in <u>the end of this world</u>."**
> *—Matthew 13:40 KJV*

> **"...what shall be the sign of thy coming, and of <u>the end of the world?"</u>**
> *—Matthew 24:3 KJV*

The King James Version is hailed as the only trustworthy Bible version. But few understand that this very translation is one of the most corrupted of all time, inserting such deliberate distortions that they reveal a blatant agenda to deceive the Church.

For example, the Greek word translated as "world" is aion (αἰών). Now, does this Greek word mean "world," or anything even close to that meaning? Not at all. The word aion simply means a *timeframe*—a period within a series of timeframes that together make up eternity. So Jesus was not referring to the end of the world, but He simply announced the end of a timeperiod. What timeperiod? The timeperiod of the old covenant.

The same goes for the apostles. Not one of the authors in the New Testament talked about the end of the *world*—they discussed the end of the *age*. That is why the apostles declared *they* were in the last days.

> **"...in <u>these last days</u> has spoken to us in His Son,"**
> *—Hebrews 1:2*

Apostle Paul used the term "last days" to refer to the period in which Christ had revealed the message of the Kingdom to them. Those were the last days—but the last days of what? Of the old covenant. The old era was about to fade away, and a brand new era was dawning: the new covenant in Christ.

So the term "last days" has nothing to do with the destruction of Brussels, Tokyo, Washington or Johannesburg in the 21st century. It is, quite simply, a term used by the apostles who lived during the final days of the age of the old covenant. They were living in the last days of that era.

In his letter to the first church in Corinth Paul stated:

> **"...they were written for our instruction,**
> **upon whom the ends of the ages have come."**
> *—1 Corinthians 10:11*

Upon whom came the end of the ages? The first Christians!

This is where the term "end times" is derived from, the end of the ages. It has zero connection with our time, thousands of years later.

We are *not* in the end times. We do not live in the last days of the human race. Our world is not about to be evaporated. Our cities will not be swallowed by the earth. Our capitals will not be blown to pieces. We have no reason to fear the end of the world.

If anything is ending, it is the reign of deception in Satan's Little Season. *That* era is coming to an end.

So in a way, we are in some sort of "end times"—but not in the way we were told. We are in the final stages, I believe, of the rule of evil, and are about to experience a major breakthrough of truth and restoration.

"But didn't Jesus say that first the gospel would be preached to the whole world, and that then the end would come? This is one of those arguments I heard often from evangelists, who claimed that the end of the world is about to come upon us because nearly every remote tribe—even in the Amazon jungles—has finally heard the gospel."

—Josh

Yes, it's what I heard for decades as well. And once again, this idea is rooted in a violation of the Scriptures and an ignorance of the historical culture in which they were written. When we abuse the Word of God, we can literally make it say anything we want—did you know that? That's why I place such strong emphasis on learning to read the Bible respectfully instead of manipulating it. When we do that, an entirely different picture always begins to emerge... So let's read what Jesus actually said, place it in the proper biblical and historical context, and then see what we discover.

This is what the Lord told His disciples:

> **"This gospel of the kingdom shall be preached in the whole world as a testimony to all the nations, and then the end will come."**
> — *Matthew 24:14*

First of all: Jesus spoke these words to the very people in Jerusalem to whom He announced the end of the old covenant and the end of Israel as a covenant nation—events that would culminate in the destruction of Jerusalem and the temple. So this has nothing to do with the end of the world. That is the first plain and simple fact that (can you believe the insanity of this?) almost not a single so-called high and lofty theologian or scholar ever seems to consider.

They twist, shift, and manipulate the Scriptures while ignoring the most basic principles: Who was the biblical audience? What is the biblical context? What is the historical setting? And so on. I keep saying this because it boggles my mind that I even have to write a book about it. These are such simple, foundational truths that they should be common knowledge for every pastor: *don't rip what Jesus said out of context.*

First look at whom He was speaking to. What event was He discussing? When did He say it would happen? What did His words mean in that culture? That's how you read the Bible.

You don't take a pair of scissors, cut out a single line, and then build your entire worldview, and religion upon it. Yet that's exactly what people do all the time—nonstop.

May we please end this habit.

Now that I've said that, let's go a little deeper. When Jesus told the Jewish believers in Jerusalem that the end would come once the gospel of the kingdom had been preached to the whole world, what was He referring to? Remember, He was not speaking to modern-day people in the 21st century who have access to the internet and can travel to Tokyo, Johannesberg, Amsterdam, or Stockholm. Christ was addressing people who, in most cases, never set foot outside their small, familiar world—primarily Israel. Some may have traveled by boat, but that was the exception.

So what was "the whole world" to them?

In the first century, expressions like "the whole world" were commonly used to describe the Roman Empire, not the entire globe in the modern sense. The Greek term oikouméne ("the inhabited world") referred to the civilized, known world centered around Rome. This is clearly seen in Luke 2:1, where a decree from Caesar Augustus is said to go out to "all the inhabited earth"—yet it obviously applied only to the Roman realm. Contemporary writers such as Strabo and Pliny the Elder used similar language to describe the Roman-dominated world as the extent of the "inhabited earth." In that cultural and linguistic context, "the whole world" was naturally understood as the Roman world system, the sphere in which people lived, traveled, and communicated.

Now, did the gospel indeed go out into the whole world, as they understood it? Let's see what Apostle Paul said:

> **"...the gospel... in all the world also is constantly bearing fruit and increasing..."**
>
> — *Colossians 1:6*

Hey, isn't that interesting? According to Paul, the gospel was bearing fruit in all the world—just as Christ said. He even wrote:

> **"...the gospel that you have heard, which was proclaimed in all creation under heaven..."**
>
> —*Colossians 1:23*

> **"Their voice has gone out into all the earth, and their words to the ends of the world."**
>
> —*Romans 10:18*

Et voilà—once again we see that when we respect the Word of God instead of abusing and manipulating it, the truth becomes brilliantly obvious. Jesus was speaking to the Jews about the end of the old covenant system, using the language and understanding of their culture when He spoke of the gospel being preached to the whole world.

Now, I need to say this: I am no better than anyone else. I also abused the Scriptures shamelessly for years when I first began ministering. I simply didn't know any better—it was how I had been shaped in the Church. But now that we know the truth, let's put an end to that harmful habit and learn to read God's Word correctly, shall we?

CHAPTER 23

The Rising Of The Sons

"Wow! We are not approaching the end of the world, but the end of the reign of Satan and his evil pawns. What a different outlook that is. I was always told that everything is going to get worse and worse, until Christ has to remove us from the Earth because evil has become too strong. But it's actually the opposite. The reign of evil will come to an end. Hallelujah! What good news. Now I can see why the gospel is called 'good news,' haha!

But this means that the Church has been lied to concerning what the message of the Bible is. Can you tell me, Mr. Sörensen, what is the true message of the Scriptures, in a nutshell?"

—*Josh*

Finally! This is my favorite topic. I honestly do not enjoy exposing what Satan is doing, nor do I love correcting the Church for its idolatry.

I much rather rejoice in revealing the beautiful future we all have. This is what matters most of all: what does our amazing, loving heavenly Father have in mind for all of us, and for this beautiful world?

And what role does He want *us* to play in it?

First of all, we must firmly understand *why* God created us in the first place. That is the foundation for everything else. Did He make us to be cowards who wait for a rapture to escape from the world God created, while He destroys it behind us as we safely cruise in the skies? Or, did He make us to be His heroes who bring healing and hope to His creation?

After reading the previous chapters, we know the answer already, as I have mentioned it multiple times.

The reason why God created us, is to be His ambassadors.

God made this crystal clear from the very moment He formed Adam. He said Adams purpose was to *rule* over all of God's creation:

> **"Then God said, 'Let Us make man in Our image,**
> **according to Our likeness; and let them rule**
> **over the fish of the sea and over the birds of the sky**
> **and over the cattle and over all the earth,**
> **and over every creeping thing that creeps on the earth.'"**
> —*Genesis 1:26*

David reaffirmed this divine mandate to rule:

> **"You have made him a little lower than God,**
> **And You crown him with glory and majesty!**
> **You make him to rule over the works of Your hands;**
> **You have put all things under his feet."**
> —*Psalm 8:5–6*

This is the original mandate that God never withdrew. On the contrary, He reaffirmed it through Jesus Christ when He said to go out, cast out demons, and heal the sick.

> **"Whatever city you enter and they receive you, ...**
> **and heal those in it who are sick, and say to them,**
> **'The Kingdom of God has come near to you.' ...**
> **Behold, I have given you authority... over all the power**
> **of the enemy, and nothing will injure you."**
> — *Luke 10:19*

Christ doesn't turn us into spectators who wait to go to Heaven.

He came to restore God's original plan and redeem our mandate to bring His authority over all creation: to turn deserts into paradises, to cast out evil spirits, to heal the broken, to bring solutions to the needs of mankind—and so much more.

It is the true calling of all of us — not to be religious oddities who sit around in churches waiting either to die and go to Heaven, or for Christ to come and take us there. That is the great lie that has been exported worldwide through what we call "the religion of Christianity."

The divine calling is that we rise up in the Spirit of God, and do what Christ instructed us to do. When we do that, the power of Satan falls to the ground.

God asked me loud and clear one day:

"David, why are the wicked reigning?"

I didn't know, so He continued:

"Because the righteous aren't!"

The Lord then shook me wide awake:

**"But I never appointed the wicked.
I appointed the righteous!"**

Suddenly it dawned in my heart: God never blessed the wicked to reign over His beautiful creation. He gave His royal mantle to His children, placed a scepter in our hands, a ring on our fingers, and a crown upon our heads. He pours His anointing oil over us and fills us with His Spirit. He gives us His Word and grants us His kingdom. He commands His angels to serve His children and offers all His riches to His beloved. He invites us to walk with Him, so that we may sit with Him on His throne and put an end to all injustice on Earth.

That is the message of the Scriptures, from beginning to end.

God's children were made to reign with Him!

But Satan stole it from the Church, so he could reign instead.

The true kings and queens of the Most High have been cast down, robbed of their royal garments, stripped of their vision and dreams, and locked up in the basement, so the wicked — who have no authority and no anointing — could run the world instead, during Satan's Little Season.

Then Satan used Darby and Scofield, funded and empowered by the Jewish elites, to accomplish this subversion of the Church.

Certain Jews believe they should rule mankind, so they stole the divine mandate from those in the Kingdom of Christ and started a worldwide campaign to destroy Christian culture, massacre countless millions of Christians, and pervert the survivors with pornography and other poisons, while corrupting their leaders, silencing all opposing voices, and mind-controlling everyone.

But God never gave His kingdom to those who hate Christ. He gives His kingdom to those who accept Christ.

The way we reign with Christ is the *opposite* of how these Jews rule the world. We are not called to spread death and destruction, wickedness and perversion, deception and mind control. Our mission is to heal humanity, cast out all evil, liberate the people, uplift the weak, and let the truth out. As Isaiah said:

> **"The Spirit of the Lord GOD is upon me,**
> **Because the LORD has anointed me**
> **To bring good news to the afflicted;**
> **He has sent me to bind up the brokenhearted,**
> **To proclaim liberty to captives**
> **And freedom to prisoners."**
> —*Isaiah 61:1*

One day the Lord again spoke to me, and said:

> "David, there are two main forces in this world. The first force is *slavery*. This force *enslaves* humans through pornography, violence, deception, toxic food, trauma, financial bondage, and demonic oppression, etc.
>
> The second force is *sonship*. That is what I give to people. I bring *freedom* to every aspect of humanity, healing them sexually, financially, emotionally; setting them free from unhealthy foods; revealing to them the truth that frees their minds, and so on. By doing this, I raise people up as My sons. They receive My blessing in every aspect of their life, which empowers

them, lifts them up, and makes them abundantly fruitful. They become *true* children of Me, the Father."

**The wicked, who hate Christ,
are on a mission to enslave humanity.**

**The righteous, who love Christ,
are on a mission to liberate humanity.**

That is where the answer lies to how God's creation will be restored. Christ said that if we obey His voice and turn from our evil ways, we will sit with Him on His throne and reign with Him, just as He reigns with the Father:

**"He who overcomes, I will grant to him
to sit down with Me on My throne, as I also overcame
and sat down with My Father on His throne."**
— *Revelation 3:21*

That's why the Apostle Peter called those who are in Christ "royal":

**"But you are a chosen race, a royal priesthood,
a holy nation, a people for God's own possession,
so that you may proclaim the excellencies of Him
who has called you out of darkness
into His marvelous light."**
— *1 Peter 2:9*

John declared that we are a "kingdom," and therefore we reign:

**"You have made them to be a kingdom and priests
to our God; and they will reign upon the earth."**
— *Revelation 5:10*

This was also prophesied by Isaiah:

**"Behold, a king will reign in righteousness,
And princes will rule with justice."**
—*Isaiah 32:1*

The Prophet David also announced it:

"The sons of God sit on thrones
'Your many sons will be kings, just like their Father.
They will sit on royal thrones all around the world.'"
—Psalm 45:6,16 (TPT)

Is the truth starting to dawn in your mind?
The Spirit of God speaks to us and says:

"Return to Jesus Christ.

He alone is the fulfillment of My promises.
He alone is the King of kings who reigns.

I do not build a kingdom with guns and rockets.
I do not sexually blackmail leaders.
I do not bribe pastors.
I do not mind-control humanity.
I do the opposite of all that.

I speak truth, loud and clear, to expose the works of the wicked,
the sins of the people, and the idolatry of the Church.

I raise My voice like a trumpet to call back the Bride of Christ
to become the brilliant light she is meant to be.

I restore the mandate of My sons and daughters on the Earth
to reign with Me and end the rule of evil in this world.

Now the time has come to end the Little Season of Satan
and initiate a New Day — the never-ending dawn of My light
that will heal the nations, deliver the people,
and restore all of My creation.

It is time for My children to take back their authority
and start reigning with Me, so the rule of Satan comes to an end,
and a New Day breaks forth for My creation."

When we listen to these words from the Spirit of God, restoration will come to all of God's creation. Then we will see fulfilled what Apostle John described as what happens after Satan's Little Season:

> **"Then I saw a new heaven and a new earth;**
> **for the first heaven and the first earth passed away,**
> **and there is no longer any sea.**
>
> **And I saw the holy city, new Jerusalem,**
> **coming down out of heaven from God,**
> **prepared as a bride adorned for her husband.**
>
> **And I heard a loud voice from the throne, saying,**
>
> **"Behold, the tabernacle of God is among the people,**
> **and He will dwell among them,**
> **and they shall be His people,**
> **and God Himself will be among them,**
> **and He will wipe away every tear from their eyes;**
> **and there will no longer be any death;**
> **there will no longer be any mourning,**
> **or crying, or pain; the first things have passed away."**
> —*Revelation 21:1-5*

We saw earlier that this does not refer to a *physical* new creation, but to the *new covenant* in Jesus Christ. I have been pondering and praying for a long time about how this fits the time we are now in—the end of Satan's Little Season. Although I don't claim to have all the answers yet, as the Spirit of God continually guides us into deeper understanding, I do believe that there is an extended fulfillment of this passage.

The new creation started when Christ ended the old covenant, and initiated a new era of His eternal kingdom in 70AD. But when Satan was released after a thousand years, he unleashed a full-blown assault on the Kingdom of Christ. According to Revelation, this is followed by a *permanent removal* of Satan. This time he is no longer temporarily locked up, but eliminated for all eternity. He will never return (Rev. 20:10).

And then Revelation speaks about the new creation.

I believe this new creation comes forth when the sons of God are rising up to become God's vessels for the restoration of His creation.

It's not something that falls out of the sky, but a gradual process of renewal as the children of the heavenly Father begin to reign with Christ.

That process is confirmed when we look at the Greek word kainós (καινός), used in Revelation to describe the "new" Heaven and "new" Earth. It does not mean brand-new in the sense of something newly created from nothing. Instead, kainós refers to something *renewed*, transformed, or made new in quality and condition. It describes an *existing* reality that has undergone *restoration* and purification, not replacement.

This Greek word choice reveals a core biblical pattern: God does not abandon His creation, but redeems it—just as a believer becomes a "new" creation in Christ while remaining the same individual.

This core biblical pattern leads me to believe that the choice of the word "new" is critically important. God does not hand us a perfect paradise in a split second; He calls us to be part of His process of renewing (kainós) all creation. We are not *spectators*, but *participants*. We are not immature babies, but mature sons called to carry responsibility.

Revelation 20:9 says that fire comes down from Heaven to judge Satan and his allies, which leads to their ultimate doom and the deliverance of humanity.

> **"And they came up on the broad plain of the earth and surrounded the camp of the saints and the beloved city, and <u>fire came down from heaven and devoured them</u>."**
> —*Revelation 20:9*

This is not a physical fire, of course. It is similar to the fire that came down from Heaven at Pentecost. It is a *supernatural* fire from God that burns within people, causing His will to be performed through them.

What we must understand very clearly is that the removal of the wicked from places of authority around the world means those same seats of power need to be filled again, by the sons and daughters of God.

As I said: the children of God are blessed to rule over His creation, not the children of Satan. This means that the children of the Most High must return to their abandoned seats in healthcare, education, politics, entertainment, media, sports, and every other realm of human society.

The deep deception that has gripped the mind of the Church during Satan's Little Season, is the belief that we must step away from human society and simply tell everyone about Christ and His "soon return." This is what the Nicene Creed established: it placed the Church in a perpetual waiting mode. It wasn't entirely successful, because despite this attempt to obstruct the Kingdom of Christ and turn it into a passive, controlled religion, it continued breaking through worldwide. Yet, it did so with clear restraint, as countless Christian leaders continually told their flock: "*Wait for Christ to return.*"

So on the one hand, the power of God remained at work, but on the other hand, it was restrained from full release due to the worldwide infiltration of the enemy.

Especially in the past two centuries, with the next wave of invasion launched through Darby and Scofield, the Church was hijacked even more than ever, and hundreds of millions of believers were literally shifted into full-blown passive waiting mode. Even to the point where some of the biggest names in Evangelical Christianity, like John F. MacArthur, stated in a 2020 sermon that it is useless to try to improve this world:

> **"Our hope is not in fixing the world,**
> **our hope is in the return of Jesus Christ."**
>
> *—John. F. MacArthur, "Final Justice: The Return of Christ, Part 1"*

Also theological giants like Billy Graham may have led many to Christ, but the deeper effect was that the Church was constantly told that Christ was about to return any moment now. Billy Graham is praised as the greatest evangelist of all time, yet during nearly every crusade he proclaimed the imminent return of Christ—a return that, of course, *never occurred.*

So even while Graham was celebrated as a powerful evangelist, he was also a false prophet who caused unspeakable damage to the Church, shutting her down more than ever, due to his constant false prophecies.

The false message in the Church for the past decades has been: "Repent, for Jesus is coming soon and the world will end."

But now, the Spirit of Truth is roaring like the mighty Lion of Judah:

Return to Christ, for He has made all things new. Enter the new covenant and welcome the presence of Christ in your midst. Rise and reign with Him to restore all of God's creation.

In 2020 the Lord called me to start StopWorldControl.com, a platform that exposes government corruption, and equips people to build a better world. Shortly after I launched this new initiative, I was contacted by well-meaning Christians who said:

"David, why are you doing this type of work—exposing the crimes of governments and revealing how the wicked are destroying humanity? You shouldn't be doing any of this. All you must do is tell people about Jesus Christ."

That sounds very nice and religious: "Only speak about Jesus." But it is a lie. Because it was Jesus Himself who told me to do this mission. We shouldn't only *talk* about Jesus—we must also *do* what Jesus tells us to do. If that means running for governor, or starting a healthcare organization, or writing new books for education, or becoming a powerful news reporter, and so on, then we must obey that calling.

The Church has been crippled by a blind focus on church ministry, while the true mission is outside of the church. We are not called only to speak on platforms about Jesus. We are called to step away from those platforms into the real world, where we don't merely talk about the kingdom—we manifest it.

Christianity has become a religion of words.
The Kingdom of God is a power that changes everything.

It's time that believers around the world stop living this life where all we do is talk and never do anything in the real world.

Of course it's important to tell humanity about the King of kings, who saves us and brings us into His presence and kingdom. But if talking about it is all we do, then what good is it?

Once we learn who Christ is and enter into His kingdom, the next essential step is to reveal Christ and His reign in human society.

I believe the greatest prophets and apostles are those who operate in the realms of business, finance, technology, government, real estate, entertainment, etc. and who represent Jesus Christ in all those areas. That is where the real shift in the Church must happen.

Step away from church ministry and enter the real world. Stop just *talking about* Jesus and start *doing what Jesus tells you to do.*

What use is it to always talk in church about being a light, and then go home and never shine that light in the real world? What nonsense! Yet that is the main habit of the Church. All we have are sermons—nothing else.

Let's shift from a culture of sermons
to the transformation of society.

Similarly, many churches constantly pray for revival, but they fail to understand that revival is futile without a shift in our mindset that leads to the transformation of society.

I believe churches should be places where people encounter the presence of Jesus Christ, receive healing and deliverance, experience the renewing of their mind, and are empowered to become world changers. A church should be a powerhouse of transformation—first for the individual, then for the community.

I envision prayer groups of powerful men and women all around the world who gather to pray together before they venture out into their mission fields in government, finance, agriculture, and beyond. I envision an army of soldiers of Christ who do not speak for the applause in churches, but who plow the fields of the real world, where it truly matters—those who run for senator, mayor, commissioner, sheriff, school board, and who change their communities with blazing truth, justice, love, and courage.

Christ calls us to rise up in His Spirit and in love, so that we may reign with the King of kings and Lord of lords, and bring restoration to all of creation. And that brings us right back to the original mandate the heavenly Father gave to the very first humans:

> **"God said to them,**
> **'Be fruitful and multiply, and fill the earth,**
> **and subdue it; and rule…'"**
> — *Genesis 1:26–28*

The Hebrew words are deliberate and strong: הָדָר (radah) means *to rule or exercise dominion*, and שַבָּכ (kabash) means to subdue—*to bring something under order.* This was a commission of *authority*. Adam was appointed as God's vice-regent on Earth—entrusted to govern creation on God's behalf, under His authority, and in alignment with His will, not as an independent ruler but as a steward-king reflecting the rule of the Creator.

Just as Jesus said, "If you have seen Me, you have seen the Father" (John 14:9). Christ set the example for all of us. He brought forth Heaven on Earth—and then instructed us to do the same.

Shall we turn back to Christ and obey Him?

CHAPTER 24

What About Israel?

"What a revelation this is! I am not saved by Jesus just to wait until I can go to Heaven, but so I can be restored to my original calling: to become a king with Christ, a royal son of God, an ambassador of Heaven—one who casts out evil and establishes Heaven on Earth. That is so flabbergastingly powerful! It's the radical, diametrical opposite of the idea that we have to wait for Jesus to come back, and until that day everything will only grow darker and darker. That is one of the most disempowering beliefs anyone could ever have.

I now see that this is indeed *the heart of the enemy*. Satan has stolen the treasure from the Church—robbed us of our crown and placed it on his own ugly head—so that he could reign on Earth instead of us, the royal, blessed, anointed children of the Most High God. Wow…

But this raises a huge question mark about Israel. If Jesus will not return to Israel to rule the world from there, then what is the true meaning of this state? Can you give me a sound biblical answer to this, Mr. Sörensen? And please—give it to me straight. I am done with the lies, the twisting, and the manipulation. Open up this can of worms all the way. I want the truth, the whole truth, and nothing but the truth—no matter how much it hurts."

—Josh

Well, Josh… that's quite a request you're making here. Do you realize that what we're about to open is not just a can of worms — it's more like raising hell itself?

This is one of those topics where the Almighty God of Heaven and Earth spoke to me in a loud, thundering voice that shook every fiber of my being and turned my entire life upside down.

Let me tell you how it happened...

Years ago, I was visited by a prophetic minister from America, who was joined by two young men. I had invited them to minister at a conference in a church I had planted in Europe. One evening, as we prayed together, one of the young men received a prophetic word for me:

> **"God is going to align you**
> **with an ally from North Holland.**
> **Together you will be an arrow of the King**
> **that will pierce the very heart of the enemy."**

It was a strange prophecy, but I treasured it in my heart.

For the next ten years, nothing seemed to come of it. No ally appeared from North Holland. The prophecy faded into the background.

During those years, the Spirit of God led me on a long and lonely journey of breaking down all the lies I had been taught and rebuilding me from the ground up with His blazing truth. He taught me one truth after another, preparing me to release what He was revealing.

At that time I had a well-established Christian ministry. I had written several books, planted churches, and organized conferences where thousands of people were powerfully touched, healed, and delivered by the presence of Jesus Christ. My mailbox overflowed with testimonies from people whose lives were totally transformed—whether through miraculous physical healing, emotional restoration, or spiritual deliverance. Marriages were restored, people broke free from sexual addictions, and hope was revived. It was wonderful.

My artwork was displayed in churches across Europe. I was being interviewed by Christian television, radio, and magazines, and I was loved and respected for the touch of God, the love of the Father, and the gifts of the Spirit flowing through my life. Many considered me an example of pure dedication to Jesus Christ, and a true vessel of His love for mankind.

But then everything changed...

The Lord told me it was time to reveal what He had shown me. And I knew exactly what that meant: the end of my successful Christian career. From that moment on, I would be hated and rejected.

Through the years, I had learned one unspoken rule in ministry: there are some things you simply do not touch. You can preach about the love of God, the power of the Spirit, repentance, holiness, miracles, healing — all of that is fine. But don't ever question the demonic doctrines that have been inserted into the Church by Darby and Scofield. Touch that, and all hell breaks loose. It's like entering Satan's bedroom and pouring a bucket of gasoline over his fiery head. Can you imagine the explosion?

The night before I was about to release an in-depth study on these revelations, I had my own Gethsemane moment. I tossed and turned in bed, sweating and gasping for air. Fear gripped me like a vice.

"They're going to cut my head off," I thought. "This is it. I'm done."

In that desperate hour, I cried out to the Father for help.

And then it happened.

His voice thundered into the room like a terrible explosion.

A massive blast of unspeakable power that shook me to the core. It roared like a tornado through the air:

"THIS IS THE HEART OF THE ENEMY!!!"

After this thunderclap I lay there trembling, breathless. Then it hit me like lightning—the prophecy from ten years earlier:

"Together you will be an arrow from the King that will pierce... THE HEART OF THE ENEMY."

The "heart of the enemy" was *this very doctrine*, this corrupted theology that had hijacked the Church for generations. It was this false teaching that turned the Church away from Jesus Christ and His Kingdom, and focused her instead on the military state of Israel. This same doctrine told Christians to stop healing humanity and instead wait for Jesus to return to Jerusalem to set up a political "kingdom" there.

That is the heart of the enemy!

Since this new belief system hijacked the Church, the army of Christ across the world came to a screeching halt, and in that vacuum, evil surged back into human society. The rightful rulers, called to reign with Christ, stepped down from their posts and began staring at the sky, waiting for a rapture, while the wicked gladly took their place.

As the Church retreated, darkness advanced. Our communities and nations were handed back to forces Christ had already defeated.

Our world was dragged once again toward the same ancient corruption and cruelty He had delivered humanity from.

That is the heart of the enemy.

As I lay there in stunned silence, the weight of God's words pressed deep into my spirit. And then, to my utter amazement, I remembered something absolutely astounding:

That prophecy had said I would find an ally in *North Holland*—a province in the Netherlands—and that *together* we would become this arrow of the King, piercing the heart of the enemy.

Suddenly I realized: that is exactly what had happened this past year!

While preparing the great revelation of the truth for the Church in the Netherlands, I had been greatly helped by a theologian who lived in... *North Holland!* He had answered many of my toughest questions and encouraged my search for truth. He didn't even realize it, but he had been walking beside me in the very fulfillment of that decade-old prophecy.

He was the ally God had promised!

Together, we were that arrow of the King prophesied to pierce the heart of the enemy.

Excited beyond words, I called him the next day to share everything. After I finished explaining, there was a long silence on the other end of the line. Then he spoke quietly and said,

"David... do you realize the name of my publishing company?"

I paused for a moment. And then it hit me. My eyes widened. My mouth dropped open.

His Christian publishing company was called—ARROWZ.

The prophecy had been fulfilled in every detail:

"God will give you an ally from North Holland.
Together you will be an arrow from the King
that will pierce the heart of the enemy."

I was overwhelmed. Moments like these strengthen us for the battles ahead. God often gives us divine confirmations when we're about to face the fiercest opposition. And opposition came—oh, it came.

In 2014, I published a first online version of this message in Europe. And as I said before, *all hell broke loose.* I was attacked, accused, slandered, smeared, and even threatened with death. It was brutal. The backlash was unlike anything I'd ever experienced.

Satan, having hijacked the Church, roared like a possessed lion, desperately guarding his mental stronghold over the minds of believers, knowing that once the deception broke, his rule would collapse.

But God sustained me through it all.

When I later moved with my family to America in 2016, I knew I had to write this book for the whole world. Yet for years, fear held me back. I knew what it would cost. I had already paid the price once. For almost ten years I waited. Then, at a conference in Denver—held in a church called Bridgeway—a prophetic minister gave me a word from the Lord. He knew nothing about me. He had no idea that God had been calling me to write this book. And yet, by the Spirit of God, he spoke words into my life that would alter my destiny—and, in time, help change the course of the world:

"Write the book, David. Write it. Just write it."

That's it. I had to obey. Come what may. No more delay.

Through betrayal, slander, misunderstanding, and fear I wrote what God told me to write.

And that is the book you are holding in your hand.

The razor-sharp truth in these devastating pages is a fiery arrow, forged in the burning flames of the heart of God Himself and aimed straight at the heart of Satan, to reclaim the hearts of believers with a rekindled passion for Jesus Christ. No more idolatry of a political, military state that denies Jesus Christ and exalts itself above Him. No more bowing to the counterfeit kingdom Satan has dangled before the Church's eyes. No more supporting Satan's plan for a one-world government based in Jerusalem meant to enslave all of mankind. No more denying Jesus Christ as the fulfillment of everything God promised.

This time, we return to Jesus Christ.

We have been told to wait for the return of Christ. A return of a world savior in a political state. But the Spirit of God is calling us back to the true Messiah. Not a military world leader. Not a political dictator. Not some kind of United Nations WorldTeacher.

We are being called back to the true Savior of all creation, the Lord Jesus Christ. He does not save the world through tyranny and oppression. He does not mass murder thousands of children. He does not bribe politicians, nor does He sexually blackmail them, the way Israel does.

Jesus Christ rules by His Spirit, who transforms us in our hearts and makes us true children of God. He ends the hostility between Jews and Gentiles and creates a whole new humanity, where there is no distinction, but *all are equal as children of one Father.*

He brings peace through love.

He heals this world by sending His servants everywhere to end the rule of Satan and restore all of creation.

We are being called back to Him, in whom all of God's promises have become reality. Not through military force, but by His Spirit, who brings love and goodness into the hearts of men. They lay down their weapons, remove all hatred from their souls, and embrace one another with a brotherly love that comes straight from the very heart of our loving Father in Heaven.

This is the real Kingdom of Heaven.

When you ask me, Josh, to show you the truth about Israel, then this is it. It's not about a military state; *it's about the Kingdom of Christ, in the Spirit of God.* It's not about Jews who donate billions of dollars to organizations in America to ensure political support for Israel. It's about the Spirit of love convicting the hearts of people to accept Christ as the Messiah and to allow Him to turn them into healers of humanity—not through organized religion, not through corrupt politicians, not through military violence, but through the life-changing and life-saving love of Christ that is being poured out into their hearts.

But when you say this, all hell breaks loose. The demons roar in fury, because it shatters all their plans.

Can you understand that it is no small thing to satisfy your plea, "So open this can of worms all the way, Mr. Sörensen"? Do you even imagine the attacks I will face by granting your request?

But, I will not shy back. I am willing to pay the price. As long as you have the courage and honesty yourself, Josh, to accept the biblical truth I am going to reveal.

So let's go even deeper and compare the raving-mad illusions injected into the heart of the Church with the crystal-clear truth of the holy Scriptures, and liberate the hearts of all truthful, honest, and humble children of God.

May the Holy Spirit of truth enlighten our hearts and minds, so we may see clearly, without the fog of Satan that blurs our sight.

Before we step into even greater realms of devastating revelation, I urge you to submit yourself once more to the Lord, for He alone can open our eyes and lead us into the truth.

Heavenly Father,

You alone are my Guide, my Shepherd and my Helper.

I pray that You shine Your light so bright into my heart
that no scheme of Satan can succeed.

I surrender myself once again to You.

Speak to me, Lord, and deliver me from the evil one.

Show me who Jesus Christ truly is,
and reveal to me the fullness of Your glory in Him.

Shatter every stronghold of the enemy in my mind.

No matter how difficult it may be for me,
I choose to become a true child of You.

Not a renegade who opposes Your words
and twists them to defend false beliefs,
but a true child who listens to the Father.

Open my heart Lord, so I will be able to see Your truth
without any form of confusion from the enemy.

You alone are my God, nobody else.

Now be My Light and My Teacher.

I submit mysef wholly to You.

In Jesus' name.

Amen.

"Thank you very much Mr. Sörensen for helping me understand what the Bible truly says about the state of Israel. So here comes my first question: why is everyone who moves to the modern state of Israel suddenly considered one of 'God's chosen people'? It doesn't matter whether they come from Africa, Europe, Asia, or the Americas. The moment someone moves to Israel and adopts a Jewish identity, they are treated as if they now hold a special status and inherit every blessing and every promise—apart from Jesus Christ. This is why we feel obligated to send them money, never criticize them, condemn anyone who disagrees with Israel, and even excuse violence and bloodshed in the Middle East—because we have been told that the inhabitants of the modern state of Israel are all 'chosen by God'. What does the Bible really say about that?"

—*Josh*

Let me tell you, Josh, as honest and blunt as you asked me to be: the phrase "chosen people of God" has become one of the most weaponized expressions in the entire Bible. It was carefully chiseled out of its Biblical context and strategically manipulated to serve the political ambitions of the Zionists, who envision a future world government, centered in Israel. As Darby proclaimed:[1]

"That government will extend over the whole earth,
but the royal nation and the seat and centre of government
will be the Jewish people.
To Jerusalem, as the centre alike of worship
and government, all nations will flow."

Scofield doubled down on this proclamation, consistently declaring that a future political rule of a Jewish Messiah would be established in the nation of Israel as the center of a one world government:[2,3,4,5]

"In the last days... the mountain [Zion] shall be
established as the center of divine government,
and all nations shall flow unto it."

"This is the establishment of the kingdom on earth,
with Jerusalem as the center."

"Israel is restored to her land and to her place as the head
of the nations, and the Gentiles come to her for light."

"The Gentile nations are subordinate to restored Israel and serve her in the kingdom."

Scofield even taught:[6,7]

"No nation that will not serve Israel shall survive. Jerusalem becomes the earthly center of the divine kingdom; Christ reigns there in visible glory."

"The nations are ruled through restored Israel."

When you read what John Nelson Darby and C. I. Scofield taught, does it not become obvious why they needed to convince us that everyone who lives in the state of Israel is "chosen by God"?

"Wow, that is shocking... I had no idea this nefarious political agenda was behind it. But it does raise a question: what then does the Bible mean with this expression that the Jews are God's chosen people?"
—Josh

Let me unpack it for you, Josh.

From Genesis to Revelation, God's dream has always been to have a family of His very own children who truly love Him and who come from every tribe, tongue, and nation under heaven. This is why Revelation 7:9 gives us such a beautiful picture of God's heart:

"After these things I looked, and behold,
a great multitude which no one could number,
of all nations, tribes, peoples, and tongues,
standing before the throne and before the Lamb,
clothed with white robes, with palm branches
in their hands."
— *Revelation 7:9*

Can you see how wonderful this is? God speaks of a family from all nations, tribes, peoples and tongues. No ethnic superiority, not one group elevated, but one grand family of God.

His heart was, and always will be, for *all of humanity.*

Yet what have we been taught in so many churches? That God is basically the ultimate cosmic racist — that He looks down on the billions of people across the Earth with a holy scowl and only lights up with joy when He glances at the little patch of land called Israel. And that is exactly what the elites want: that all of mankind thinks this political Israel is highly exalted above all other nations, so everyone would gladly surrender their nation to it, when the time arises.

To prove to you how some in the state of Israel have an outspoken supremacist ideology, I will provide several world famous quotes. These aren't fringe radicals whispering in dark corners. These are mainstream voices, shaping national policy, backed by military power, and broadcast without shame.

There is, for example, Rabbi Ovadia Yosef, who served as the Chief Rabbi of Israel and was one of the nation's most revered spiritual authorities. This top leader of Israel declared in a sermon:[8]

> **"Non-Jews were born only to serve us.**
> **Without that, they have no place in the world."**

This supremacist attitude is not limited to religious figures. It also comes from the very top of Israel's political leadership. Prime Minister Benjamin Netanyahu has openly called non-Jews "wild beasts":[9]

> **"In our neighbourhood, we need to**
> **protect ourselves from wild beasts."**

Another prime minister of Israel, Menachem Begin, stated that Palestinian people are "beasts":[10]

> **"The Palestinians are beasts walking on two legs."**

Israeli defense minister Yoav Gallant agreed publicly that the Palestinian families are indeed "human animals":[11]

> **"We are fighting human animals**
> **and we are acting accordingly."**

The Talmud, Judaism's central text alongside the Torah, contains verses that demote non-Jews to subhuman status. Yebamoth 61a states:

> **"the Jewish people, are called men [adam]**
> **but gentiles are not called men [adam]."**

"NON-JEWS WERE BORN ONLY TO SERVE US. WITHOUT THAT, THEY HAVE NO PLACE IN THE WORLD."
— CHIEF RABBI OF ISRAEL, RABBI OVADIA YOSEF

Tractate Shabbath 32b decrees that each Jew will have 2,800 non-Jewish slaves, when their Messiah comes:

> **"Anyone who is vigilant in performing the mitzva of ritual fringes merits that two thousand eight hundred servants will serve him in the World-to-Come."**
> —*Shabbath 32b,6*

The same Talmud declares that non-Jews should be killed, when they study the Torah, because Jews claim exclusive rights to read Scripture:

> **"And Rabbi Yohanan says: A gentile who engages in Torah study is liable to receive the death penalty; ... The punishment of a gentile who studies Torah ... is execution by stoning."**
> —*Sanhedrin 59a, 2-3*

Jews are even made equal to God, as the Talmud states:

> **"And Rabbi Hanina says: One who slaps the cheek of a Jew is considered as though he slapped the cheek of God. ... Such a violent person has no remedy but burial."**
> —*Sanhedrin 58b*

A prominent Israeli rabbi, Rabbi Yitzhak Ginsburgh, told New York Jewish Week that he would "probably allow" a Jew to seize a non-Jew, and cut out his liver, in order to save the life of a Jew who needs a liver transplant. Why? Because...[12]

> **"There is something infinitely more holy and unique about Jewish life than about the life of any other people."**

This supremacist worldview stands in direct opposition to the message of Jesus Christ who tears down every wall of division:

> **"A renewal in which there is <u>no distinction</u> between Greek and Jew, circumcised and uncircumcised, barbarian, Scythian, slave, and free, but Christ is all, and in all."**
> —*Colossians 3:11*

Jesus Himself modeled this by ministering to Samaritans, Romans, and other so-called "outsiders" whom the Jews despised. He shattered cultural barriers and called His followers to love their enemies, not dominate them. As Paul declares in Romans 2:11:

"For there is no respect of persons with God."

And again in Romans 10:12:

"For there is no difference between Jew and Gentile — the same Lord is Lord of all and richly blesses all who call on Him."

Peter confirmed this when the Holy Spirit fell on Gentiles in Acts 10:34–35:

"I now realize how true it is that God does not show favoritism but accepts from every nation the one who fears Him and does what is right."

Even the Old Testament warns Israel against the idea that they are somehow superior. Amos 9:7 is a striking examples, where God says:

"Are you Israelites more important to me than the Ethiopians? Did I not bring Israel up from Egypt, the Philistines from Caphtor, and the Arameans from Kir?"

Apostle John drives the point home in John 1:12–13:

"As many as received Him, to them He gave the right to become children of God, to those who believe in His name, who were born, not of blood, nor of the will of the flesh, nor of the will of man, but of God."

John could not make it more clear: *nobody* becomes a child of God through birth, blood, flesh, or the will of man. Only those who believe in the name of Christ receive the right to become children of God.

Jesus even confronted the racist superiority mindset of the leaders of Israel, by bluntly stating they were in fact children of the devil:

> **"You are of your father the devil, and you want to do the desires of your father. He was a murderer from the beginning, and does not stand in the truth because there is no truth in him. Whenever he tells a lie, he speaks from his own nature, because he is a liar and the father of lies."**
> —*John 8:44*

Christ then clarified who the true chosen people of God are: those who listen to His words and obey them.

> **"For whoever does the will of God, this is My brother, and sister, and mother."**
> — *Mark 3:35*

All who obey God are His children, no matter where they come from. It has nothing to do with race, DNA, culture, politics, or religion. For that same reason, the Apostle Peter called *the followers of Christ* God's holy nation and His royal people:

> **"But you are a chosen race, a royal priesthood, a holy nation, a people for God's own possession, so that you may proclaim the excellencies of Him who has called you out of darkness into His marvelous light."**
> — *1 Peter 2:9*

Apostle Paul stressed that not the physical descendants of Abraham receive the promises, but the spiritual descendants, which is all who have faith in Christ:

> **"Therefore, be sure that it is those who are of faith who are sons of Abraham."**
> — *Galatians 3:7*

> **"So then those who are of faith are blessed with Abraham, the believer."**
> — *Galatians 3:9*

"For you are all sons of God through faith in Christ Jesus.
... There is neither Jew nor Greek,
there is neither slave nor free,
there is neither male nor female;
for you are all one in Christ Jesus.
And if you belong to Christ,
then you are Abraham's descendants,
heirs according to promise."
— *Galatians 3:26–29*

It's all about one thing, and one thing only: *faith in Christ.* Not faith in Israel, not faith in the Jews, not faith in Jerusalem, not faith in the Law, not faith in rabbis, and not faith in feasts. Those who have faith in Christ are the sons of Abraham, they are the blessed ones, the heirs of the promises, and the true people of God.

The chosen people of God is all who are in Christ.
Not all who are in Israel.

Nobody in all of history destroyed Israel's spiritual elitism more than Jesus Christ. He took a sledgehammer to their arrogance when He said to their face:

"The Kingdom of God will be taken away from you
and given to a people who will produce its fruit."
— *Matthew 21:43*

Do you grasp the monumental weight of this terrifying statement of Jesus Christ? No—it is not those who are in Israel, or who are Jewish, or who stand with Israel, who are blessed and receive the kingdom. On the contrary, God took it all away from them and gave it to another people who would honor it.

In John 8, the Israeli leaders boasted about being Abraham's descendants, but Christ shut them down with holy fire:

"If you were Abraham's children,
you would be doing the works Abraham did...
You are of your father the devil,
and your will is to do your father's desires."
— *John 8:39, 44*

Apostle Paul said that, in fact, the one true descendant of Abraham is Jesus Christ — nothing and nobody else:

"Now the promises were spoken to Abraham
and to his seed. He does not say, 'And to seeds,'
as one would in referring to many,
but rather as in referring to one, 'And to your seed,'
that is, Christ."
— *Galatians 3:16*

"But Mr. Sörensen, you are missing something crucial. Don't you know that Apostle Paul clearly stated in Romans 11 that *all of Israel will be saved?* That means they are a special, elect group of people after all. It doesn't matter what they do — God will save them anyway. See for yourself:

"And so all Israel will be saved."
— *Romans 11:26*

I know, Josh. Again, it is a disturbing example of how Christians in our time shamelessly manipulate the Word of God to spread ideas and beliefs that violently oppose the true message of Scripture. Because what did Paul explain all throughout that same book of Romans?

"For all have sinned and fall short of the glory of God."
— *Romans 3:23*

Paul declared that Jews have sinned, just like everyone else, and they are no different from other people. God is no respecter of persons.

"For there is no partiality with God."
— *Romans 2:11*

"For there is no distinction between Jew and Greek;
for the same Lord is Lord of all,
abounding in riches for all who call on Him."
— *Romans 10:12*

He even declares that, although there are many sons of Israel, only a small number—a remnant—is saved.

"Though the number of the sons of Israel
may be like the sand of the sea,
it is the remnant that will be saved."
— *Romans 9:27*

In the rest of this famous letter to the Romans, Paul reveals that not all Jews are truly Jews. Only those who are circumcised in their hearts through faith are considered true Jews.

"For he is not a Jew who is one outwardly,
nor is circumcision that which is outward in the flesh.
But he is a Jew who is one inwardly;
and circumcision is that which is of the heart,
by the Spirit, not by the letter."
— *Romans 2:28–29*

He goes deeper, teaching that this means only those born of the Spirit are children of God.

"That is, it is not the children of the flesh
who are children of God, but the children
of the promise are regarded as descendants."
— *Romans 9:8*

And he says that only believers who walk in the footsteps of Abraham are the true descendants of Abraham.

"Know then that those who are of faith,
these are sons of Abraham."
— *Galatians 3:7*

"If you belong to Christ,
then you are Abraham's descendants,
heirs according to promise."
— *Galatians 3:29*

Paul explains clearly that those who are circumcised in their hearts by the Spirit, and who walk in the faith of Abraham, are the true Israel. They are the "noble olive tree". That's why they will be saved, *through their faith in Christ.* But Paul also stated unequivocally that the vast majority of ethnic Israel—numbered like the land of the sea—was not truly Israel. They rejected God, denied Christ and ran after demons.

To twist Paul's words into meaning that anyone who moves to the land of Israel is automatically saved is outrageously false.

"But if God isn't interested in specific lineage or DNA, why then did He choose Abraham? Surely he was superior to other humans, right?"
—*Josh*

Absolutely not. The only reason the Eternal Lord of Heaven and Earth came down from His throne of glory to form a covenant with Abram was this: *Abram had kept himself pure in a world drowning in evil.*

You must understand Josh, that the entire Earth at that time was submerged in unimaginable wickedness — brutal demon worship, child sacrifice, witchcraft, sorcery, blood rituals, and every form of evil you can think of. Humanity had completely surrendered to the rule of Satan. Violence and perversion covered the planet like a thick, choking fog.

And yet, in the midst of that overwhelming darkness, there stood one man who refused to bow.

Abram remained faithful to the one true Creator. While everyone else worshipped darkness, Abram walked in the light. While nations offered their children on fiery altars to bloodthirsty demons, Abram offered his heart to the Lord.

Abram's faithfulness was the only reason God chose him. Nothing else.

And when the eternal, Almighty Lord of glory came down to seal His covenant, He placed His own name into Abram's name. Abram became Abra-ham — with the sacred "H" (Hebrew hey, representing God's breath) inserted into his very identity.

Abraham now carried God's dream of having a family of His own, a people who would love Him deeply and walk in His ways, just like Abraham did.

From that moment, God's vision was set in motion — not to create a political nation-state, but to raise up a spiritual family, a nation of individuals from every tribe and tongue, who would stay pure and faithful in the midst of a corrupt world.

Abraham was never called to be the father of the Jews, the father of Israel, or the father of Zionism. Abraham is "the father of all who believe" (Romans 4:13, 16) regardless of their race, language, or nationality.

The natural descendants of Abraham rejected this divine calling. Instead of walking in Abraham's footsteps, they trampled them. They indulged in every form of satanic ritual, including human sacrifice, sexual perversion, and worship of demons. Whenever God sent His prophets to call them back, they persecuted or even murdered them.

> **"Jerusalem, Jerusalem, you who kill the prophets
> and stone those sent to you..."**
> —*Matthew 23:37*

Their hearts were hardened against the Lord, and their rebellion was total. Over and over again, God described them in devastating terms:

> **"This is a rebellious people, deceitful children,
> unwilling to listen to the Lord's instruction."**
> —*Isaiah 30:9*

> **"For the Lord has a charge to bring against the people
> who live in the land: There is no faithfulness, no love,
> no acknowledgment of God in the land.
> There is only cursing, lying and murder,
> stealing and adultery; they break all bounds,
> and bloodshed follows bloodshed."**
> —*Hosea 4:1-2*

The wickedness of Israel made it look as if God's dream of having His own people would never come to pass. But the Almighty had a plan. He would send a Messiah through whom He would accomplish every dream He had carried since the dawn of time. This Savior would not compel obedience through laws carved in stone, nor would He use political or military power to force nations to bow before Him. Instead, He would transform people from the inside out. By His Spirit, He would remove their hearts of stone and give them tender, responsive hearts of flesh.

> **"I will give you a new heart and put a new spirit
> within you; I will remove your heart of stone
> and give you a heart of flesh.**

And I will put My Spirit in you and move you
to follow My decrees and be careful to keep My laws."
— *Ezekiel 36:26-27*

The Messiah would cause such a profound transformation inside the hearts of those who believe that they would become a new creation, filled with the very Spirit of God. As a result, they would truly become children of God. They would be His true Israel, His chosen nation, His heavenly Jerusalem — the city of peace where His presence would dwell. They are the apple of His eye. Not an elect group of people who happen to live in Israel, but all His children around the world who truly love Him.

"All the nations you have made will come
and worship before you, Lord;
they will bring glory to your name."
— *Psalm 86:9*

"Many nations will be joined with the Lord
in that day and will become My people.
I will live among you and you will know
that the Lord Almighty has sent Me to you."
— *Zechariah 2:11*

"Nations will come to your light,
and kings to the brightness of your dawn."
— *Isaiah 60:3*

Jesus came to fulfill these prophecies. He is the One who gathers the children of God around the world into one family:

"He died not only for that nation
but also to gather into one the children of God
who are scattered abroad."
— *John 11:52*

This is why Paul proclaimed there is a new humanity in Christ:

"His purpose was to create in Himself one new humanity
out of the two, thus making peace."
— *Ephesians 2:15*

When the apostles finally understood this revelation, they were transformed. Paul declared that his previous Jewish heritage and religious credentials were worthless garbage compared to knowing Christ:

> **"I consider everything a loss because of**
> **the surpassing worth of knowing Christ Jesus my Lord,**
> **for whose sake I have lost all things.**
> **I consider them garbage, that I may gain Christ."**
> — *Philippians 3:8*

Peter, who once denied Jesus out of fear, became a bold warrior of the faith, willing to die for his Lord. And Paul, who once hunted and killed Christians, became their greatest leader. They saw that Jesus is the true seed of Abraham, the fulfillment of every promise God ever made.

This revelation shook them so severely that they endured unimaginable persecution. The Jews who demanded a political, military Israel responded with demonic rage: they killed Christ, tortured the apostles, burned Christians alive, and crucified them upside down.

But those who had received the Spirit's revelation of God's true kingdom were so overwhelmed by divine glory that they gladly suffered for the sake of Christ.

The Spirit of Truth testifies about Jesus Christ—the all in all, the One and only, the Name above all names, the Yes and Amen, the Beginning and the End, the King of kings and Lord of lords, the joy of the Father. He is the true apple of God's eye.

He is the Chosen One. He is the Son of God, the beloved of the Father. In Him we receive all blessings; from Him flows all glory. Through Him we are saved from the curse.

May we all turn from our wicked ways
and return wholeheartedly to Jesus Christ.

"I see the truth now, Mr. Sörensen... how could I not? It is as clear as the bright midday sun. But still, I am sorry to say, I'm struggling with something that honestly terrifies me. It haunts me like a shadow that won't let go. I keep hearing my pastor's voice thundering in my mind: 'If we don't support Israel, God will curse us! Only Christians who bless Israel will receive God's goodness. Anyone who questions Israel will face His fury!' What am I supposed to do with that?"

—*Josh*

Yes, it's incredible to what lengths they went to force everyone to side with the modern military state of Israel. It is their primary weapon:

"You must stand with Israel, or God will curse you!"

It is horrifying, Josh. Because the truth of Scripture is so clear: we have received every blessing of God *in Christ.* He is the fullness of God, and in Him we share that fullness. Every blessing flows from Him — and in Him we are heirs of every promise. All blessing, all riches, all spiritual inheritance flow through Christ alone.

"Blessed be the God and Father of our Lord Jesus Christ,
who has blessed us with every spiritual blessing
in the heavenly places in Christ."
— *Ephesians 1:3*

"For of His fullness we have all received,
and grace upon grace."
— *John 1:16*

"In Him you have been made complete,
and He is the head over every ruler and authority."
— *Colossians 2:10*

"For all the promises of God find their Yes in Him;
therefore also through Him is our Amen
to the glory of God."
— *2 Corinthians 1:20*

And yet... pastors across the world claim that all of this is lost unless we send our dollars and loyalty to the state of Israel. The insanity of it is beyond words. It shows how far the Church has fallen when its leaders no longer understand even the most basic truth of the Gospel that God's blessing comes through Christ, not through a military state.

I pray that we will open our hearts to the Spirit of God, who is the Spirit of truth and who testifies about Jesus Christ.

"The Spirit of truth ... will testify about Me."
— *John 15:26*

Never in the New Testament does any Apostle, or the Lord Jesus Christ, say that we all have to turn back to a national Israel. On the contrary, they denied their religious and national heritage and traded it in for a far more glorious one:

a new name given by Christ Himself. A new heart, born from the Spirit. A new identity, affirmed by the Father. A new kingdom, not by ethnicity but by the Spirit. A new worship, no longer in Jerusalem, but in Spirit and truth.

The apostles and disciples in Israel who opened their hearts to the truth about Jesus Christ became so overwhelmed by this new creation, this glorious fulfillment of God's promises to Abraham, this supernatural, heavenly dimension in which demons were cast out, hearts were utterly transformed, sins were forgiven, and healing flowed like a river, that they gladly suffered for their Lord and Savior, Jesus Christ.

They stepped out of the dark shadows of the night and gladly entered the new day, in which all things were made new, to the glory of Jesus Christ—the Yes and Amen, the beginning and the end, the hidden mystery revealed by the Spirit, the object of all worship, the joy of heaven, and the fear of the demons.

That's why Revelation says all Heaven rejoices at the feet of Jesus Christ. Every knee bows before His name. He is exalted far above all others, in Heaven, on the Earth, and underneath the Earth.

He is truly the King of kings and Lord of lords.

It is high time that the Church in our day returns to this true King and abandons the idols that have taken His place.

CHAPTER 25

Two Different Israels

"That is truly beautiful, Mr. Sörensen. In my heart, I don't want to be a racist who condemns all the nations of the world to eternal submission under one group of people. I agree that in Christ we are all one big family of equal children of the heavenly Father.

But this does, of course, raise the question: if the military state of Israel is not the divine nation I was told, then *what* is it really?"

—*Josh*

In order to comprehend the true nature of the modern state of Israel, we must understand that the Bible speaks of *two different Israels*: the "Israel according to the **flesh**" and the "Israel of **God**."

The highly esteemed Pharisee Saul, one of the leading experts in the Jewish religion of his time, was thrown off his high horse by Jesus Christ, taken into Heaven, and shown this distinction (2 Cor. 12:2–4, Eph. 3:3–5). When Saul returned from the heavenly realms, he became known as Paul and stepped forward to boldly declare one of the most shocking revelations in all of Jewish history:

not everyone who descends from Israel is Israel.

**"They are not all Israel
who are descended from Israel...**

**it is not the children of the flesh
who are children of God,**

**but the children of the promise
are regarded as descendants."**
— *Romans 9:6–8*

This one declaration by the Spirit of Truth, in the Holy Scriptures, should be enough to settle all our questions about the state of Israel.

The respected Jewish teacher delivered a devastating message to the world, which shattered the idea that Jews are the chosen people:

the children of the flesh are not the children of God.

Paul clarified that besides the Israel of the flesh, there exists a far more important Israel: the **"Israel of God".** He declared the blessings of God upon this entirely different Israel:

"Peace and mercy be upon... the Israel of God."
— *Galatians 6:16*

According to this respected Jewish expert, who was transformed after being taken into Heaven with Christ, the Israel of God refers to those who rejoice in Christ:

**"We are the circumcision, who worship God in the Spirit,
rejoice in Christ Jesus, and have no confidence in the flesh."**
—*Philippians 3:3*

Being a former Pharisee of the highest order, it became the backbone of his message to mankind: we have no confidence in the flesh, because only in Christ is there forgiveness of sins, sonship, blessing, and the inheritance of God's promises.

**"Jesus Christ, who has blessed us with every
spiritual blessing in the heavenly places in Christ."**
— *Ephesians 1:3*

Even the Apostle Peter, who was a Jew from Galilee, did not boast in his Jewish blood, but contrasted the natural seed, which is perishable, with the spiritual seed, which is imperishable:

> **"...for you have been born again**
> **not of seed which is perishable but imperishable,**
> **that is, through the living and enduring word of God."**
> — *1 Peter 1:23*

To the people who were born of the Spirit, he said that *they* were the actual people of God, His holy nation—in other words, the true Israel:

> **"But you are a chosen people, a royal priesthood,**
> **a holy nation, a people for God's own possession."**
> — *1 Peter 2:9*

Millions of believers have quoted this proclamation by Peter to encourage one another, without understanding what these incredible words are really saying. Peter, a Jew, wrote to the followers of Christ that *they* are God's chosen people, *they* are God's holy nation, *they* are His royal priests. Not the Jews who rejected Christ and sought a powerful military Israel, but those who are in Christ and have accepted His true Israel of God, which is built by the Spirit of God.

The distinction between the Israel of the flesh and the Israel of God is such a basic revelation of the New Testament that it is utterly mind-blowing that almost not a single preacher, pastor, or prophet in the Church of our day knows about this. It shows how deep the Church has fallen into the depths of darkness, because it has sold out to the military nation of Israel, which pays handsome amounts to major Christian leaders who will openly support their political nation-state instead of pointing to Christ.

One significant aspect of the Israel of the flesh is that it violently persecutes the Israel of God. The apostle Paul was stoned, Peter was beaten, John was arrested, and the early church was fiercely hunted down by Jewish authorities. And, as we all know, they also handed over Christ to the Romans to be tortured and killed by means of brutal crucifixion.

The Israel of the flesh not only denies the Israel of God, but also seeks to destroy it—either through *violence* or through *infiltration*. Many Jews infiltrated the churches, trying to lure the followers of Christ back to the Israel of the flesh, as we can see in Paul's letter to the Galatians.

"For there are many rebellious men, empty talkers and deceivers, especially those of the circumcision."
— *Titus 1:10*

"But it was because of the false brethren secretly brought in, who had sneaked in to spy out our liberty which we have in Christ Jesus, in order to bring us into bondage."
— *Galatians 2:4*

Paul called these infiltrators "dogs" and "evil workers," and exposed their traditions as false:

"Beware of the dogs, beware of the evil workers, beware of the false circumcision."
— *Philippians 3:2*

Throughout Church history, the Israel of the flesh has continued its infiltration of the Israel of God, even to this very day. In fact, never before has there been such a widespread effort to draw the followers of Christ back to the Israel of the flesh, which is now more clearly manifested than ever through a rebuilt political state that openly rejects Jesus Christ and has even proposed laws that would make the public preaching of Christ punishable. Meanwhile, agents of this state are invading churches around the world, seeking to convince believers to financially support it—even declaring the curse of God over those followers of Christ who refuse to submit to their manipulation.

"I can surely attest to that infiltration, Mr. Sörensen. But the problem is that they do it with great persuasiveness, juggling isolated verses from the Bible like magicians, causing people to be hypnotized by such a display of wizardry. And most Christians simply lack the required in-depth understanding of Scripture to defend themselves against this treacherous trickery. How can Christians stand strong against this invasion of deception?

Is there a way to have an unshakable foundation of understanding that the military state of Israel is indeed not the Israel of God?"
—*Josh*

You are so right, Josh. I am also amazed at how some well-known preachers, like John Hagee, and countless others, spin verses from their biblical context to wind their audiences around their finger and get them to donate billions of dollars to support the wars of Israel.

And I love your question: how can we defend ourselves against this powerful mind control that happens in our churches? The answer is plain and simple: first of all, go back to the Scriptures I just quoted—they should make it all as plain as daylight. But there is yet another truth that adds to that, which is the historic origins of the state of Israel. When we look at how it was founded and by whom, it settles every lingering doubt.

The story of the modern state of Israel begins in the late 1800s, with a movement called Zionism, a *secular* project that sought to establish a Jewish state through political action, diplomacy, and military force.

The man most credited with launching modern Zionism was Theodor Herzl, a secular Jewish journalist and political activist from Austria. Herzl was not a man of faith. He didn't believe in the God of Abraham, Isaac, and Jacob. In fact, he rejected Judaism as a religion altogether. In his diary from 1895 Herzl noted:[1]

> **"I do not know whether I believe in God or not...
> But I do know that I do not believe in the Jewish God."**

At the First Zionist Congress in 1897 Herzl confirmed:[2]

> **"Zionism is a national movement, not a religious movement."**

It is important to understand the weight of these words, as Herzl claimed to be the man responsible for realizing a Jewish state:[3]

> **"At Basle, I founded the Jewish State."**

Many of the early Zionist leaders were outspoken atheists who openly mocked faith in God. The first president of Israel, Chaim Weizmann, said:[4,5]

> **"I am a Jew by birth, but I am not a religious Jew."**

> **"The Jewish people, for all their religiosity,
> are not a religious people."**

David Ben-Gurion, Israel's first prime minister, often hailed as the "founding father" of the state, declared:[6]

THE FOUNDER OF ISRAEL,
THEODOR HERZL, REJECTED GOD,
AS DID SEVERAL OF THE OTHER
FOUNDERS OF ISRAEL.

"Since I invoke Torah so often, let me state that I don't personally believe in the God it postulates ... I am not religious, nor were the majority of the early builders of Israel believers."

Moshe Sharett, Israel's second prime minister, explained:[7, 8]

"Secularism is not a negation of Judaism, but a new way of being a Jew."

"I am not a believer in the God of the Torah, but I believe in the Torah as a source of our national identity."

Golda Meir, Israel's fourth prime minister, reinforced the same principle. For her, Jewish history had nothing to do with God:[9]

"I have never thought of Jewish history as a religious one."

This secular nationalism also shaped the ideology of Israel's most influential intellectual architects. Among them was Vladimir Jabotinsky, the fiery founder of Revisionist Zionism, whose ideas deeply influenced Israel's military, political, and cultural direction. Jabotinsky did not hide his indifference toward the God of Israel:[10]

"Religion is not the most important factor in Jewish life."

And yet, paradoxically, he also appealed to Scripture to legitimize the Zionist project, while denying its Author:[11]

"The Bible is a book of national history, not of religious dogma."

For Jabotinsky, the future of Israel would not be secured by faith, prayer, or covenant — but by military violence:[12]

"Zionism is a colonizing adventure and therefore it stands or falls by the question of <u>armed force</u>. It is important to build, it is important to speak Hebrew, but, unfortunately, <u>it is even more important to be able to shoot.</u>"

One of Jabotinsky's disciples was a fiery young militant named Menachem Begin, the leader of Irgun, a paramilitary Zionist group labeled a terrorist organization by the British for its bombings and assassinations designed to drive them out of Palestine.

Under his command came one of the most infamous attacks of all: the 1946 bombing of the King David Hotel in Jerusalem, which killed 91 people of various nationalities. Yet decades later, this violent terrorist would stride onto the world stage as prime minister of Israel and, in one of history's great ironies, receive the Nobel Peace Prize in 1978. He denounced God's involvement in establishing the state of Israel:[13]

"We are a nation that came home by our own strength."

The Zionist movement was massively supported by banking elites. One name towers above the rest: Lord Jacob Rothschild. As we have seen in the previous chapters, the Rothschild family—who openly display their involvement in satanism—has been at the center of world finance for centuries, amassing unimaginable wealth through banking, war profiteering, and the manipulation of governments. They control more wealth than entire nations combined and positioned themselves as puppet masters of the global financial system.

The Rothschild agenda was never simply to be rich. Their ultimate goal was the establishment of a world government headquartered in Jerusalem. Exactly as Darby and Scofield proclaimed:[14,15]

"That government will extend over the whole earth, but the royal nation and the seat and centre of government will be the Jewish people."

"No nation that will not serve Israel shall survive."

Thanks to their enormous financial superiority the Rothschilds were able to use the military power of the British Empire to accomplish their goal. During World War I, Britain needed funds to continue fighting. In exchange for Rothschild support, the British government issued the Balfour Declaration in 1917, pledging to help establish "a national home for the Jewish people" in Palestine. This was a geopolitical transaction, deeply tied to Britain's colonial interests and its desire to control the Middle East — especially the oil-rich regions that were becoming the lifeblood of modern empires.

AN EARLY FOUNDER OF ISRAEL, VLADIMIR JABOTINSKY, SAID THE MOST IMPORTANT ELEMENT OF FOUNDING ISRAEL WAS THE ABILITY TO KILL PEOPLE.

Arthur Balfour himself, who signed the declaration, was a high-ranking member of Freemasonry, and many of the political elites involved were also Masons.

"Can we pause here for a minute, sir? I really need to process this.

In church, I was always taught that the military state of Israel was nothing but a divine miracle of God, who gathered the Jews from the diaspora back to their own homeland. And now I learn that the historic reality reveals the exact opposite: this state is the result of atheists who openly resent God, deny His Word, and manipulate it for their own political ambitions.

And they were even Freemasons—one of the darkest spiritual networks in the world. Worse still, Palestines invasion was funded by the Rothschilds, who don't even hide their involvement with satanism.

I am sorry, but I do need a break. I know I asked you to pull the lid off and blow the truth out in the open. But I didn't expect this..."

—*Josh*

I feel your struggle, Josh. I was furious after I discovered how graveley I have been lied to all my life. Especially when I started understanding that these lies are used to justify the torture and mass slaughter Israel inflicts upon millions of Palestinian people. We've all been convinced that these people are evil demons, but they're daddies and mommies, children and families, just like all of us. They are not the super villains, while Israel is the holy cow to be worshipped by all the Church. We're talking about normal human beings—uncles and aunts, grandmas and grandpas, families seeking happiness for their loved ones. Fathers working hard to provide for their kids. Mothers nursing their babies and playing with them in the garden. Friends having fun at the beach. Farmers enjoying God's creation as they prune vineyards and olive trees.

There's nothing nefarious about these people. Yet the lies being spread throughout the Church, every single day on social media, all over the Internet, in thousands of Bible studies, by countless books, through Christian television—allow Israel to murder these beautiful people, who are just as much dearly beloved children of God as anybody else.

Did you know that an estimated 200,000 innocent people have been brutally slaughtered by Israel since they invaded the land of Palestine? And did you know Israel has killed approximately 30,000 children, who have done nothing wrong?

Palestinian people are
precious children of God,
deeply loved by Christ,
no different from other
people in the world.

"Excuse me, Mr. Sörensen, did you just say that Israel has killed hundreds of thousands of people? Isn't that a vast exaggeration?"

—Josh

When you examine the documented casualties of every major conflict involving Israel since 1947 — the 1947–49 war, the 1950s border raids, the 1967 and 1973 wars, the 1982 Lebanon invasion, the First and Second Intifadas, and the repeated military campaigns against Gaza — the cumulative death toll becomes undeniable. Responsible historical estimates, grounded in UN records, human-rights investigations like B'Tselem and Human Rights Watch, and scholarly analyses, place the total number of Arabs and Palestinians killed around 200,000.

This number doesn't even include the millions of Palestinian people who died through starvation, lack of medical care, psychological torture, suicide, and other reasons. The indirect death toll is in the *millions.*

What is happening in Israel is exactly what the early founder of the Jewish state, Vladimir Jabotinsky, publicly proclaimed:

"It is even more important to be able to shoot."

Israel's colonization of Palestine also resulted in the staggering deaths of thousands of Palestinian children. Since 1948, estimates suggest that 30,000 children have been killed, with 4,000 alone dying in the 2023 Gaza attacks. The UN reports that Israeli violence has orphaned tens of thousands more. These numbers make it impossible to look away. They show just how heavily Israel's military actions fall on Palestinian children—and why people around the world are condemning it.

According to UNICEF 28 children are killed by Israel, every single day. That's the size of a large classroom.[16]

The horror gets even worse, as Israel stands among the few nations on Earth where hundreds of children are systematically *tortured in prison.* According to Amnesty International, Israeli authorities have carried out "harrowing torture and other ill-treatment of Palestinian detainees, including children," describing beatings, sleep deprivation, and prolonged solitary confinement.[17] The UN Committee on the Rights of the Child report states:[18]

"The Committee is gravely concerned by reports

of routine cruel, inhuman, and degrading treatment of Palestinian children during arrest, transfer, and interrogation."

Hundreds of Palestinian minors are arrested every year, often dragged from their beds in night raids, blindfolded, and shackled.

Human Rights Watch has likewise accused Israel of:[19]

"systematically mistreating Palestinian children in military detention, subjecting them to physical violence and threats."

These children are not terrorists or soldiers—they are schoolboys and girls whose only "crime" is being born on the wrong side of a military fence. How different is this from what Jesus Christ said:

"But when Jesus saw this, He was indignant and said to them, 'Permit the children to come to Me; do not hinder them; for the Kingdom of God belongs to such as these.'"
—Mark 10:14

"But, but, but... Mr. Sörensen, you got it all mixed up! Israel isn't the bad guy, it's all the fault of Hamas! They are the ones attacking Israel, and all Israel does is defend itself! Hamas are the bad guys, not Israel!"
—Josh

Oh, Josh, I know that's what Israel always tells the world. But don't you know that Hamas was literally created, and has always been heavily funded by Israel? Zvi Barel, a famous Israeli journalist who worked for Israels most respected newspaper Haaretz, revealed:[20]

"Hamas, to my great regret, is Israel's creation."

Avner Cohen, a former Israeli intelligence officer confirmed:[21]

"Hamas, to a large extent, was Israel's creation."

The official reason Israel created Hamas, was to weaken the PLO, but in reality Israel could, thanks to Hamas, always play the role of "victim," and nobody would ever suspect that Israel is the actual aggressor. That is why Israel has continued funding Hamas.

For years on end the Israeli government *sent $30 million to Hamas every single month*[24], with Prime Minister Netanyahu confirming in 2023 that these payments were facilitated through Qatari intermediaries.[25] IDF officials have even described Hamas as a "key partner" in Gaza.[26] Leaked documents from 2025 revealed the Israeli government secretly funnels funds to Hamas, contradicting its claims of combating terrorism.[27]

Israel has even funded other major terrorist organizations, like Al Qaida, ISIS and the Muslim Brotherhood.[28] The Wall Street Journal reported, for example:[29]

> **"Israel's intelligence agency, Mossad, has been secretly funding Al-Qaeda fighters in Syria to weaken Assad."**

And the BBC documented:[30]

> **"Israel has provided medical treatment to ISIS fighters in its hospitals, effectively supporting their operations."**

Despite its public stance against Iran, Israel has been secretly funding Iranian-backed militias in Syria, as revealed by The New York Times in 2019.[31] Prime Minister Netanyahu later confirmed these payments in 2020, exposing a web of strategic alliances.

Meanwhile, the U.S. Department of State has labeled Iran the "world's leading sponsor of terrorism," with Tehran serving as a hub for groups like Hezbollah and Hamas.

Once you understand that Israel created Hamas and continues to fund it to this day, while the Israeli Defense Forces openly describe Hamas as their "strategic partner," the entire narrative of "Israel is the victim of Hamas" no longer holds.

The most shocking revelation in this context came from two former Israeli soldiers who publicly testified on camera that it was Israel who opened the gates for Hamas to enter on October 7, 2023. Their explosive testimony is documented in my film "The Mystery of Israel" (StopWorldControl.com/israel).

HAMAS WAS CREATED BY ISRAEL AND HAS BEEN FUNDED BY ISRAEL EVER SINCE. FOR YEARS ON END ISRAEL GAVE HAMAS **$30 MILLION EVERY SINGLE MONTH!**

"It's absolutely unbelievable. I had no idea. Why does not a single church ever talk about this? Aren't Christians called to be the guardians of human rights? How is it possible that Christians support these crimes"?

—Josh

The answer is simple. If your creed is no longer what God says:

"Vindicate the weak and fatherless;
Do justice to the afflicted and destitute."

—Psalm 82:3-4

...and instead the compass of your life has become:

"We must support Israel, no matter what,
otherwise God will curse us."

...then you are no longer able to live guided by love and compassion, but you are forced to shut down your heart, close your eyes, and become fully complicit in all the injustices and atrocities of the state of Israel.

All Israel has to do is play the role of the *eternal victim*, and millions of Christians will support even its cruelest horrors.

"I don't get it. Isn't Israel always the true victim? I mean, Jews suffered worse than any other people in all of history during the Holocaust! Six million Jews died, is what we're told."

—Josh

We've indeed all been told that "six million Jews died during the Second World War" and because of this Holocaust, they now have the "right" to brutally massacre other people and build a "safe homeland" for themselves. But did you know there is a large number of scholars, writers, and researchers worldwide who have raised questions about various aspects of Holocaust history? They claim that many elements of this story are historically inaccurate. Most of these investigators were imprisoned, because laws were pushed that make it a crime to investigate the Holocaust. In all of the following nations you can end up in jail for publicly revealing factual inconsistencies in the Holocaust narrative: Austria, Germany, France, Belgium, Netherlands, Switzerland, Italy, Spain, Poland, Czech Republic, Slovakia, Hungary, Luxembourg, Romania, Lithuania, Latvia, Moldova, Israel.

This brings us to another question: why is it not allowed to express disagreement with the actions of Israel? Why is it always labeled "antisemitic"? Former Israeli cabinet minister and Israel Prize laureate Shulamit Aloni said in a 2002 interview with *Democracy Now!*:[30]

> **"Well — it's a trick. We always use it.**
> **When from Europe somebody is criticizing Israel,**
> **then we bring up the Holocaust.**
> **When in this country people are criticizing Israel,**
> **then they are antisemitic."**

This is one of Israel's highest political leaders admitting outright that both the Holocaust and the word "antisemitism" are weaponized as a trick to silence legitimate questions and sincere criticism.

On the other hand, hundreds of films about the Holocaust have been produced by Hollywood to tell all of humanity how the Jews suffered during World War II. But, how many of us are aware that Hollywood was built from the ground up by mostly Jews? Men like Carl Laemmle (Universal Pictures), Adolph Zukor (Paramount Pictures), Louis B. Mayer (MGM), Samuel Goldwyn, and the Warner brothers founded the studios that would define American cinema. Later Jews — including Steven Spielberg, Woody Allen, Mel Brooks, Joel and Ethan Coen, and Barbra Streisand — continued to shape storytelling and film culture worldwide.

Now let's go back to the previous chapters, where you learned about the official agenda to control the mind of mankind—and to ensure that no one thinks outside the box of the prescribed narrative.

How far do you think this mind control goes?

We saw that people at the highest levels of our societies not only tell everyone what to believe, but also go to great lengths to hide what they don't want anyone to be aware of. I will give you one example of this that will shake you to the core...

In 1917 an event took place in our world that was so diabolical and so horrifying that it dwarfs World War II. An estimated 60 million people were violently massacred during this indescribable atrocity. It is many times more horrific than both World Wars combined. Yet, astonishingly, Hollywood has *never* produced a single film about this disaster.

What is probably the most nightmarish chapter in all of human history has been meticulously erased from our collective memory.

It has become "forbidden history."

What cataclysmic event am I referring to?

The Russian Bolshevik Revolution of 1917, which erupted in the same era as the first World War. During this Revolution nearly 60 million Christians were brutally murdered. It was an all out attack on the Christian Church in Russia, followed by the establishment of communism.

For nearly a thousand years, Russia was the largest center of Eastern Christianity on Earth — a civilization shaped and sustained by the Orthodox faith. The dazzlingly beautiful Christian cathedrals and churches, which were world-famous for their grandeur and splendor, are witnesses to this. Russia was a herald of Christ to the world.

But in 1917, Russia was overthrown and dozens of millions of Christians were slaughtered in the most brutal ways. The terror that swept across Russia during the Bolshevik Revolution stretches far beyond the boundaries of human expression.

Nobel laureate Aleksandr Solzhenitsyn, who lived through the aftermath and chronicled its horrors, tried to warn the world, yet even he admitted that language strains under the weight of such cruelty:[31]

> **"The cruelty of that revolution was unbelievable.**
> **The Bolsheviks were not merely indifferent**
> **to human suffering— they gloried in it."**

As Solzhenitsyn observed:[32]

> **"With the Bolsheviks, hatred of God and hatred of men fused into one."**

The indescribable cruelty of the Bolshevik Revolution was studied in great depth by the French scholar Stéphane Courtois. This renown historian stands as one of the most unflinching witnesses of the twentieth century — an academic researcher who dared to open the darkest archives humanity ever produced.

After decades of research across Soviet, Chinese, Cambodian, Eastern European, and African communist records, he uncovered a reality so vast and monstrous that even seasoned scholars recoiled.

Courtois found that communism alone claimed more than ninety million lives in the twentieth century — not through war, but through cold, calculated ideological murder: executions, artificial famines, forced labor camps, purges, and the annihilation of entire populations.

The majority of these victims were followers of Christ — Orthodox Christians, Catholics, Protestants, and people of every faith tradition — crushed under regimes that viewed God as a direct threat to the State.

Courtois concluded that no other modern ideology unleashed such a tidal wave of deliberate human destruction. As he wrote in *The Black Book of Communism:*[33]

"The Bolsheviks killed more people in cold blood than any other regime in history."

If there was ever a political movement in which the face of Satan shone through with haunting clarity, it was the movement of Bolshevism, followed by communism. Its leaders did not merely oppose the Church — they set out to *eradicate* it.

The severity of this attack on the Russian Church was confirmed by the testimony of a man who stood at the very heart of the Soviet system. Dimitri Volkogonov was a Soviet general, a guardian of Marxist ideology, entrusted with the highest secrets of the USSR. For forty years he believed the Soviet gospel. But when glasnost opened the archives of the KGB, Party, and military to him, he discovered *a systematic war against Christ and His people.* Volkogonov saw the orders, the signatures, the internal reports of executions, torture, desecrations, and the planned annihilation of the Church. The truth was so devastating that it shattered the ideology he had preached his entire life. And when he emerged from those archives, he uttered a sentence that should shake every soul awake:[34]

"The Bolsheviks destroyed the Russian Orthodox Church as an institution."

Now I need to point out a remarkable historic fact about this event. Dishonest people can frame the following information as a form of antisemitism, which it is *not* by any means. It is merely a historic *fact*. And it needs to be mentioned for the sake of understanding the dynamics in our world. The historic fact is that the Bolshevik Revolution was greatly influenced by certain Jews. The Soviet Politburo, created in 1917, became the highest policy-making authority of the Communist Party of the Soviet Union. The first Bolshevik Politburo consisted of seven members, and among them were Leon Trotsky, Grigory Zinoviev, Lev Kamenev, and Grigori Sokolnikov—all of whom were of Jewish background.

These individuals, along with other Jews like Mikhail Kaganovich, Genrikh Yagoda, and Lavrentiy Beria, implemented policies that led to the systematic slaughter of almost 60 million Christians.

This was confirmed by the Nobel laureate Aleksandr Solzhenitsyn:[35]

> **"We cannot state that all Jews are Bolsheviks. But without Jews there would never have been Bolshevism."**

Aleksandr Solzhenitsyn (1918–2008) was a Russian novelist, historian, and moral philosopher, best known for exposing the Soviet Union's system of forced labor camps (the Gulag) and for his defense of truth, conscience, and spiritual responsibility. Because Solzhenitsyn devoted his life to dismantling ideological falsehoods and documenting historical reality—often at immense personal cost—his analysis of Jewish dominance in the early Bolshevik leadership is regarded as serious, well-researched, and grounded in historical documentation. He revealed that the Bolsheviks anti-Christian genocide was unprecedented in scale and cruelty, with methods including forced starvation, mass shootings, mass rape, live burnings, sexual mutilations, and other cruel forms of torture.

But the attack on the kingdom of Jesus Christ didn't end there.

Right after the Bolsejvik Revolution *communism* was installed, not just in Russia but in several nations around the world. Under communism, Christians were further persecuted, tortured and tens of millions more followers of Christ were violently murdered.

I know the next revelation will again shock certain readers. Nevertheless, we cannot ignore the historical record that reveals significant influence of certain Jewish individuals in the founding of the Chinese Communist Party (CCP). Jewish revolutionaries like Sidney Rittenberg, Israel Epstein, and Morris Cohen played pivotal roles in seeding the Chinese Communist Party. Rittenberg became Mao's personal translator and confidant, while Epstein edited the People's Daily. Morris Cohen trained Chinese communists in Moscow. Their fingerprints are on the 1949 takeover that plunged China into decades of bloodshed, where millions of Christians were slaughtered.[36]

This pattern echoes in America.

Charlie Kirk was one of the heroes of the Christian faith, who went to college campuses and universities to preach Christ. Charlie was ruthlessly killed after he began exposing how the woke movement, LGBTQ+ perversion, and Marxism in America are all heavily funded by Jewish billionaires. Kirk revealed:[37]

"You know who's funding the Marxist takeover of America? Soros, Steyer, Bloomberg—Jewish billionaires. They're funding this anti-American, anti-Christian, anti-white revolution."

Even the atheist movement in the Western world has been significantly shaped by certain Jewish intellectuals.[38] One prominent figure in this trend is Sam Harris, born in 1967 to a Jewish family. Harris gained recognition with his 2004 book *The End of Faith*, which critiques religious dogma and advocates for a secular worldview. Harris has aggressively attacked the Scriptures, stating:[39]

"The Bible is one of the most immoral books we have."

He openly ridiculed faith in God:[40]

"Religion is a failed science of happiness."

Many leading voices in American atheism have Jewish backgrounds. For instance, Isaac Asimov, a renowned scientist and writer, declared:[41]

"I don't believe in God. I am an atheist."

Christopher Hitchens, who culturally identified with Jewish heritage, called religion:[42]

"a poison that corrupts everything."

The same happened in Europe where many of the loudest voices in atheism have emerged from Jewish intellectual circles. Pioneers like Baruch Spinoza, Karl Marx, and Sigmund Freud promoted the denial of God. Their ideas have profoundly reshaped Western philosophy, psychology, and politics, steering Europe toward a worldview grounded in the rejection of God, and the destruction of the heritage of the Church.

The moral foundations of Christianity—such as healthy marriages and the sanctity of sexuality—were also replaced in our culture by the radical sexual ideologies of the LGBTQ+ movement. And once again, this is mostly thanks to the efforts of some Jewish individuals. Magnus Hirschfeld, George Weinberg, Frank Kameny, Leslie Feinberg, Joel Simkhai, Jazz Jennings, Harvey Milk, Gayle Rubin are just some of the names of Jews who laid the foundation of the LGBTQIA+ ideology.

Brenda Howard is the "Mother of Pride" for her leading role in coordinating the first LGBT pride march in 1970. Leslie Feinberg laid the groundwork for much of the terminology and awareness around gender studies, and was instrumental in bringing these issues to a mainstream audience. Joel Simkhai founded Grindr, a social networking and dating app for LGBT people. It is the most popular gay mobile app in the world. Gayle Rubin's essay *Thinking Sex* is widely regarded as a founding text of gay and lesbian studies, sexuality studies, and queer theory.

The same can be said about the porn industry. From Samuel Roth, who legalized pornography through the landmark Supreme Court case Roth v. U.S.A., to Reuben Sturman, the "Walt Disney of Pornography," certain Jewish figures have dominated every aspect of the porn industry. Sturman created an underground pornography empire and became the biggest distributor of porn magazines in the U.S. in the 1960's.

Al Goldstein became the first to publish hardcore pornography, while Steven Hirsch grew into one of the top adult film producers.

The list of Jewish porn moguls is staggering: Bobby Hollander, who pioneered the "shot-on-video" genre. Mark Spiegler, founder of the elite talent agency Spiegler Girls, often regarded as the industry's top recruiting agency. Joe Francis, aka Jonah Frankel, who launched the Girls Gone Wild empire; Seth Warshavsky, dubbed the "Bill Gates of Pornography" for his early internet porn ventures, an early pioneer of internet pornography who founded the Internet Entertainment Group, and fought for web pornography rights in court.

Al Goldstein's, one of the founders of the porn industry, explained what drives some Jews to push porn on humanity:[43]

> **"The only reason that Jews are in pornography is that we think that Christ sucks. ... Pornography thus becomes a way of defiling Christian culture."**

It is also a few Jewish individuals who created the four largest dating apps, designed to drive children into sexual relationships. The founders of Tinder, Bumble, OkCupid and Hinge—Sean Rad, Whitney Wolfe Herd, Sam Yagan, and Justin McLeod respectively—all acknowledged their Jewish heritage.[44]

The subversion of Christianity even included hijacking Christmas. Jewish composers and lyricists have dominated Christmas music, transforming the Christian holiday into a secular celebration of materialism and idolatry. Iconic songs like "White Christmas", "Rudolph

"THE ONLY REASON THAT JEWS
ARE IN PORNOGRAPHY IS THAT
WE THINK THAT CHRIST SUCKS.
PORNOGRAPHY THUS
BECOMES A WAY OF DEFILING
CHRISTIAN CULTURE."
—AL GOLDSTEIN

the Red-Nosed Reindeer", and "Santa Baby" were all written by Jewish songwriters. By flooding popular culture with such songs, they have effectively removed Jesus Christ from Christmas.

Now, is it antisemitic to state these facts? Of course not. It reveals a historical reality confirmed throughout the Scriptures: Christ came to the Jews first, yet many rejected Him and persecuted His followers. However, that doesn't apply to all Jews, as some did accept Jesus Christ and became apostles who spread the good news to the whole world. But both the Bible and history document that a certain group of Jews became enemies of Jesus Christ. This animosity against Christ and His kingdom continues to this very day and some Jews, like Goldstein, publicly declared their war against the Church by defiling it through the promotion of pornography.

Certain Jews also started, promoted, and globally distributed the horror film industry[45]. Horror movies traumatize millions of people for life by exposing them to horrifying scenes of people being tortured and slaughtered in gruesome detail.

In the mid-20th century, the CIA documented that extreme trauma fractures the human psyche, making it more suggestible, dissociated, and programmable—a fact exposed through programs such as MK-Ultra, where victims were subjected to terror, pain, and psychological shock in an attempt to break the will and overwrite the mind.[46]

The intelligence agencies known for trauma-based psychological experimentation have had deep, ongoing relationships with Hollywood for decades. That's not a conspiracy theory—it's documented. U.S. intelligence agencies, including the CIA, have openly acknowledged liaison offices, script approval programs, and behind-the-scenes cooperation with major Hollywood studios.[47] They guided what audiences would see, and how they would feel about it.

When you look at declassified documents, whistleblower testimony, and official acknowledgments, they all point in the same direction:

there is a deliberate strategy behind the production of countless movies that spread violence, perversion, adultery, war, death, the occult, magic, satanism, and even outright terror and horror—assaulting the human soul with pure terror no human being was ever created to behold.

Satan has used the Hollywood industry to unleash the same horrors of the ancient past—horrors that Jesus Christ removed from the world—and reintroduce them on a massive scale, straight into the hearts and minds of billions of people.

I repeat that this doesn't mean all Jews are evil. The vast majority of people who identify as Jewish—whether religiously, culturally, or geographically—have *no idea* about any of this. I am fully convinced that most Jewish people harbor no hatred against Christ. I have several dear friends who are Jewish. They are wonderful people.

My goal by unveiling these historic facts is not to cast a dark shadow over the Jewish people as a whole. They are just as precious as anyone else. But history does reveal that the main attack on Christ and His kingdom came through the same type of people who historically hated Christ, killed His apostles and tortured His followers.

However, Jews who did accept Jesus Christ, became powerful instruments of healing and restoration to all of mankind. They abandoned the idea of a political Israel and stepped wholeheartedly into the heavenly Kingdom of Christ.

Other Jews who rejected Christ took a whole different direction. They became the ones who have been working relentlessly to build an earthly world empire.

One of their efforts has been to exert control over the global field of education. A striking example is Robert Maxwell (1923–1991) — the British media tycoon who built one of the most powerful publishing empires on Earth. Through his company Pergamon Press, Maxwell shaped what entire generations of students would believe.

His textbooks filled classrooms, while his scientific journals dominated university libraries and his encyclopedias became the "official" sources that teachers trusted. Maxwell decided which ideas would be taught and which information would quietly disappear from the academic world.

The worldwide scope of Maxwell's influence has been documented by Aileen Fyfe, a respected historian of science and publishing, and professor at the University of St Andrews, known for her authoritative research on the power structures of academic publishing. She writes:[48]

> **"Pergamon Press had become one of the world's largest and most influential publishers of scientific and technical journals, giving Maxwell unparalleled leverage over the dissemination of scientific knowledge."**

The implications of this power have also been analyzed by Geoffrey Crossick, a distinguished historian and former senior academic leader. In his work on scholarly publishing, Crossick explains:[49]

"Maxwell understood earlier than almost anyone that controlling journals meant controlling the currency of academic life. Pergamon's dominance gave him enormous power over what research was visible and what was not."

Maxwell's influence was further confirmed by Gordon Thomas, a renowned investigative journalist and biographer whose meticulously sourced works on intelligence, media power, and global elites made him a credible chronicler of Maxwell's life and reach. Thomas concluded:[50]

"Maxwell exercised a degree of influence over scientific communication unmatched by any other individual publisher of his time."

In short, Robert Maxwell was one of the world's architects of what humanity would be taught in schools and universities—and what knowledge would be carefully withheld from the human race.

The question is: did this man act alone, or was he merely an extension of a far more powerful hidden force?

The answer began to surface shortly after his death.

In 1991, Maxwell's sudden and mysterious demise cracked the façade wide open. Seymour Hersh's *The Samson Option* (1991) and his 1992 reporting in *The New Yorker* revealed Maxwell's deep entanglement with Israeli diplomatic and intelligence networks.[51]

The picture grew even sharper when Rafi Eitan, a former chief of operations of the Israeli intelligence agency Mossad, openly admitted how important Maxwell was to Israel. The former Mossad operations chief referred to Maxwell as "a good friend" who "helped us a lot."[52]

Further investigative works literally called Robert Maxwell "Israels Superspy".[53] In other words: the man who determined what knowledge humanity was allowed to study—and what had to remain hidden from the world—was one of Israel's most powerful agents.

The Mossad, the Israeli agency behind Maxwell, is also known as the "World's #1 Killing Machine." No entity in this world has killed more opponents than the Mossad. They boast in this reputation with their slogan: *"We will find you, anywhere."* From Europe to the Middle East, from hotel rooms to quiet streets, they have left a long trail of corpses—militants, scientists, political figures, and critics of the Israeli state. Authors such as Ronen Bergman (Rise and Kill First), Gordon Thomas, and Seymour Hersh revealed that no other intelligence organization has

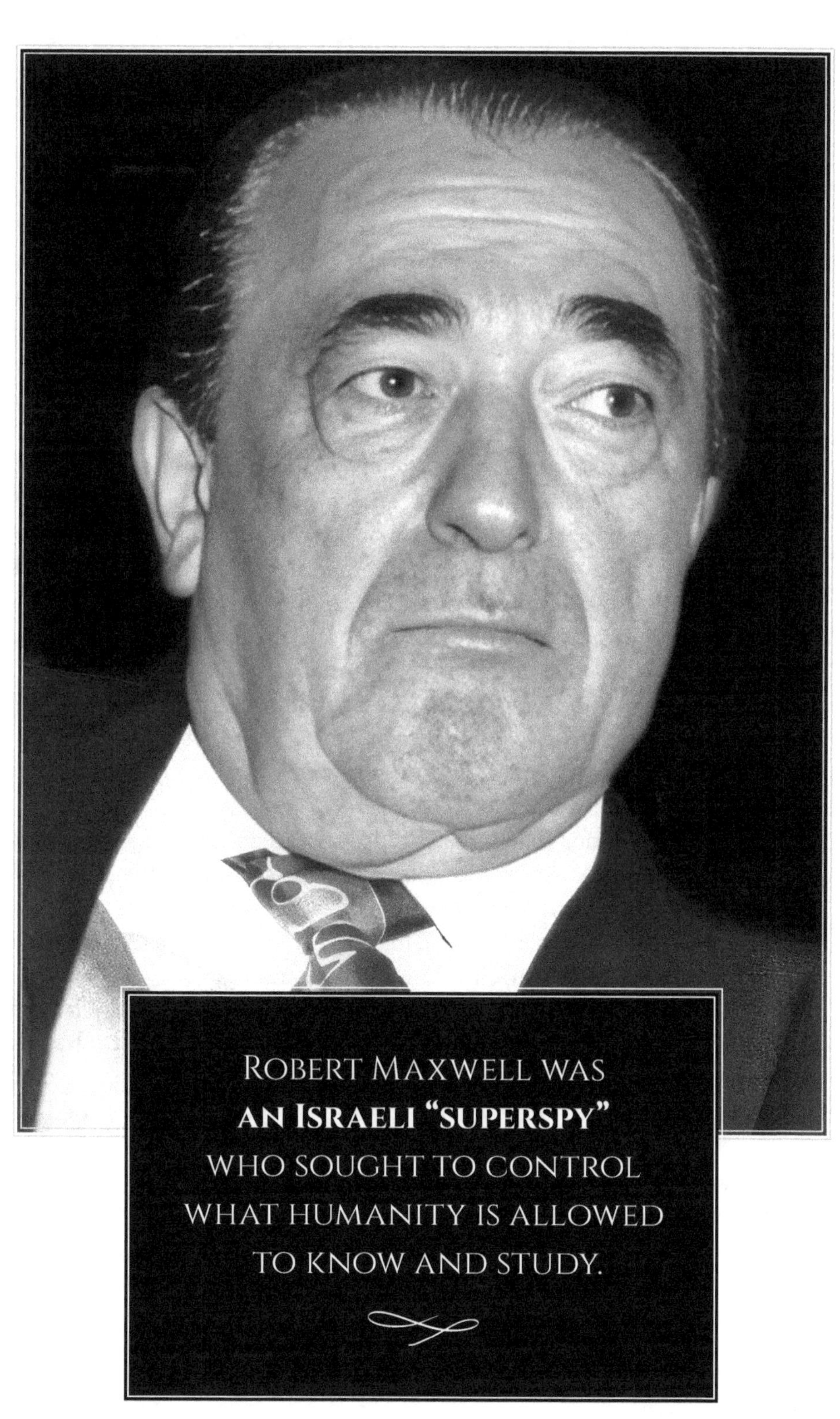
ROBERT MAXWELL WAS
AN ISRAELI "SUPERSPY"
WHO SOUGHT TO CONTROL
WHAT HUMANITY IS ALLOWED
TO KNOW AND STUDY.

carried out as many confirmed extrajudicial killings over such a long period of time.[54]

> **"In recent years Israel has assassinated more people than any other country in the western world."**

Former officials have openly talked about "kill lists" and even approving assasinations before those victims became a threat. In Israels worldview, assassination is a routine instrument.

But mind control and murder aren't the only tools Israel uses to spread out its tentacles of control over the world. A method even more effective is *sexual blackmail.* This technique involves inviting influential leaders from every sphere of life to secure locations, where they are offered sexual interaction with children. These crimes are then secretly recorded on video and used to ensure lifelong obedience to Israel's agenda. It's a well known and widely documented technique to gain full and unwavering control over powerful people.

This practice gained worldwide attention through Jeffrey Epstein. His right hand was Ghislaine Maxwell, the daughter of Robert Maxwell. Together they operated one of the most extensive sexual-compromise networks the modern world has ever seen. Epstein's "black book" contained over 1,500 names of powerful men, including politicians, CEOs, and Hollywood stars.[55]

For the third time I insist that this doesn't mean all Jews are wicked. But we do see that history repeats itself. What is described in the New Testament, is also plainly visible in our time: certain Jewish individuals reject the kingdom of love, peace and justice from Jesus Christ and choose to build their own kingdom, through other means.

This brings us to the question: who are the good Jews, and who are the bad ones? What causes some of them to choose evil? I do not have a satisfactory answer to this, and therefore choose not to go deeply into it. If I cannot provide a comprehensive insight, I would rather not meddle with it.

All I know is that the invitation to become true children of God—to become part of His actual chosen people—is extended to all the people of this world. Every human being is welcome into the Kingdom of Christ, where we learn to love one another and lift each other up. There is no bribery, blackmailing, abuse, or mind control in the Kingdom of Christ. I invite all who read this to turn wholeheartedly to this kingdom of love and unity.

A final word needs to be said about the great confusion surrounding what a Jew is and who the true "Jewish people" are. I believe the term "the Jewish people" is one of those misused expressions that often lacks substance. Because what are the Jewish people anyway? Is it everyone who moved to the state of Israel? Is it all who converted to Judaism? The fact is that the vast majority of people who call themselves Jewish have no direct genetic connection to the original Jews. A 2019 study published in the journal *European Journal of Human Genetics* found that 98% of Ashkenazi Jews have no ancient Hebrew DNA.[56] Most Jews are descendants from people in different nations who converted to Judaism, over the past two thousand years. In America alone there are approximately 185,000 "Jews by choice"—Americans who decided to become Jewish.[57] A Stanford University publication states that between 10,000 to 19,000 individuals annually undergo Jewish conversion, suggesting that over the past century alone, up to two million people could have adopted Jewish identity.[58] Anyone can move to Israel and become a "Jew". Israel offers significant financial incentives to do so. Any American, African, Asian or European can migrate to Israel, "convert" to Judaism and as a result be loaded with financial benefits, like impressive tax breaks, government grants, rent assistance, health insurance, etc.[59]

But no matter how anyone became part of the "Jewish people", I pray they will all wake up to what is going on in their belief system.

I invite all Jews to look at the true Messiah, who removes all ideas of superiority or inferiority, who ends all wars and terrorism, who expels all corruption and satanism, and who unites all the people of the world into one beloved family of one heavenly Father.

He is truly the Prince of Peace, who brings peace between all Jews and Gentiles, and makes us into children of God who love one another.

Christ doesn't inspire us to enslave other people, but was an example for us on how to serve one another. In His kingdom, we don't expand our influence through violence and oppression, but through love, goodness, and mercy. We accept suffering ourselves in order to save others.

His kingdom truly is not *of* this world—but it does *transform* this world, once we allow Christ to work through us with His Spirit.

Jesus Christ is the hope for all of mankind, Jews and Gentiles alike. He saves us from our wicked hearts, gives us a brand new divine nature of love and compassion, and renews our minds with His truth. In Him, we find one another to be dearly loved brothers and sisters, not enemies or slaves. We are all children of the same loving heavenly Father.

Let's return to Christ, shall we?

EPILOGUE

Enter His Kingdom

After writing such a vast amount of information, I would like to return to the simplicity of the true biblical message—the core declaration of both the prophets of old, and the apostles of the new covenant:

In Christ, all things have been made new.

We are not called to cling to the old, like trying to revive a rotting corpse. We are invited to leave the darkness of the old covenant behind, and step into the brand-new reality that Jesus Christ has opened for us.

Christ did not come to delay or postpone God's promises, leaving generations of believers waiting endlessly for His presence and kingdom. His message was clear: He established the reality of a powerful, supernatural Kingdom of Heaven in our midst—a kingdom we enter through childlike faith, leaving our old mindsets behind.

This glorious invitation is also extended to all of us today.

Lay down the lies and deceptions that have been spread with great force by the enemy of Christ, and return to the core message of our Lord and Savior. He is the fulfillment of all of God's promises. That is why Heaven and Earth bow to His name, angels worship Him, and demons flee from His glory. He is exalted by the Father and given the Name above all names, the King of kings and Lord of lords.

Jesus Christ is the mystery God had hidden for ages, but He was revealed by the Spirit of prophecy two thousand years ago.

Today the Spirit of Truth is reminding us of who Jesus Christ is.

The mission of the Church today is not to keep waiting—waiting, and always waiting—for Christ to return. He came exactly as He and His apostles said, during the time of God's judgment over Israel and the closing of the old covenant era. In that moment, judgment was executed, and a new era was established—bought and paid for by the blood of Jesus Christ. A new covenant in which the presence of Christ and the Father is no longer distant, hidden in an unreachable Heaven or confined to a closed-off temple, but is now in our midst.

The presence of Christ is the greatest power any human being can encounter. It transforms our innermost being and empowers us to become sons and daughters of God.

That is the essential difference between the Kingdom of Christ and human religion. In man-made religion, the Church is taught to wait for the presence of Christ and His kingdom. This disempowers believers and opens the door to a constant stream of false prophecies that repeatedly announce His return, and always fail, resulting in confusion and a Church unable to rise.

The Kingdom of Christ is the opposite.

It reveals that Christ is the King of kings and Lord of lords *right now*, and that we are called to walk in His authority. Our mandate is to establish His reign, not only in our churches, but in every sphere of human society: government, finance, business, healthcare, agriculture, entertainment, education, and beyond.

The Church is not called to stand apart from society, waiting for escape, but to be at the very center of human culture, bringing transformation through truth and love.

When that happens, the power of darkness is utterly defeated, which is why Satan has gone to such great lengths to hide these critical truths of the Kingdom of Christ.

The invitation to all of us is this:

Turn with all your heart to Jesus Christ. Not with the belief that He is far away somewhere, but with the full realization that He is here with us. We are His temple—His dwelling place.

He is our daily companion, and He longs to lead us into an ever-increasing awareness of His presence. These truths are not grasped by the human mind, but revealed to our spirit. It is a heavenly, supernatural kingdom which we enter, perceive, and experience by the Spirit.

This kingdom will never morph into a geopolitical, military power that forces all nations into obedience. It grows through the Spirit of God, who convinces the hearts of people to surrender to the love and goodness of the heavenly Father. It works through faith and love, not through coercion and violence.

God wants children who love Him, not slaves who are oppressed by Him.

This is such a profound difference, yet the majority of Christians and Jews alike have been led to believe that Christ or the Messiah will come down to force everyone, against their will, to worship Him. That is slavery, not love. It is tyranny, not family.

God is a loving Father, not a brutal tyrant. Even that basic understanding should shatter all false doctrines in our minds about a coming world rule by Christ as a global dictator.

His kingdom expands through His Spirit, who touches, heals, and transforms people deep in their hearts, causing a wondrous and authentic transformation.

I welcome you to pray one final prayer with me, with all your heart. May this be a prayer that transforms our hearts and lives, making us true sons and daughters of the Most High God, who walk in His presence and become world changers through His Spirit.

Heavenly Father,

I thank You for loving me so deeply that You sent Jesus Christ
to forgive my sins and welcome me as Your beloved child.
I accept your invitation and open my heart for You.
I confess that I have walked in rebellion against You.
I regret that and now choose to embrace Your love.

Fill me with Your Holy Spirit and plant within me
a deep hunger to know You more and to walk with You
every day of my life.
Come and dwell inside of me,
that I may become Your holy temple.

In Jesus' name.
Amen

LIBERATING THE CHURCH

"Now that I've read this entire book, I have to say: I'm burning inside. Part of it is anger, because I now see how deeply I've been deceived for my entire life.

But there's another fire burning too. It's a fire to *speak*. To shout this truth from the rooftops. Everyone needs to know this!

But at the same time... I am terrified.

I tremble when I think about the reaction I'll face.

Do you have any advice for me? Any wisdom on how to share this truth with other Christians, without being burned at the stake?"

—Josh

I understand your hesitation, Josh. But I beg you, not to be the next coward and traitor. As I said before, the son of a large Christian publishing company once called me and said, "Many pastors know this, but they are afraid to speak up because they don't want to lose finances."

When I was under severe attack in Europe for speaking the truth—when Christians openly called for my death, when preachers went from pulpit to pulpit slandering me, and when my very name became a curse in churches simply because I called the Church back to Jesus Christ—

I often thought to myself:

How different would it be if every Christian who knows the truth would actually stand up and speak it? The Church would awaken in an instant. The sound of truth would become so loud, that it could no longer be silenced or ignored.

We have a responsibility to restore truth to the Church.

Christ did not hide in Heaven either, did He? Jesus came down and spoke the truth bluntly, fearlessly, without apology. He confronted the leaders of Israel, exposed their corruption, laid bare their wicked hearts, and then set before them a clear path to redemption: turn from evil and put your trust in Me—Jesus the Christ.

I hope all of us will have the courage to follow Jesus just as He obeyed the Father.

Paul did not hide from his own people. Neither did Peter, John, Mark, or Matthew. They spoke with boldness, and the result was nothing less than worldwide deliverance. Millions upon millions were pulled out of darkness and into the light.

It will be hard—because this is war. We may be hated, attacked, mocked, and slandered. But if we all stand up, then this beast will be driven out of the Church in no time. And when it is, Jesus Christ will be brought back to the center—along with His healing kingdom of truth, freedom, and love—not only in America, but throughout the world.

We truly have no idea what the worldwide impact of that will be. Just imagine: two billion Christians who start bringing the truth and love of Christ into their communities. That won't be a revival, but a massive worldwide renaissance of the Kingdom of Christ. Everything will be transformed by His light!

Shall we go for it?

"Yes! I want to be part of this army of God that will bring back the true gospel to the Church. What a glorious mission! Once I was blind, but now I can see, and I want others to be set free as well. So, what can I do to help the cause, Mr. Sörensen?"

—Josh

The first thing I want to ask you is very simple, but it can have a big impact: go to my book on Amazon, and give it a five-star review.

Why is that so powerful? Because Amazon relies heavily on reviews to decide whether it will show this book to other people or not. The more five-star reviews it receives, the more Amazon will determine that this book is worth showing to its visitors.

So please go to Amazon and take a moment to give my book a five star review. It can have a huge impact.

Second, I want to encourage you to order extra copies of the book to give to pastors, ministry leaders, Christian influencers (ask ChatGPT how to contact these people), and even school directors and teachers.

We have to understand that the deception that stole the presence and Kingdom of Christ from the Church was spread worldwide through enormous efforts and the investment of billions of dollars. Entire Christian schools, universities, seminaries, Christian TV stations, Bible study networks, and many other institutions were bought or established to spread these satanic lies, and they continue to do so to this very day.

We may not have billions of dollars, but we can all place a few copies of this book into the hands of other people.

To make this easier, we offer a 50% discount on all orders of 10 books or more. Go here to place your bulk order of 10, 25 or 50 books:

TheReturnToChrist.com/bulk

There is an epic project I invite you to become a part of: I want to place a copy of this book into the hands of thousands of pastors, leaders, and ministries across this nation. We can make it happen, when we all make an effort. If you want to be part of this mission, then go to:

TheReturnToChrist.com/support

Let's reverse the satanic invasion of the Church and liberate her, so the Bride of Christ can once again shine her brilliant light of truth and salvation into every aspect of human society, worldwide.

The worst thing we can do is become like Judas: refusing to do what is right in order to protect ourselves. That is a betrayal of both Christ and His beloved people.

We all have a responsibility to help where we can. I encourage you to step over your hesitation and spread the truth.

Art That Reveals Christ

At the conclusion of this book I would also like to share something entirely different with you. When I came back to Jesus Christ in my early adulthood, I had dramatic encounters with His love and glory. He became the most beautiful reality there is to me.

But when I looked at the overall Christian culture worldwide, I was disappointed to discover that so few people seemed to know the Lord in this way. Most Christian artwork, for example, did not display His majesty the way I experienced it.

Being an artist myself, I decided to create a series of Christian artworks to reveal to God's people how wonderful He truly is—art that would touch people in the depths of their souls.

During this time, I began to receive visions of how certain artworks were supposed to look. God literally showed me what to create.

As these artworks began to be released, I received incredible testimonies. One lady wrote to me that her husband had left her for another woman. The woman was so heartbroken that she needed therapy just to survive. One day she came across a piece of art I had created that portrays the overwhelming love of God for us. It shows a giant hand reaching down from Heaven to lift a person into His presence. She wrote:

"Every morning as I walked down the stairs, I looked at this artwork. I stood still in front of it and absorbed God's love for me. This has healed me more than all the therapy."

A youth leader also shared his story with me:

"I was addicted to alcohol and became so desperate that I decided to end my life. On the way to kill myself, I felt God speak to me, telling me to look in the back of my car. There was a piece of art from you, and it revealed God's love for me. I broke into tears and turned around. Your art literaly saved my life! Now I am a youth leader, helping others find Jesus."

I encourage you to explore my art collection and share it with others. Besides Christian artwork, I also offer beautiful nature prints to help you experience the glory of God's creation.

Lion of Judah
LAMB OF GOD
Behold, the Lion of the tribe of Judah, the Root of David, has prevailed to open the scroll and to loose its seven seals.
Jesus Christ
And I looked, and behold, in the midst of the throne and of the four living creatures, and in the midst of the elders, stood a Lamb.
Revelation 5:5-6

References

When doing research, it is crucial to understand that AI, Google, Wikipedia, and most mainstream sources are programmed to hide many of the truths revealed in this book. Especially in an age of easily accessible information, it is more important than ever to personally verify sources and learn proper investigation. The sources provided here are only a starting point. Instead of relying on Google, consider using Yandex.com; and instead of YouTube, use BitChute to do a deep search for truth.

Chapter 20: Satan's Little Season

1. Ferguson, Niall. The House of Rothschild, Volume 1: Money's Prophets, 1798–1848. New York: Viking, 1998, 342–345.
2. Collier, Peter, and David Horowitz. The Rockefellers: An American Dynasty. New York: Holt, Rinehart and Winston, 1976, 123–126.
3. "Rothschild Family." Encyclopædia Britannica. Encyclopædia Britannica, Inc., 2022.
4. Sizer, Theodore R. Horace's Compromise: The Dilemma of the American High School. Boston: Houghton Mifflin, 1984.
5. Carnegie Foundation. Annual Report / Bulletin. Early 1900s.
6. Rhodes, Cecil. Confession of Faith. 1877. Online primary-source archive.
7. Quigley, Carroll. Tragedy and Hope. New York: Macmillan, 1966, 324.
8. Quigley, Carroll. Tragedy and Hope, 324–325.
9. Quigley, Carroll. Tragedy and Hope, 950.
10. Quigley, Carroll. Tragedy and Hope, 950.
11. Garfield, James A. The Works of James Abram Garfield. Vol. 1. 1882, 456.
12. Jefferson, Thomas. Letter to John Taylor, May 28, 1816.
13. Wilson, Woodrow. The New Freedom. New York: Doubleday, 1913, chap. 8.
14. Lippmann, Walter. Public Opinion. New York: Harcourt, Brace and Company, 1922.
15. Lippmann, Walter. Public Opinion. New York: Harcourt, Brace and Company, 1922.
16. Lippmann, Walter. The Phantom Public. New York: Harcourt, Brace and Company, 1925.
17. Bernays, Edward L. Propaganda. New York: Horace Liveright, 1928.
18. Russell, Bertrand. The Impact of Science on Society. London: George Allen & Unwin, 1952.
19. Rees, John Rawlings. Strategic Planning for Mental Health. 1940.
20. Wells, H. G. The Open Conspiracy: Blue Prints for a World Revolution. London, 1928, chap. 14.
21. Wells, H. G. The Open Conspiracy: What Are We to Do with Our Lives? London, 1928.
22. Lucis Trust. "The Great Invocation." https://www.lucistrust.org/the_great_invocation.

Chapter 21: How the Church Was Hijacked

1. Darby, John Nelson. Collected Writings. Prophetic No. 1.
2. Darby, John Nelson. Commentary on Deuteronomy 32.
3. Darby, John Nelson. Synopsis of the Books of the Bible, Matthew 24.
4. Darby, John Nelson. Jerusalem as the Centre of Worship and Government.
5.Lyon, Mark. "Leap Castle Ghost Story." Irish Central.
https://www.irishcentral.com/roots/history/leap-castle-ghost-story.

6.Lyon, Mark. "Leap Castle Ghost Story." Irish Central.
7.MouseHouseLife. "A Lovely Day Out, Part 1 – Leap Castle." October 12, 2019. https://mousehouselife.wordpress.com/2019/10/12/leap-castle/.
8.Superstitious Times. "Beyond the Haunting: Leap Castle Special." https://superstitioustimes.com/beyond-the-haunting-explores-irelands-infamous-leap-castle-for-te-special/.
9.Darby, John Nelson. On the Faithful Witness.
10.Darby, John Nelson. The Humiliation of Christ.
11.Darby, John Nelson. On the Death of Christ.
12.Liberty to the Captives. "Occult Words and Phrases in the Writings of John Nelson Darby." https://www.libertytothecaptives.net/darby_writings_occult.html.
13.Tregelles, Samuel Prideaux. Remarks on the Prophetic Views of J. N. Darby.
14.Spurgeon, Charles H. The Sword and the Trowel. 1864.
15.Jones, John. Letters on the State of the Church. 1872.
16.Hannah, John D. "Scofield, Cyrus Ingerson." American National Biography Online, February 2000.
17."C. I. Scofield." Wikipedia. https://en.wikipedia.org/wiki/C._I._Scofield.
18.Scofield, C. I. Scofield Reference Bible. Note on Isaiah 2.
19.Acton Institute. "C. I. Scofield: God's Self-Made Man."
20.Scofield, C. I. Scofield Reference Bible. Note on Ezekiel 43:7.
21.Scofield, C. I. Scofield Reference Bible. Notes on Ezekiel 45–48.

Chapter 24: What About Israel?

1.Darby, John Nelson. Jerusalem as the Centre of Worship and Government.
2.Scofield, C. I. Scofield Reference Bible. Note on Isaiah 2:2.
3.Scofield, C. I. Scofield Reference Bible. Note on Isaiah 2:3.
4.Scofield, C. I. Scofield Reference Bible. Note on Isaiah 60:1–3.
5.Scofield, C. I. Scofield Reference Bible. Note on Isaiah 60:10–12.
6.Scofield, C. I. Scofield Reference Bible. Note on Ezekiel 43:7.
7.Scofield, C. I. Scofield Reference Bible. Notes on Ezekiel 45–48.
8.Ynet News. "Rabbi Ovadia Yosef: Gentiles Exist Only to Serve Jews." October 18, 2010.
9.Netanyahu, Benjamin. Speech, Eilat, February 9, 2016.
10.Begin, Menachem. Interview, Jerusalem Post, June 25, 1982.
11.Gallant, Yoav. Press briefing, October 9, 2023.
12.Ginsburgh, Yitzhak. Interview, New York Jewish Week, April 1996.
13.Darby, John Nelson. Jerusalem as the Centre of Worship and Government.
14.Scofield, C. I. Scofield Reference Bible. Note on Ezekiel 43:7.

Chapter 25: Two Different Israels

1.Herzl, Theodor. The Complete Diaries of Theodor Herzl. Vol. 1. New York: Herzl Press, 1960, 7.
2.Cohen, Israel. The Zionist Movement. London: Frederick Muller, 1945, 63.
3.Weizmann, Chaim. Trial and Error: The Autobiography of Chaim Weizmann. New York: Harper & Brothers, 1949, 29.
4.Herzl, Theodor. The Complete Diaries of Theodor Herzl. Edited by Raphael Patai, translated by Harry Zohn. Vol. 1. New York: Herzl Press, 1960, 4.
5.Weizmann, Chaim. The Letters and Papers of Chaim Weizmann. Vol. 1. Jerusalem: Israel Universities Press, 1968, 123.
6.Ben-Gurion, David. Memoirs. Cleveland: World Publishing Company, 1970, 113.
7.Sheffer, Gabriel. Moshe Sharett: Biography of a Political Moderate. Oxford: Clarendon Press, 1996, 176.
8.Sharett, Yaakov, ed. Personal Diary. Vol. 3. Tel Aviv, 1978, 102.
9.Meir, Golda. My Life. New York: G. P. Putnam's Sons, 1975, 44.

10.Jabotinsky, Vladimir. The Jewish War Front. London, 1940, 15.
11.Jabotinsky, Vladimir. The Story of the Jewish Legion. New York: Bernard Ackerman, 1945, 22.
12.Jabotinsky, Vladimir. "The Iron Wall (We and the Arabs)." Rassvyet (Paris), November 4, 1923.
13.Begin, Menachem. The Revolt: Story of the Irgun. New York: Henry Schuman, 1951, 378.
14.Darby, John Nelson. The Hopes of the Church of God in Connection with the Destiny of the Jews and the Nations as Revealed in Scripture. London: G. Morrish, 1840, 134.
15.Scofield, C. I. Scofield Reference Bible. Oxford: Oxford University Press, 1909, Appendix Note 4, 1345.
16.UNICEF. Post on X (formerly Twitter), August 4, 2025.
https://x.com/UNICEF/status/1952399722586538085
17.Amnesty International. Israel and Occupied Palestinian Territories 2021. London, 2022.
18.United Nations Committee on the Rights of the Child. Concluding Observations on the Second to Fourth Periodic Reports of Israel. CRC/C/ISR/CO/2-4, 2013.
19.Human Rights Watch. Israel: Security Forces Abuse Palestinian Children. New York, 2019.
20.Barel, Zvi. "How Israel Helped to Spawn Hamas." The Guardian, June 18, 2002.
21.Cohen, Avner. Israel and the Bomb. New York: Columbia University Press, 2004, 273.
22.Al Jazeera. "Israel to Transfer $30 Million to Hamas Monthly." August 2022.
23.Associated Press. "Netanyahu Confirms Israel Transfers Qatari Cash to Hamas." March 2023.
24.Haaretz. "IDF: Hamas Is 'Key Partner' in Gaza." June 2024.
25.Jerusalem Post. "Israel Secretly Funds Hamas." February 2025.
26.Wall Street Journal. "Israel Funded Al-Qaeda in Syria." 2013.
New York Times. "Israeli Intelligence Helped Al-Qaeda in Syria." 2014.
BBC News. "Israel Treats ISIS Fighters in Hospitals." 2015.
Al Jazeera. "Israel Secretly Funded ISIS." 2016.
Associated Press. "Israel Funded Muslim Brotherhood in Egypt." 2013.
Haaretz. "Netanyahu Meets Muslim Brotherhood Leaders." 2017.
27.Wall Street Journal. "Israel Funds Al-Qaeda in Syria." 2013.
28.BBC News. "Israel Treats ISIS Fighters in Hospitals." 2015.
29.New York Times. "Israel Secretly Funds Iranian Militias in Syria." June 12, 2019.
Haaretz. "Netanyahu Confirms Israel Paid Iranian Proxies in Syria." August 20, 2020.
30.Aloni, Shulamit. Interview on Democracy Now!, August 14, 2002.
31.Solzhenitsyn, Aleksandr. The Gulag Archipelago. Vol. 1. New York: Harper & Row, 1973.
32.Solzhenitsyn, Aleksandr. The Gulag Archipelago. Vol. 2. New York: Harper & Row, 1974. Courtois, Stéphane, et al. The Black Book of Communism. Cambridge, MA: Harvard University Press, 1997.
33.Acts of the Russian Orthodox Church, 1918–1922.
34.Volkogonov, Dmitri. Lenin: A New Biography. New York: Free Press, 1994.
35. Solzhenitsyn, Aleksandr. 200 Years Together: A History of the Jews in Russia (1795-1995). Moscow: Russkii Put', 2001.
36.Spence, Jonathan D. The Search for Modern China. New York: W. W. Norton, 1999.
Terrill, Ross. Mao: A Biography. Stanford: Stanford University Press, 1999.
Vogel, Ezra F. Deng Xiaoping and the Transformation of China. Harvard University Press, 2011.
37.Kirk, Charlie, The Daily Beast, "Charlie Kirk Calls Jewish Billionaires 'Anti-Christian' in Viral Video," October 2019
38. Jones, E. Michael. The Jewish Revolutionary Spirit. Fidelity Press, 2008, 234-236.
39.Harris, Sam. The End of Faith: Religion, Terror, and the Future of Reason. New York: W. W. Norton, 2004.
40.Harris, Sam. Letter to a Christian Nation. New York: Knopf, 2006.
41.Asimov, Isaac. I. Asimov: A Memoir. Bantam, 1995
42. Hitchens, Christopher. God Is Not Great. New York: Twelve Books, 2007.
43. Al Goldstein quoted in Luke Ford, XXX-Communicated: A Rebel Without a Shul (2004)
44. · The Jerusalem Post, "Tinder Founder Sean Rad: 'Judaism is very important to me'", 2015

· Forbes, "Whitney Wolfe Herd: The Queen Bee of Dating Apps", 2016
· The New York Times, "A New Dating Site for the Modern Woman", 2011
· The Washington Post, "Hinge's CEO wants to make dating less painful", 2019
45. · The Jewish Contribution to the American Horror Film by Jeffrey Shandler (2003)
· Universal Horrors: The Studio's Classic Films, 1931-1946 by Tom Weaver (2007)
· The Horror Genre: From Beowulf to Blair Witch by Paul Tremblay (2008)
· German Film and Literature: Adapations and Transformations edited by Eric Rentschler (2012)
· The New Jewish Horror: A Collection of Jewish Horror Stories edited by David Agranoff (2020)
46. "MK-ULTRA." Encyclopædia Britannica Online. Last updated November 17, 2025.
47. · Central Intelligence Agency. "Office of Public Affairs — Entertainment Industry Liaison." CIA.gov.
· Central Intelligence Agency. "Examples of CIA Entertainment Industry Outreach." Declassified FOIA document, CIA.gov Reading Room
48. Aileen Fyfe et al., Untangling Academic Publishing (University of St Andrews, 2017)
49. Geoffrey Crossick, discussion of Robert Maxwell's control over academic journals and the power of scholarly publishing, in analyses of twentieth-century academic publishing and higher education.
50. Gordon Thomas, Robert Maxwell: Israel's Superspy (1996)
51. Seymour M. Hersh, The Samson Option: Israel's Nuclear Arsenal and American Foreign Policy (New York: Random House, 1991).
52. Rafi Eitan, interview quoted in Ma'ariv (Tel Aviv), December 12, 1991.
53. Gordon Thomas and Martin Dillon, Robert Maxwell: Israel's Superspy (New York: Carroll & Graf Publishers, 2002).
54. Ian Black, "Rise and Kill First: The Secret History of Israel's Targeted Assassinations – review," The Guardian, July 22, 2018.
55. According to Alfredo Rodriguez, Epstein's former butler, the black book contained "hundreds of names of important people" who visited Epstein's properties (Rodriguez, 1).
56. Oppenheim, A. (2019). Genetic studies of Ashkenazi Jews reveal no ancient Hebrew DNA. European Journal of Human Genetics, 27(9), 1234-1238. DOI: 10.1038/s41431-018-0311-3
57. Jewish Council for Public Affairs. "The Conversion of American Jewry." Jewish Council for Public Affairs. Accessed December 24, 2025.
https://jcfa.org/article/the-conversion-of-american-jewry/.
58. Phillips, Bruce A. Jews by Choice: A Quiet Revolution. New York: American Jewish Committee, 2005.
https://www.bjpa.org/content/upload/bjpa/jews/JewsByChoiceAQuietRevolution.pdf.
59. Native Israel. "Benefits of Moving to Israel." Native Israel. Accessed December 24, 2025.
https://www.nativeisrael.com/blog/benefits-of-moving-to-israel.

www.ingramcontent.com/pod-product-compliance
Lightning Source LLC
LaVergne TN
LVHW010851110826
845149LV00005B/1384

* 9 7 9 8 9 9 6 0 8 8 4 0 9 *